CLARK McGINN was born and brought up in Ayr, being educated at Ayr Academy where he spoke at his first Burns Supper. He then studied at Glasgow University where he graduated MA (Hons) in Philosophy in between a barrage of debating and speaking where he was twice-elected Convener of Debates, founded the World Debating Competition, won (with the late, great Charles Kennedy) the *Observer Mace,* and represented the UK on the ESU Debating Tour of the USA. After a near 30-year career in corporate and investment banking in London and New York, he left the City to capitalise on his experience in financing helicopters globally, holding senior executive positions in the then largest helicopter operating company and the largest independent specialist helicopter leasing company.

He has performed over 200 Immortal Memory speeches in 32 cities in 17 countries, travelling nearly a dozen times around the globe in the process. He was President of the Burns Club of London during the Burns 250th Celebrations in 2009, when he gave the Eulogy at the National Service of Thanksgiving for Burns at Westminster Abbey. In 2014, he was awarded a PhD by the University of Glasgow for his research into the history of the Burns Supper and has had several peer-reviewed articles published on various aspects of Burns. Among his books *The Ultimate Burns Supper Book* and *The Ultimate Guide to Being Scottish* have both been published in several editions by Luath Press as was *Out of Pocket: How Collective Amnesia Lost the World Its Wealth – Again,* a detailed study of financial crisis. His other hobby is writing letters to the *Financial Times*, where he holds the record of 59 letters printed to date.

Clark lives with his wife, Ann, in Harrow-on-the-Hill and Fowey. Their three daughters live outside London and New York.

The Burns Supper

A Concise History

CLARK McGINN

Luath Press Limited

EDINBURGH

www.luath.co.uk

First published 2019

ISBN: 978-1-912147-83-0

The paper used in this book is recyclable. It is made from low
chlorine pulps produced in a low energy, low emission manner
from renewable forests.

Typeset in 10.5 point Sabon by Lapiz

Printed and bound by Martins the Printers, Berwick

To Lucy
who needs to prepare for 2059

Contents

Acknowledgements

THIS BOOK HAS been long in thought and represents a small and hopefully digestible portion of my larger, comprehensive history of the Burns Supper. In its anterior (or stand-up before an audience) life, the initial thesis grew through many Burns Supper speeches since 1975. To all those many friends, my thanks for allowing me to explore the poet's work in your convivial company and for not shouting out 'heard it before'– even if you had. I am only sorry that some, including my father George L McGinn and my dear, gifted friend Charles Kennedy will not be here to read this.

In its posterior (or seated in front of the laptop) life, I am grateful for the insights and friendships of the team at the Centre for Robert Burns Studies at the University of Glasgow: Professors Gerry Carruthers and Kirsteen McCue could not have been more helpful and supportive supervisors, helping one who knew the language of Burns but less about the grammar of academia. Thanks also go to my examiners Professors Nigel Leask and Chris Whatley. Murray Pittock remains (as ever) an old friend and a wise scholar. I have particular thanks for the staff of Ayr's Carnegie Library, and East Ayrshire Museums. This is a neat segue to Dr William Zachs whose exceptional kindness in permitting me to work with his private collection allowed the first Immortal Memory to be discovered through his characteristic generosity. Throughout those two phases stand knowledgeable friends whose opinions and thoughtfulness reflect the greatest traditions of the Burns Club: Frank and Susan Shaw and Jim Henderson (remembering Wendy fondly) who are always consistently encouraging. It is a pleasure to be working with Gavin at Luath on another project together.

Appropriately in the Burns context, I could have accomplished nothing without my 'lassies'. Ann, forever inspirational and essential; and Claire, Eleanor and Emma – as wonderful, engaging and infuriating as only a trio of much-loved daughters could be (and my salutations to their lovely husbands, too). History books are (paradoxically) often about the future, and so I dedicate this book to our first grandchild, hoping that the burden of learning 'To a Haggis' will not impinge on the many happy years ahead of us.

Introduction

THIS IS THE FIRST detailed study of the unique phenomenon known as the Burns Supper.[1] This annual celebration of the life and works of the poet Robert Burns is held in Scotland and increasingly globally around the anniversary of the poet's birthday in the form of a convivial dinner with particular, some may say peculiar, ritual traditions. There is no similar literary or national celebration dedicated to a poetical or heroical figure held with broadly recognisable ritual around a given annual date. St Patrick's Day in an unstructured fashion comes close and while many figures are revered at their birthplaces or during their centennial celebrations, it is only Robert Burns who captures international interest each year on (or about) 25 January when Scots amongst others including their families and descendants, diasporic Caledonians, communists, inhabitants of former outposts of the British Empire and folk throughout the USA share in a dinner in memory of Scotland's national poet, celebrating his charismatic life and his memorable poetry, and what each of those legacies mean to that particular audience. As one early biographer put it, Burns has achieved 'every honour except canonisation'.[2]

The history starts with that biographer, the minor Ayrshire poet, cleric and Freemason, the Reverend Hamilton Paul (1773–1854) who organised the first Burns Supper in Alloway on the fifth anniversary of Burns's death. The number of Burns Suppers held has grown virtually every year since then such that around nine million people (about one and a half times the population of Scotland) participated in Burns Suppers, or Burns Nights as they are sometimes called, in the 250th anniversary

year of his birth in 2009. Like the global use of the English
language, the celebration of Burns Night is *of* Scotland but is
(happily) not insulated *from* global ownership.

This growth was spontaneous on the whole and broadly
adopted the rituals created by Hamilton Paul. These core
elements have been relatively consistent features in the Burns
Supper over its 200-odd year history: toasting the poet's
memory, addressing and eating a haggis and sharing in Burns's
poems and songs. To these at various times, other conventions
have been added, but were the proposer of today's Immortal
Memory to be exchanged in time and place with Hamilton
Paul in 1801, each would recognise the form and structure
of the event they were enjoying. There is a cliché of a Burns
Supper being the domain of elderly, kilted Scotsmen, guzzling
in a fug of whisky fumes and misogyny. The research in this
volume shows a wider and significantly more diverse story.
Over the years, the Burns Supper has been held at various levels
of social formality, bringing together dukes and dustmen, from
Scotland and across the globe, as hosts, guests and performers.
Many Suppers have involved the consumption of heroic
quantities of alcohol, but there have been many douce events,
sometimes even on strict temperance lines, and, while no
formal dinner in 1801 would have had women present (unless
cooking or serving) within a few decades women had begun to
attend Burns Night, as spectators, then at table, and ultimately
as complete equals. Above all the Burns Supper has exhibited
every shade of political opinion (and none) and so has very
rarely been used as a political agenda.

The success of the format is three-fold. First, the Burns
Supper remains a social and convivial party that should be a
pleasure to attend. Fellowship and community are key themes
in Burns's works, so this is an apt vehicle for his celebration.
Secondly, there is a greater flexibility in how it can be arranged
than is often recognised; and finally, the few mandatory
elements are key to understanding Burns's own imperative to be

recognised as the 'Bard'. The original Burns Suppers recognised this and utilised Burns's most performative verse to capture the spirit of his oeuvre. By incorporating that bardic quiddity, the Burns Supper after two centuries still shares that fundamental experience which is essential to its immediacy and integrity as a vehicle for the appreciation of Robert Burns. While other contemporary societies and annual literary dinners have fallen into desuetude, the Burns Supper has exhibited longevity and scale that is exceptional. Its key elements will each be discussed in turn in the chapters below, showing that the event is, and has been from the beginning, more multi-faceted and open than critics have generally given it credit for.

Thirdly, the Burns Supper has developed in national and international scope with audiences composed of Scots of birth, heritage or inclination mixing with people the world over. In fact, certain rituals we take for granted as Scottish inventions have received embellishment abroad contributing to an organic development of the patters of performance within the 'standard' Burns Supper.

Academic research into the Burns Supper has been hindered by one practical issue and two category mistakes. The practical point is the sheer volume of ephemeral sources. The growth of the phenomenon was spontaneous without an underlying governing body: so, for every Burns Club which kept records, there would be other groups holding events, possibly with some press notice, but by-and-large leaving no footprints in the sand. This thesis has attempted to start a rigorous capture of newspaper and other anecdotal and biographical reports to round out the corpus of formal club minutes, with over 3,200 recorded Burns Suppers from 1801 to 1859 arising out of the research for this book.

The first category error arises out of those records. The last two or three years have seen some rewarding research around the great Burns Centenary of 1859 as documented by James Ballantine, whose massive *Chronicle of the Hundredth Birthday of Robert Burns* which reported on around 1000 Burns celebrations. The depth (and availability) of this compendium has encouraged many commentators to see 1859 as the keystone of the Burns Supper bridge.[3] However, despite centennials being a very appealing study, the Burns Supper had almost 60 years of development prior to that year and it has to be seen and analysed as both annual and polycentric in its approach. The concept can only be truly engaged with by looking at the early events which established the recognised form, and then seeing how the global publicity of 1859 accelerated an already established and growing phenomenon.

The second, more negative and more long-standing, category mistake was the growing confusion arising out of the polemics of Hugh MacDiarmid (1892–1978) which carried into the 1970s and 1980s. This conflates the Burns Club movement with the Burns Supper itself. While the very nature of the Burns Supper is born out of the clubbable life of Burns's time, the popularity of the Burns Supper is linked to a wider range of social and national groups than the one narrow target of Grieve's diatribes. So, while it is accepted that the formalisation of the Burns Clubs into the Burns Federation and then, pejoratively, into the 'Burns Cult' brought with it an often stultifying self-belief in the form of the ritual of the supper and in a sub-kailyard orthodoxy, there were many other suppers based on fresher approaches to the poet. The possibility of arranging one to suit a particular group's politics, location or social views was open to all and was consistently taken up; MacDiarmid personally attended Burns Suppers virtually every year from 1918 to his death 60 years later, which effectively proves this latter point of accessibility.

These errors were magnified and maintained by a mutual distrust which grew in the 20th century between the remaining professional, yet numerically declining, cadre of Burns academics on one hand and the growing amateur world of the Burns enthusiasts on the other. The former looked upon the latter with the *de haut en bas* approach of a modern Hugh Blair, asserting that their appreciation of the poet 'smelt of the smithy', while the latter disregarded the former as impractical spinners of wool 'so fine that it is neither fit for weft nor woof'. Fortunately, a rapprochement over the last 15 years had taken most of the heat out of that false debate with a mutual recognition that Burns appreciation is a complex area and in consequence can be handled in different but equally effective ways without compromising one's tribal standards.

It is also enlightening to see how broad the adoption of the Burns Supper was in geographical terms. For the traditionally Scotto-centric Burnsian, it will be a shock to find that there were Burns Suppers held in Sunderland before Paisley, in Oxford before Kilmarnock, in Philadelphia before Dumfries and in Tasmania before Irvine. The success of the concept across the world comes from its affinity with the way Burns enjoyed his own poetry. As evidenced in his works, his enjoyment of good company and how he saw his own poetical legacy are key themes of importance to Burns. In creating an anniversary dinner at the behest of Burns's old patrons, Hamilton Paul matched these two particular tropes of Burns's life and works to the convivial club atmosphere of the period, imbued with Masonic inspired ritual. Paul readily found what Robert Crawford has called the 'performative' and 'bardic' qualities of Burns, and that empathy crystallised key points in the dinner to echo position statements made by Burns in his own poems about how he saw his own national and bardic inheritance. As Crawford sums it up: 'Burns wanted to shape how audiences would regard him' so the dinner was deliberately built on a structure of a toast to him who's far awa' with 'Auld Scotia' feasting on her haggis and her dram while making the most of a rowth o' rhyme, sangs and clatter to while away care.[4] Literally hundreds of other societies from that clubbable time waned while the Burns Supper waxed and there is a logical reason for that – it was the way Paul introduced key resonances from Burns himself, in what could be called Burns's bardic DNA into the format ensuring its longevity. Paul thus combined a basic ritual with sufficient flexibility to allow it to cross boundaries (be they geographical, political, national or, in time, of gender) yet remaining true to a celebration of a great poet and a complex man.

The development of the Burns Supper can be described using the construct of Max Weber's sociological analysis to frame its growth patterns. Starting with a 'Charismatic' period between 1801 and to around 1826, where Burns Suppers were driven by friends, Freemasons and mainly minor poets who had been directly influenced by the dead Bard; then a 'Traditional' period from then to the founding of the Burns Federation in 1885 which saw the widening *ad hoc* growth of Burnsian celebration now seen as an established and recognisable tradition; next a 'Bureaucratic' period from 1885 to 1996, covering the period of the growth of the Burns Federation (and a period of many dull, rigidly righteous, Burns Suppers); and finally, the modern, 'Global' period (following the relatively unsuccessful 1996 bicentenary) when modes of Burns Suppers multiplied but with each being still recognisable in essential terms.

Prior to that Global period, and still occasionally today, academic, nationalist and left-wing critics sniped at the phenomenon. Tom Devine famously hits two coconuts with one shy in his put down: 'the Burns Supper School of Scottish History', but that is ill informed as there can surely be no complete understanding of Scottish cultural history without seeing Burns and his writings in context and in terms of the people's reception of them. Given the popularity of Burns as poet and icon, alongside the widespread support of the Burns Supper, this is an important part of how Scottish literary heritage has developed in the last two centuries, so it should not be lightly dismissed.[5] It is instructive to think of what the Burns Supper has enabled: from after the Second World War, the academic study of the works of Burns had been in steady, apparently irreversible decline, yet during that same period, the number of people attending a Burns Supper increased, showing an inverse correlation between the scholarly and the popular reception of Burns.[6] It is no part of this thesis to claim that the quality of the analysis of Burns's work in Burns Supper speeches on average was, or is, of consistent, rigorous, academic quality but care should be taken to avoid Voltaire's fallacy of 'the best being the enemy of the good' by assuming that any lack of academic tone or critical apparatus in an Immortal Memory speech automatically invalidates its worth or insight.

At bottom, the concept of the Burns Supper is about people meeting around the dinner table, enjoying and thinking about the poems of Burns in a context that reminds them of Burns's self-desire to be remembered as an immortal bard. The Burns Supper has been an inclusive international phenomenon: with greater female participation, more encouragement of other poets, and less drink consumed than its critics would have believed. As with all amateur (in both senses) movements, enthusiasm has at times exceeded critical judgement and the fear of change was, for some time, self-defeating. By a mutual recognition that the Burns Supper, like Burns's poetry, is not in the ownership of one nationality, one political party or any gender, the Burns Supper remains the largest literary festival in the world and shows no sign of abating.

This book examines the Burns Supper phenomenon first by looking at how Hamilton Paul took the conceits of the dining clubs of Enlightenment Scotland and embedded performative parts of Burns's work into it to create a ritual whole. Secondly, it explores the rapid growth in participation in the Burns Supper (numerically and geographically) over two centuries. Thirdly, it looks at the key elements within the Burns Supper programme, when and how they were introduced and their development over time.

In the run up to 2009 and since that 250th anniversary year, the Burns Supper's popularity has again increased as groups rediscovered that it was possible (canonical, even) to celebrate Burns in a way congenial to their own social or interest group and, in so doing to welcome to the table, through the mediation of his poetry, the poet whom Longfellow called his 'dear guest and ghost' in a fashion he would recognise and enjoy. As Burns enjoined us:

> HERE'S, a bottle and an honest friend!
>   What wad ye wish for mair, man?
> Wha kens, before his life may end,
>   What his share may be of care, man.
>
> Then catch the moments as they fly,
>   And use them as ye ought, man: —
> Believe me, happiness is shy,
>   And comes not ay when sought, man.[7]

Part One

The Creation and Growth of
The Burns Supper

CHAPTER ONE

Convivial Club Life in Burns's Time

For thus the royal *Mandate* ran,
When first the human race began,
'The social, friendly, honest man,
    'Whate'er he be,
''Tis *he* fulfils *great Nature's plan*,
    'And none but *he*'.[8]

WHEN THE REVEREND HAMILTON Paul agreed to arrange the first anniversary dinner for Robert Burns's patrons and friends in July 1801, he deliberately planted the Burns Supper seed in identifiably fertile soil: the club milieu of late 18th century Scotland. A scene not unfamiliar to the Bard himself, to say the least.[9] Hamilton Paul created his format before the particular characteristics of Regency (im)morality and the subsequent counterweight of early Victorian values changed the accidental and alcoholic nature of clubbable life into a more regimented, regulated and self-perceived respectable set of institutions. The key element of the 'convivial sociability' which reigned in the decades before, during and immediately after Burns was that Scottish people (mainly but not exclusively men) met in regular gatherings for debate, conversation or song with a modest amount of food and a large (or larger) quantum of alcoholic drink. In the 1950s the equivalently ubiquitous pastime would likely have been described as attending the cinema while smoking and now, perhaps, the commonest social activity of an evening in Scotland may well be sitting side by side on the settee half watching Netflix while posting pointless tweets: for Burns and his fellows, it was the life of clubs.

Clubbability was then a national pastime and the clubs were multiform: ranging from local tavern drinking partnerships who might meet daily or weekly through to learned societies whose activities were enshrined in Royal Charters. The interesting characteristic of Scottish clubs of that era is that the majority of them spanned adjacent social classes (they had 'vertical' dimension) yet, were not exclusive – a man might be a member of several quite different clubs according to his interests and friendships (being a 'horizontal' axis). Some care must be taken with the first of these concepts. While, for example, Freemasonry encouraged a view of classless brotherhood which allowed, in theory and to an extent in practice, a working man to participate in lodge business beside a peer, most convivial societies seem to have operated within what might be thought of as social airlocks. Here a median social class formed the bulk of membership with some members or associates joining from social strata a rank (or perhaps more) higher or lower, rather than there being a complete collection of all classes present in one society or association at any one time.[10]

The common factor with all of these clubs (and their 'social, friendly, honest' members), was the consumption of alcohol alongside meeting of the club's *raison d'être* (assuming it had one, other than drinking!). Many of these clubs were formed for the common pursuit of a leisure interest from the singing of songs to the enjoyment of sport. At the top of the vertical/social axis, the Caledonian Hunt created opportunities for horseracing and gambling, with more controversial hobbies shared by groups like the Crochallan Fencibles, with their penchant for rude wit and bawdry, or the Beggars Benison in Anstruther with their sexual interests.[11] Other societies had party-political slant, good examples being those idolising Pitt on the one hand or Fox on the other. Most of these clubs (whatever their 'unique selling proposition') enjoyed ephemeral success then terminal decline, which Peter Clark calls 'a limited shelf life' of three to four years, as the fashion or the friendships faded and the initial arranger and company died, moved on, sobered up, or found a new affinity in the next fad.[12]

A few bodies found ways to institutionalise and endure. Freemasonry was already a thriving institution in Scotland in the late 1780s and is a special case which merits separate discussion below. Of the others, 'gentleman's clubs' acquired premises independent of the tavern or ale-house and thus gained a physical definition beyond the cadre of members at any given point in time, and they keep the same mandate of practical hospitality today. Many debating societies like Burns's own Tarbolton Bachelors Club have passed away, but those associated with the universities keep that same Enlightenment tradition of free speech around university and external politics. Outwith undergraduate life, the formality of debate as a furtherance of academic endeavour can still be seen operating within the learned societies, such as the Society of Antiquaries of Scotland and the Royal Society of Edinburgh.

Beyond these forms of formal association, three additional species went further and achieved a corporate status in the parallel world view of 'self-help' within the wider community. Burns enjoyed membership of several private library societies, and these institutions inspired Andrew Carnegie's 19th century benevolence in establishing free public libraries (although it appears to be a myth that every Carnegie Library was obliged to display a bust of Burns).[13] In finance, the savings bank movement was founded by Burns's acquaintance, the Reverend Henry Duncan and despite Adam Smith's concern that 'people of the same trade seldom meet together, even for merriment and diversion, but the conversation ends in a conspiracy against the public', Glasgow's 1783 concept of a merchant's chamber of commerce morphed into an internationally recognised form of virtuous trade association.[14]

This book is more concerned with the wider and generally ephemeral social or convivial clubs, which were a recognisable and an important part of social life and enjoyments in Burns's time. By their nature, many of these societies left no records and few memories. As the recollections of the Edinburgh clubs of the period are more extensive than those of Glasgow or of the county towns most analysis tends to focus on the capital as the seat of the Enlightenment club nexus.[15] This has the risk of creating a survivorship fallacy and so care must be taken not to assume that the Cape Club with its archive at the National Archives of Scotland is the necessary standard base case of how a club was conducted. This chapter seeks to look at clubs in a pan-Caledonian fashion taking as its foundation the associational milieu during Burns's lifetime and the Charismatic period of the Burns Supper movement (say between 1801 and 1826). The ubiquity of 'convivial sociability' is striking. A 'club' could range from a bunch of tavern regulars who met for drinks on a specific (or every) night of the week, to a group who met periodically on a given weekday to dine, or those who planned a formal reunion dinner once a year. Written rules and formal membership were not uncommon but not obligatory and while there are interesting questions around why a group would choose to bind themselves in a formally written constitution (as opposed to merely gathering along customary lines) that is not a question that is material to this specific point, the agreement by action to create an associational group being what effectively binds the club together and gives it a personality.

These 'convivial' groups could be founded by definition along class or political lines, by geography of birth, or around a common interest, a favourite pub or a shared desire to play a specific sport or pastime. Corey Andrews calls this construct of life: 'drinking and thinking', wittily adding, 'the world of mid-century Edinburgh often borrowed more from the model of symposium than *trivium* and *quadrivium*'.[16] This has led many commentators to focus on the intellectual theme which runs through all Scottish Enlightenment studies and to see this club life as a highly thoughtful enterprise. However, the construct is better thought of as 'drinking and fill-in-the-gap' for the 'thinking' element took myriad forms from the truly analytical or scientific chat, through participative poetry and song, to those clubs whose sole aim was to meet for witty conversation as opposed to solemn ratiocination. The genesis of clubs was truly democratic: for if there were no clubs that catered for one's tastes, one found like-minded friends and started a new club to fill that gap. One of the notable traits in this model of creation was to choose a punning name for the group: the Boar Club, who gathered in Hogg's Tavern, the Antemanum Club who paid their bill 'beforehand' as they would be too drunk to settle up at the end of the night, or the Pious Club whose name reflected their meetings in the Edinburgh pie houses.[17]

In addition to transcending class, politics and wealth, club life had some limited ability to cross gender lines. While formal female-only clubs were unusual (the Fair Intellectual Club of Edinburgh being a rare example) the social convention of ladies making calls or attending soirées filled many of the associational needs that club life provided and the Assembly Rooms as centres of mixed conviviality in major towns is familiar to any reader of Jane Austen.[18] The mingling of the sexes was not easily countenanced; there were etiquette challenging events such as Edinburgh's Order of the Horn in the early 18th century which was later described as a notorious 'species of masquerade in which the sexes were mixed, and all ranks confounded'.[19] So some element of gender mixed conviviality apparently could not be utterly frozen out even in Calvinist Scotland. Another good example is the Oyster Frolics which James Grant censoriously describes as 'little better than orgies', where 'ladies and gentlemen alike indulged in unrestrained manner in sallies and witticisms, observations and jests, that would not have been tolerated elsewhere.[20]

The formulae of clubs are capricious – like-minded people finding a common purpose of enjoyment (would the use of the word 'clubbing' today be the same thought albeit a very different activity?). The underlying principle is clear: any group regardless of size, or class and to a limited extent, gender, can form a club. In Hans Hecht's words, Burns had stumbled on:

> The great intimacy which existed at that time throughout the literary world in Scotland. A brotherly bond seemed to unite its members; they were constantly meeting, in parties, in the daily discharge of their official duties, or in the numerous and varied clubs where they passed a considerable part of their spare time. They had the same habits, the same interests, the same amiable virtues and vices.[21]

A noticeable feature of clubbable life was the horizontal axis – the fact that most men would be members or affiliates of several often quite diverse clubs. Peter Clark estimated that 'three or four... were probably close to the maximum for most people, given the constraints of time and money'. One often-found feature of Scottish club life was a maximum spend on food and drink which allowed someone to be associated with more clubs than the national average.[22] Mark Wallace provides an invaluable review of the integrated nature of Edinburgh clubs, cross-referencing major men and their affiliation.[23] According to contemporary records, James Cumming of the Lyon Office (the heraldic court of Scotland) had sufficient time to be a noted antiquary, a subscriber to Burns's First Edinburgh Edition, and reputedly the most clubbable man in eminently clubbable Edinburgh.[24] He was an active member of at least 15 clubs including:

The Cape Club
(as 'Sir Nun and Abbess' he served as Sovereign
1783–84)
The Jolly Society
The Canongate Catch Club
The Royal Company of Archers
The Society of Fair Anglers
Thistle Lodge No 64
Gormandising Club
The Royal Order
The Royal Oak
The Society of Teachers
Mrs Hamilton's Club
The Society of Antiquaries (Secretary)
Johnie Dowie's 'Circle'[25]

And that is merely a list of where we know he went to drink formally.

Burns enjoyed (literally) a similar scope of formal, informal and honorary memberships.[26] In addition to his famous Batchelors Club and his Freemasonic affiliations (he served as Depute Master in Tarbolton, Senior Warden in Dumfries, while accumulating four honorary Lodge memberships),[27] he was a paid-up member of the Crochallan Fencibles and an honorary member of the Royal Company of Archers in Edinburgh. In Dumfries, he acted as secretary of the Monklands Friendly Society library, enrolled in the Loyal Dumfries Volunteers and was made an honorary burgess of Dumfries, and five other burghs. He freely gave songs and poems to his Freemasonic brethren, famously being recognised by the Grand Master Mason as 'Caledonia's Bard'.[28] As 'poet laureate' he contributed the verse expected at a range of dinners and Clubs, whether grudgingly, for Buchan's Thomson Club or enthusiastically for the 'proto-celebration' of the Haggis Club supper. He was even-handed, writing for his government colleagues in the

Excise and for a party of Jacobite gentlemen celebrating Bonnie Prince Charlie's birthday in Edinburgh'.[29] Even allowing for an element of lionising, Burns can be seen as enjoying significant stimulation through the spectrum of associational engagement, both structured and less structured, in a defined, enjoyable social environment. The creation of that shared environment is key.

Freemasonry can be seen as the archetypal club of that period, spanning rank and geography internally in Scotland, but also including a network across the three kingdoms and beyond the seas such that it could be seen as the broadest associational network, absent the Kirk, in Scotland at that time. The Craft had recently evolved from the merchant guilds of stone masons ('the operatives') into the Enlightenment movement of the 'speculative' Freemasons who used allegories of the ancient craft skills, projected onto the Biblical story of the building of Solomon's Temple, to create a rule of life around a belief in an unspecific Supreme Being and an all-encompassing fraternal duty of charity and mutual support. There is a strong adherence (particularly in Ayrshire) to the belief that Freemasonry came into this post-mythological existence through agency of the stone masons who built Kilwinning Abbey. To this day, Lodge Kilwinning has special status within the Grand Lodge of Scotland as 'Mother Kilwinning', heading the roll of lodges as Lodge No. o.

As an ancient house, Kilwinning formerly had the power to charter new lodges including several of the lodges with Burns affiliations, notably Canongate Kilwinning No.2 in Edinburgh. This lodge effectively operated as the embassy of Ayrshire in the nation's capital. The leading men of the county were prominent members, including Sir James Hunter Blair (the city's Lord Provost and quondam MP whose banking fortune prospered after the Ayr Bank collapse) and Sir John Whitefoord (who lost his estates in that same debacle), James Dalrymple of Orangefield, the Earls of Eglinton (on the rise) and of Glencairn (on the decline), and in literature, Professor Dugald Stewart of Catrine and James Boswell of Auchinleck.

Any discussion of Freemasonic history is a challenging debate, but it would seem common ground that the Masonic fellowship certainly implies not only respectful working practices, but beyond that a social contentment amongst brethren. As Mark Wallace astutely comments: 'Freemasonry has too often been viewed from a strictly Masonic context that frequently ignores its wider impact and influence on Enlightenment sociability'.[30] Certainly in Burns's time, the Freemasons embodied Corey Andrew's 'thinking and drinking' concept. As they were not confined to a particular locality or to a class, Freemasons met firstly in the ritual of their lodge meeting ('thinking') then afterwards to dine together ('drinking') with no apparent dichotomy. For example, the minutes for Roman Eagle Lodge, No. 160 in Edinburgh record:

> What with eating and drinking and appropriate conversation... passed the time with much good humour and sparkling wit till past eight o'clock in the evening. Finally, after several songs in Latin, French, Italian, English, and Gaelic, the Lodge was closed in the usual manner.[31]

The important thing to remember is that the working of the masonic ritual was always followed by the social interaction around 'the festive board', which in the Scottish Masonic tradition is called the 'harmony', connoting both the custom of interspersing toasts with songs and more broadly the over-arching concept of fraternal bonding conducted after each regular lodge meeting.

That second part of a Masonic evening was scarcely different to the range of convivial societies popular at the time but what made Freemasonic Harmony different was that the philosophy of universal brotherhood amongst Masons gave any visiting Mason from out of town the right to join his brethren (after confirming his *bona fides* through word, sign and grip) in a way that could not happen in mainstream clubs. That is not to say that there exist some examples of societies which established offshoots: the Cape Club blessed daughters in Glasgow, Manchester and London and possibly in Charleston, and The Beggar's Benison permitted meetings outwith Anstruther in Edinburgh. However, these have the feel of core members from the mother club moving away from home and being granted a dispensation to hold meetings rather than them sending out missionaries or embassies to found a new branch *in partibus infidelium* where old friends from home might never visit.

Freemasons were the only body to have that franchise concept as an integral part of the organisation at this time. This was heightened through the new Grand Lodge of Scotland which recognised 49 lodges at its foundation in 1736, some 267 by 1785 and a total of 330 by 1800.[32] The members had a dual commitment of local loyalty and simultaneously an inherent bond to the wider masonic community. An important part of the successful growth of the movement during this period was the relatively straightforward ability for a group of master masons to obtain the charter for a new lodge to fill a geographical or – importantly – social gap. The creation of the Grand Lodge of Scotland still left individual lodges a great deal of freedom to express an individual character in non-ritual practices and this approach, combined with the ban on discussion of the two then divisive topics of Scottish life – politics (effectively, who should be the King) and religion (how should the Kirk be governed) – which made the institution highly appealing to the broadest range of Scotsmen. It would be wrong, however, not to see that Freemasonic model as a part of the convivial associational whole, albeit the most highly developed and ultimately the most replicable and sustainable over centuries.

The associational life of 'drinking and thinking' was a defining element of the culture of Scotland in Burns's time, and Burns grasped that part of life with both hands. His portfolio of club involvement was triple: a core commitment to Freemasonry, a periodic attachment to formal clubs where he lived and a popular 'freelance' role as poet laureate at large to many differing groups. As a participant and as a provider, Burns was a child of those clubbable times.

CHAPTER TWO

The Creation of the First Burns Supper

The posthumous fame of Burns is without parallel in the annals of poetry. Soon after his death, meetings were held in various parts of the British Empire, commemorative of his excellencies as a son of inspiration.[33]

Alloway, July 1801

IT WAS WITHIN this social and intellectual milieu of 'drinking and thinking' that John Ballantine of Ayr, called on Reverend Hamilton Paul, himself a well-known and clubbable man, to arrange for 'a select party of the friends of Burns... to dine in the cottage in which he was born, and to offer a tribute to the memory of departed genius'.[34] Thus the fifth anniversary of the death of Robert Burns, 21 July 1801, saw nine gentlemen from Ayr dine at Burns Cottage, Alloway in commemoration of the life and works of their fellow Ayrshireman: the Bard of Coila, the Bard of Ayrshire, and a man who was being increasingly recognised as the Bard of Scotland.

If the sole thing that Hamilton Paul had done was create an annual dinner anchored in their poet's veritable birthplace in Alloway that would be the end of a much shorter story. Many other birthplaces had such commemorations. What was to prove unusual, arguably unique, was the way in which the format immediately de-linked from the poet's physical birthplace and spread through the West Coast, then across the remainder of Scotland and England and thence throughout the British colonies,

trading posts and expatriate Scots communities. In a timescale
shorter than the life of the poet, it was to become a globally
recognised and annually enacted 'convivial' memorialisation of
Robert Burns over a dining table by all modes and manners
of men. This has been a neglected area of study and where
academics and Burnsians have addressed it, they have conflated
two distinct social incidents: the Burns Supper on the one
hand and the formal Burns Clubs on the other. As there have
always been more Burns Suppers than Burns clubs, writing the
history of popular celebration of the Bard by focussing on club
activities and structures and, latterly, the Burns Federation,
necessarily limits the understanding of the spontaneous and
popular appeal of the Burns Supper. A much wider grouping
of Scots by birth, descent, affiliation, or residence along with
other national and political groups use the Burns Supper as
a re-confirmation of shared values through the prism of the
life and poetic works of Robert Burns. Just as the convivial
clubs of Scotland in Burns's time ranged from the formal to the
occasional in constitutional terms, so Hamilton Paul's creation
of a ritual format could be adopted by different groups with
whatever level of written obligation or even cultism that might
appeal to the particular participants. The creation of the first
Burns Supper was at one level a spontaneous mark of affection
by a former patron of Burns to mark the fifth anniversary of his
protégé's death and, at another level, it occurred not long after
the first nationwide publication of his complete works and life
story, as edited by Dr James Currie. One a localised channel of
memory, the other international.

The first commemoration of Burns's life and works was at
his birthplace in Alloway which had recently become a rather
shabby ale house.[35] The form of the dinner, and the nine men
who attended it, are entirely typical of the period. The poet's
patrons were represented by 'Provost John' Ballantine and
Robert 'Orator Bob' Aiken who were joined by others who had
assisted the poet, such as Patrick Douglas of Garallan (who

found Burns potential albeit now controversial employment on his Jamaican slave estate) and William Crawford (whose uncle had employed the poet's father as his master gardener). The town community was reflected in a local banker, David Scott, who had been a financial assessor in the Lochlie arbitration between Burns's father and his landlord; Captain Primrose Kennedy, a Carrick landowner, friend of George Washington and hero of the American War of Independence (whose unusual Christian name spawned the occasionally repeated error that a lady attended); the Rector of Ayr Academy, Dr Thomas Jackson and the town's barrack-master, Captain Hugh Fergusson. These friends were brought together by Hamilton Paul who wrote, looking back on the successful dinner, that 'the party was such as Burns himself would have joined with heartfelt satisfaction'.[36]

Hamilton Paul was a well-liked man in Ayr who, in his student days at Glasgow University had studied with the poet Thomas Campbell and remained his lifelong friend. Paul was well-known as a social man, a versifier and a wit, whose obituary in the *Ayr Advertiser* (a publication he had edited and partly owned for a time) described his talent in an affectionate but pointed judgement: '[h]is compositions are characterised by great elegance, but they exhibit versatility of talent and facility of versification rather than capacity to reach the higher flights of poetry'.[37] His light pastoral duties as a 'stickit minister' (he served as assistant minister to several parishes) allowed him to dedicate his gregarious nature to Ayr's myriad clubs and societies, such that he was described by a contemporary as being:

> whirled about in a perpetual vortex of business and pleasure, never a single day without company at home or abroad. If he could obtain three or four hours sleep, he was satisfied. He was a member of every club, chaplain to every society, had a free ticket to every concert and ball, and was a welcome guest at almost every table.[38]

Notwithstanding his clerical calling, through which he was well-known to be a theological liberal of the 'New Licht' wing of the Kirk, such a gregarious man was an obvious choice to arrange the first festival dinner given his literary talents, his legendary sociability, his links to Ayrshire Freemasonry and, above all, his genuine appreciation of Burns's poetry. Without a parish and with time to indulge both his love of Burns and the tastes of some of the most important men in the area, Paul looked to create a memorable occasion (with little risk to his sacerdotal preferment).

There are two sets of manuscripts which evidence the activities of the Allowa' Club. The first were acquired by the Kilmarnock publisher James McKie (1816–1891) as part of his extensive collection of Burnsiana, now held in the collections of East Ayrshire Council. He acquired the papers from David Aird, the landlord of the George Hotel, Kilmarnock who was Hamilton Paul's grandnephew and an early member of the Burns Federation management committee. These minutes are incomplete, but include notes of 10 of the 18 Burns Suppers held between 1801 and 1819.[39] The second set of 12 pages was acquired in 2013 by Dr William Zachs and, despite some water damage, contains the first ode from 1801 (lost for many years) and for four other years.[40] That last ode had been published in the *Air Advertiser* and was brought to the notice of Robert Chambers who exclaimed that 'he would give all Ayrshire' for copies of the earlier odes. Hamilton Paul obliged with characteristic generosity, sending Chambers a copy saying that he would settle for a single farm.[41] Given that both sets of manuscripts contain 1810, it is fair to assume that the McKie Mss represent Paul's papers, inherited by Aird and the Zachs Mss is part of the Chambers copy.

From these memoranda we can recognise the core of the Burns Supper celebration as still performed today. The first McKie minute records that:

> In the summer of 1801, a select party of the friends
> of Burns proposed to dine in the cottage in which

he was born, and to offer a tribute to the memory of departed genius. Two gentlemen of distinguished philanthropy and taste waited on the author of the following Odes, and requested him to produce a short poem on the occasion. The author never saw Burns, but was an early and enthusiastic admirer of his writings. The party was such as Burns himself would have joined with heartfelt satisfaction.

- William Crawford, Esq., of Doonside.
- John Ballantine, Esq., to whom Burns dedicated 'The Twa Brigs of Ayr'
- Robt. Aiken, Esq., to whom Burns dedicated the 'Cotter's Saturday Night'.
- Patrick Douglas, Esq., of Garallan, who patronised the Poet in the early stages of his career.
- Primrose Kennedy, Esq., of Drumellan.
- Hew Fergusson, Esq., Barrackmaster, Ayr.
- David Scott, Esq., Banker, Ayr.
- Thomas Jackson, A.M., Rector of the Air Academy, now Professor of Natural Philosophy in the University of St Andrews.
- The Rev. Hamilton Paul, Chaplain and Laureat.

These nine sat down to a comfortable dinner, of which sheep's head and haggis formed an interesting part. The 'Address to the Haggis' was read, and every toast was drank by three times three, i.e., by nine. A portrait of the poet, painted on wood, intended as a signpost to the cottage, which is a rural tavern, was presented to the company, to which there is an allusion in the poem, — 'When even his image in my burning breast', &c.

Before breaking up, the company unanimously resolved that the Anniversary of Burns should be

> regularly celebrated, and that H. Paul should exhibit
> an annual poetical production in praise of the Bard
> of Coila, and that the meeting should take place on
> 29th January, the supposed birthday of the poet.[42]

From this minute, it is possible to recognise, in the guise of a
typical convivial club's entertainment or Masonic harmony of
1801, the self-same elements that a modern participant would
acknowledge as characteristic of the Burns Supper:

1. It was a convivial meeting;
2. to be held annually on Burns's anniversary (typically of
    his birthday or possibly, of his death);
3. It featured 'a tribute to the memory of departed genius'
    (albeit then in the form of a poem);
4. It consisted of a 'comfortable dinner' featuring a dish of
    haggis as traditional Scottish fare, with the recitation of
    To a Haggis; and
5. It was rounded out by further toasts, songs and poems
    performed by the company and enjoyed over a drink in
    a sociable environment – 'every toast was drank by three
    times three'.

Later in the book, each of those core elements will be looked
at in depth in terms of both their importance in the event, and
their development through their introduction to other cultures.
The first topic of analysis is how Paul chose these themes and
bound them together in a coherent Burns setting.

How Hamilton Paul Bonded the Elements of the Burns Supper Together

The majority of the first guests of the Allowa' Club were
Freemasons; Paul is recorded as having performed at various

Masonic festivals, so the flavour of the Scots tradition of the 'harmony' can be felt in the agenda he built for this event.[43] Here a close group of men passed the evening in songs and toasts over a board of simple food and (it is fair to suppose) ample drink. This was an eminently replicable formula or ritual, and contributed in no small way to the burgeoning of the concept over the following 25 years without there being the necessity of a central organising body to encourage expansion or conformity beyond Paul's invention of the form of proceedings as laureate of the group (or club).[44]

The second strength in the conceit developed by Paul is that it is looking for what Burns would have desired in securing his own commemoration. When Burns feared that he would have to leave Scotland for Jamaica, he enjoined his Tarbolton lodge friends to remember him in an annual toast:

> A last request, permit me here,
>   When yearly ye assemble a',
> One *round*, I ask it with a *tear*,
>   To him, *the Bard that's far awa'*.[45]

This appeal appears true to type given Robert Crawford's key theme of Burns's desire to achieve 'bardship' where Crawford, in *The Bard*, cleverly emphasises what he calls Burns's 'articulation of a bardic manifesto'.[46] Certainly, Burns sought to define not just his works but himself from an early stage sometimes with an ironic tinge or smile, but always with purpose. Paul would have been acquainted with the preface to the *Kilmarnock Edition* (where Burns described himself as 'an obscure, nameless Bard' and talked of 'the heart-throbbing gratitude of the Bard') and similar self-references in the *First Edinburgh Edition* ('A Scottish Bard, proud of the name').[47] These clearly set out Burns's claim to a prominent position on any bardic roster that was to be created. Now after his removal by death rather than emigration, by meeting at his birthplace in the company of nine men – nine being the number of the Muses (and no doubt, additionally resonant for a Masonic 'three times three' particularly given Royal Arch symbolism around the number nine, (Paul, like Burns, was accredited to that alternative ritual branch of masonry) – it looks certain that Paul set out to cement Burns's claim and title to a posthumous national bardship. Certainly, the fact that each toast was acclaimed with open Masonic honours is consistent with an attempt to create a remembrance of ritual within the brethren.

Just as Paul chose to position Burns in the role of bard, the choice of venue and of a menu consisting of simple 'hamely fare' emphasise the ordinariness of the poet's background – connoting both the trials he faced in his upbringing, but also the ideal and idealised concept of the hardy Scottish peasant (which of course is one of the principal themes of Currie's biography and which would be the consistent interpretation of the life behind Burns's works throughout that century). Paul likely chose to recite *To a Haggis* to underscore that theme but he was likely aware of the tradition that Burns had recited at least part his poem over a physical haggis at dinner (probably as a mock Grace).

At a typical dinner of this period, including Masonic suppers, toasts were ubiquitous, either in recognising one's fellow guests through the concept of 'taking wine' with them or in toasting famous personages, great events or emotive conceits. These toasts would be frequent and any preliminary speech would be very short, often a formalised apophthegm or 'sentiment' and not usually structured as a long oration, but culminating in an invocation to toast as we would practise today. To mark the signal purpose of this Alloway dinner, Paul, as we have said a modest poet (in talent, if not confidence and output), was requested to prepare an ode to be the centrepiece of the memorial and to precede the toast to their poet's memory. He appears to have taken inspiration from the numerous anniversary elegies on Burns which sprang up in the papers at the time of, and the subsequent anniversaries, of the Bard's death.

The first dinner 'minute' (McKie MS a) does not contain the
verse recited on the day. The minute does reference 'an allusion
in the poem, — "When even his image in my burning breast"'
but the Ode was on a second page of manuscript which was
missing.[48] In his *Air Edition* of 1819, Hamilton Paul published
an 'Irregular Anniversary Ode, Sacred to the Memory of Burns',
which was a cento poem, a new work but one crafted out of
fragments of verse from many of his 18 anniversary poems
delivered to the Allowa' Club.[49] All but the first 22 lines of
this omnibus Ode matched verses published in the press
after Alloway or Glasgow dinners and so there was a strong
possibility that those opening lines could well be from the
missing First Ode. However, tantalisingly Paul failed to use the
'image in my burning breast' quotation in the *Irregular Ode* so
it was impossible to be conclusive. However, the first 'Immortal
Memory' toast was discovered in 2012 by Dr William Zachs and
authenticated by the author. In these newly discovered pages,
Hamilton Paul's first ode is structured in the highly classical
form that the reverend gentleman could generate by the yard,
and consists of 34 lines, of which 22 were the opening section
of the 'Irregular Ode'. *Ode No. 1* took as its text the debate at
Troy amongst the Greeks over who had the right to bear the
arms and armour of the dead Achilles. Odysseus wishes that
Achilles were there with them, that he might rightfully bear the
weaponry which made him famous and the hero of the Greeks,
rather than the second, lesser, tier of warriors left alive. Paul
took that and turned into a recognition that no one could bear
Burns's laurel in the field of Ayrshire – indeed Scottish, if not
all – poetry:

> Had Burns surviv'd, vain were my feeble lays,
> Himself had sung, himself had worn the bays. [50]

We do know that the Ode was met with praise on the day,
as Hamilton Paul recounted an anecdote to William Chambers

much later. Paul records that he was asked to meet Robert Aiken ahead of the first dinner, and after reading the ode, said:

> 'That will do – there are two Criteria by which
> I judge of the merit of a production of this kind.
> First my eyes are suffused – next the button of my
> waistcoat skelps.' He was dressed in a Brown coat
> and a snow white vest which actually burst open.[51]

The day was a great success, with no doubt many skelpit waistcoats. Paul, who like Burns enjoyed a happy dinner with like-minded friends, had effectively taken the style of the convivial club supper, added nods to the Freemasonic ritual the guests all shared, and inserted specific performative elements which echoed clear references in Burns's own works of the poet's own self-image. This would have been clear and persuasive to the men around the kitchen table in Burns Cottage that afternoon. Yet while the format of the event was well choreographed to reflect the themes of Burns's work within a Masonic fellow-feeling and it looks to have been an enjoyable, if somewhat sentimental, occasion, there is nothing inherently special about this first Burns Supper on that one day.

The subsequent run of suppers in Alloway or at nearby venues in Ayr mainly on or about the anniversary of Burns's birth could itself be seen simply as personal friends joined at the shared locality of the poet's birthplace, being merely a localised celebration of the bard of Coila and Ayrshire.[52] Thus being no more than a personal and finite commemoration without national or international pretension. What makes the phenomenon more interesting is the next stage of development, where Burns Suppers started to be organised by people with no personal link to Burns, or to Ayr, or even to Scotland, resulting in the transformation from a local to a national and then to a global memorialisation, which in time expanded upon the core elements of Paul's ritual feast. Paul had maintained an outward looking approach, regularly submitting reports of his Burns Suppers not just to the

Ayrshire papers but to Greenock and Glasgow, to Edinburgh and London, with several of those articles copied into the US press. Paul further recognised that expansion when drafting the appendix to the *Air Edition* in 1819, written when Burns Suppers were regular occurrences in Ayr, Greenock, Paisley, Kilbarchan, Kilmarnock, Dunfermline, Glasgow, Edinburgh, Newcastle-upon-Tyne, Sunderland Baltimore, Philadelphia and New York and where they had been held in some fashion in Aberdeen, Oxford, London, Sheffield, Jamaica and Bombay.

Central to this effective conceit stands Hamilton Paul. At once an aficionado of the club and associational atmosphere of the time and an acute (if perhaps over-zealous) proponent of Burns's work, Paul identified key themes around bardship that were (and remain) fundamental to any interpretation of the poet's importance. He chose elements that were inherently participative and which represented parts of the Burns oeuvre which call out for performance. So, just as Burns appreciated (in both senses) the associational milieu of the clubbable, so Paul both recognised that important trope in Burns's life and work and saw that it chimed with the Supper format. Burns in life enervated dinners by his participation, Paul found the way to capture that essence, a way of celebrating the real Robert Burns, in a way that Burns himself had effectively asked to be remembered.

CHAPTER THREE

The Charismatic Period

While we to our lamented Bard,
Pour forth this tribute of regard,
We seem to feel his very soul
The spirit that pervades the bowl;
And catch from every circling glass,
That's toasted to a bonny Lass,
The social, friendly, manly glow,
That brightens every shade of woe;
And tells us, Friendship, Love, and Song were given,
To render this our earth a miniature of Heaven.

Revd Hamilton Paul, Alloway 1813[53]

THE 250TH ANNIVERSARY of Burns's birth saw over nine million people attending Burns Suppers of varying size but which shared the essential ritual of the first Burns Supper held in 1801.

First, let us look at the rapid expansion in scale and geography of the Burns Supper concept beyond the direct friends of Burns and of Alloway. The obvious difference between the celebration of Burns through the disparate but similarly structured dinners contrasts with what Quinault calls 'The Cult of the Centenary', where large, uniquely located and centrally controlled events were created to commemorate major poets, playwrights, composers or nation-builders upon significant anniversaries of their births or deaths.[54] In the 18th and 19th century, several of these events were crafted on a national scale using nation-building rhetoric.[55] Centenaries were held for Shakespeare

(1769) and for Handel (1784); for Goethe (1849) and Schiller
(1853 and 1859); for Shakespeare (again) in 1864 and for Dante
(1865) and for Scott (1871).[56] Each of these to a greater or lesser
extent reflected a desire to capture national bardism, whether in
the national unification movements of Germany and Italy or in
the development of a British construct of an Imperial culture. The
difference though with all (save the *Schillerfest* and to a limited
extent the Scott Centenary) was the central and monolithic
structure of the festival, rooted in one spot for one day, both
highly specific to the honouree. Schiller was the exception, being
commemorated in a broader range of smaller regional German
festivals, but it is only for Burns that we see the annual network
of anniversary dinners linked increasingly not by locale or by
being part of the Burns story, but by being what Murray Pittock
described as 'hybridizing' 'Burns's poetic achievement... with
the quotidian life of Scots... in their convivial and associational
hours' rather than being confined to idealised (and potentially
stage-managed) centenary festivals.[57]

   The concept generated a level of journalistic interest:
Hamilton Paul was a part owner and editor of the *Air Advertiser*
(a newspaper still published today) so he was aware of the
appetite of the newspapers for 'celebrity' stories as can be seen
in how often Paul's events are reported in the press.[58] Between
1802 and 1807 there are more than 20 reports in UK newspapers
and a further dozen across the USA. This was obviously one of
the vectors of promotion of the whole concept.

   Storer and Greig's illustrated guide to Burns Country, the first
of its kind published in 1805, reported that at Burns Cottage,
now 'a snug public house... yearly on the birth-day of Burns, a
social group meet and celebrate it with festivity and rejoicing'.[59]
By 1809, an article about travelling through the south-west of
Scotland specifically referred to the already embedded tradition of
'[t]he Gentlemen of Ayr [who] with a degree of taste and liberality
that does honour to them, annually meet in this ale-house, to dine
and celebrate the anniversary of their native Bard'.[60]

By that date the celebration was held in a wider circle than merely at the site of his birth (which had assumed a position of place of literary pilgrimage by that time, independent of the annual dinner). Popular, broadly based celebration manifested itself through the Burns Supper which then became the building block for two other social enterprises, Burns clubs and monster meetings. A good way to think of the growth in the popularity of Burns Suppers is to see them coming in waves which could be categorised using a methodology similar to Max Weber's theories of management structure. In such a construct, the period initiated by Hamilton Paul in 1801 through to the dinners arranged by either John Syme and Henry Duncan at Dumfries (in 1818 and 1820), Andrew Crawford and his fellows in Dalry from 1826, Dr John Mackenzie and 'Davie' Sillar at Irvine that same year represent a charismatic foundation – dinners arranged by personal friends of the Bard or early acquirers of his books of poetry, held in venues intimately connected with his life with the entertainment. This is the 'Charismatic period' of the Burns Supper: where these men (for it would be inevitably all-male in this period) would meet in an inn or tavern on or around the time of the anniversary of the birth or death of Burns, to eat food in some way redolent of Scotland and to drink through a series of short toasts or songs.

The next phase – or 'Traditional period' – is in the hands of men like Sir Alexander Boswell and Professor John Wilson, where political and literary forces sought to mould Burns's life and works into a coherent 'national' story with a wider purpose, with an underlying element of political messaging. As discussed below in the 1832 London 'Fiasco Dinner' or looking at Wilson's contributions to the 1844 'Festival on the Doon', this contested memory could sometimes be divisive rather than unifying, as left-leaning and liberal aficionados felt squeezed out by an ultimately unsuccessful Tory attempt to arrogate the man and his life as a peculiarly traditional, anti-reform totem. This conservative/liberal tussle over any one party's ownership of the Burns Supper *per se*, died a death as the 1859–1885 period saw the Bard achieve the undisputed status of a popular and national icon, allowing different groups (by age, class, gender, nationality or political belief) to use Burns as a traditional symbol of Scotland as was, as is, and as might be for that particular group and its intrinsic philosophy with freedom of expression, the sheer number of varied events meant that, in the words of Pittock and Whately, 'the cultural memory of Burns was ultimately beyond the control of those who sought to stage-manage it'.[61]

The advent of the Burns Federation in 1885 had an unintended side effect of creating a greater ritual rigidity as its move to standardise coincided with the broader ossifying tendencies towards social formality and etiquette in late Victorian culture. These twin themes saw Burns celebrated with a greater level of formality which when combined with the well-meant (and often successful) wider activities of the Federation created a species of tradition within the Burns movement which did influence the wider celebratory community such that the formal or ritual detail of the Burns Supper became less playful and more defined or rule-like. Thus by 1896, the forms and formats of celebrating Burns often had a more socially conservative bent (even if the political colour of the organisers was more radical or liberal in outlook). Fifty years after that with the return of the troops to Britain after the Second World War in 1946, this approach morphed into a widely held, albeit non-exclusive, *bien pensant* assumption that Burns was a supporter of the Labour Party, a transformation which oddly caused little relaxation of the formal code, save perhaps in dress. So, this long century, from around 1885 to 1996, is described as the 'Bureaucratic period'.

During the late 1990's, an increased populism opened the Burns Supper beyond the formalism of Burns Clubs notably through the establishment of several large-scale Burns Suppers by groups neither being Burns Clubs, nor affiliated to the Burns Federation: such as West Sound Radio (in Glasgow) or the

Scottish Bankers and Lawyers (both in London) who created on-going suppers which were open, mixed gender dinners – oddly turning the original model on its head, with the public dinner (rather than the club) now being the open entry to memorialising Burns over dinner, in a return to a Traditional structure of management without ties or obligations to the Bureaucratic club movement. It was this theme which inspired *The Ultimate Burns Supper Book*, which was written as 'a descriptive rather than a prescriptive guide to organising a Burns Supper'.[62] This latest phase, between 1996 to date, in the history of the Burns Supper can be characterised, as mentioned above, as the 'Global period' which has encouraged a greater freedom in the interpretation and execution of the Burns Supper without losing its core around the haggis, toasting Burns's Immortal Memory and the performance of the works of the poet.

These trends can be traced through the records of the earliest Burns Suppers held. Looking back at the initial days of the phenomenon, on the same day as the Alloway dinner, some members of the Greenock Ayrshire Society (which had been founded in 1795) met under the chairmanship of Neil Dougall (1776–1862) to arrange a dinner for the following birthday of the poet, 29 January 1802. That initial July meeting in Greenock, which also featured an ode to the Bard's memory, traditionally included representations from several of Burns's close friends, including Captain Richard Brown.[63] Dougall, despite having been blinded and maimed in a naval gunnery accident was a musician of some merit. One of his hymn tunes, *Kilmarnock,* is still in today's choral church repertoire and it was he who provided the first Greenock odes. The histories of Greenock Burns Club say that the following poem was used at that first meeting, however it is of a much earlier composition and is in Dougall's collected works as 'being '[w]ritten on hearing read in the Glasgow Courier an account of the poet's death, a few days after its occurrence'.[64] Although there is no contemporary evidence, it is perfectly possible that Dougall could have read this to a wider audience at the initial meeting. Dougall consciously used a Standard Habbie verse form echoing Burns's *Tam Samson's Elegy* with some appeal, emotionally and poetically. It ties the three strands of (1) recognition of Burns as the immortal chief of Scotland's poets, (2) mourning for his untimely death, and (3) attacking the prudes and hypocrites who censure his 'frailties'.

> Ye Scottish Bards, where'er ye be,
> This simple boon, O grant to me,
> Lay bye your books and pens awa'
>   The news gae read;
> An' there in doleful lines ye'll see
>   Rab Burns is dead.[65]

Pursuant to that resolution, the first Burns Supper outwith Alloway was held in the White Hart Hotel, Greenock on 29 January 1802 contemporaneously with the second Alloway Supper which was again held at the Cottage. The format of Greenock's first supper is sketchy, given the loss of the original club minute books, however secondary sources record 'a sumptuous repast', with the chairman John Wright (who is reported to have served in the Excise at the time of Burns) reciting the anniversary ode which was reflects Dougall's deft hymnology.

> But six short years have rolled their circles round
> But six short winters have, in stormy rage,
> Poured down on men their hail and frost and snow.
> Six nimble summers with delightful breeze,
> Their flowery scents have wafted o'er the land
> Since though wert in thy lowly mansion laid,
> And, lost to men, blent with thy mother earth.[66]

The initial links or inspirations from direct contact with the Bard's life, personally or through common Ayrshire roots, through Freemasonry and particularly channelled through Dougall's love of song not only established the series of Greenock anniversary dinners but included a cycle of other club meetings through the year at the Henry Bell Tavern. At some meeting soon after, Greenock adopted the 'three times three' honours at the toast to Burns and, by 1804, as might be expected in a community with such strong links to the Highlands, they appear to have been the earliest diners to include bagpipers as part of the entertainment, albeit with a secretarial comment (still echoed at many Burns Suppers today) that the music was 'to the delight of some and the annoyance of others, who believed bagpipe playing an outdoor exercise'.[67]

Both Allowa' and Greenock Ayrshire groups dined again in January 1803 and in 1804 were joined by the first dinner held beyond the Scottish border, in Sunderland. It is surprising to find that the first Burns Supper to be held in England would appear to have been earlier than Paisley's first meeting. There is a rich tradition of celebrating Burns in the Tyne and Wear area and this likely started at Bishopswearmouth (a part of Sunderland) where a Burns Club is first mentioned in the *Tyne Mercury* newspaper in 1809 in the context of a repeated annual celebration.[68] Interestingly the club makes repeated claims to have held its first dinner in 1804. It is of interest that the *Tyne Mercury* carried a report of the Allowa' Dinner in 1803, with the editorial comment that the news 'will be received with every emotion of pleasure by all his admirers as well in England as Scotland'.[69] Was this the rallying cry that inspired the men of Bishopswearmouth to hold their own celebration in 1804? Unfortunately, no primary source has (to date) been discovered, however newspaper reports from 1809 through beyond 1828 consistently numbering their foundation from January 1804. Their chairman in 1816 captured that tradition:

> It may not be unnecessary to name, now, when
> the birth of the poet is celebrated at several places
> in Scotland, that Sunderland stands first by many

years, in declaring its admiration of that wonderful genius , by commemorating his birth-day being now twelve years since his Anniversary was first celebrated there; and it is worthy of remark, that in consequence of some of his countrymen having been introduced, they caught the flame, and actually communicated it to his native country, where his anniversary has been continued in a similar manner, with a degree of enthusiasm ever since.[70]

The annual repetition of the claim to have commenced celebrations in 1804 thus being 'the parent society of Sunderland, who first set the noble example' seems relatively convincing.[71]

In January 1805, Alloway, Greenock (for the first time independent of the Greenock Ayrshire Society) and Sunderland were joined by a new fourth celebratory group in Paisley. A higher degree of formality can be seen in the preparations for the feast of the Paisley Burns Club largely due to the talent and industry of the able local poet, Robert Tannahill (1774–1810). His verse invitation to attend the dinner was in the style of Burns's *Libel Summons* and was sent to the members of his previous literary club (primarily composed of weavers, often of a radical bent, like himself), and other locals including Masons and fellow townsmen in this new but not uncommon venture.[72]

But I, the servant of Apollo,
Whase mandates I am proud tae follow-
He bids me warn you as the friend
Of Burns' fame, that ye'll attend
Neist Friday e'en, in Luckie Wricht's,   [next, Mrs Wright's Tavern
Tae spend the best-the wale o nichts;   [the pick of nights
Sae, under pain o ha'f-a-merk
Ye'll come, as signed by me, the Clerk.[73]

Like Hamilton Paul, Tannahill actively co-opts Burns to create the atmosphere for the celebration from the very invitation using this highly recognisable poetic style. Burns's poems and politics were hugely interesting to, and influential upon, Tannahill's poetic development. Along with some other Paisley residents, notably William McLaren (a prominent radical Freemason), about 70 men met on 29 January 1805 at the Star Inn to eat and to hear both a prose toast given by the president and an anniversary ode by their clerk and then to join in communal singing of new and old Scots songs. An innovation in the format was that, in addition to the poetry and songs, William McLaren gave a prose oration to complement Tannahill's ode. Tannahill's biographer, Semple describes the first president of Paisley Burns Club as 'possessed of literary ability... his style however, was flowery and grandiloquent, and he was very vain of his abilities'. (The speech is certainly of more historical than rhetorical interest).[74] Unlike Hamilton Paul, however, Robert Tannahill had both poetic talent and an artistic self-doubt. He was part of a wide coterie of friends and versifiers in Paisley and went on to publish a single volume of his poetry and songs by subscription in 1807. His Burnsian friends were always keen to have him compose odes or to review their works and he penned not only the 1805 ode for the Paisley Burns Club and acted as clerk to the association for a year, but also supplied the words for his *Dirge* (which he had written to mark Burns's death) to be set to music for the 1806 dinner and moreover, co-creating an extensive and ambitious multi-part piece of recitation and song in 1807.[75] Initially, and for several years, Tannahill seems to have enjoyed the company of the club and the correspondence with other poets who shared an affinity and affection with Burns. After his 1807 work, however, Tannahill stressed that he had 'no more thoughts of attempting one more line on the subject [of Burns], having done what I reckon sufficient for one hand already'.[76] Yet, in 1809, despite the poet's misgivings, an old but importunate friend who had been elected president of the Paisley Burns Club caused him to promise an ode in for the next dinner, but with 'despair of being able to produce anything half so good as what has been, by different hands, given to the public'.[77] He duly delivered a production for January, but depressed by the rejection of his proposals for publication of a new edition of his poems, Tannahill drowned himself in May 1810. The Paisley Burns Club has consistently and aptly honoured the memory of their first clerk ever since on their toast lists.

Interestingly, the newspaper report of the Greenock dinner of 1810 began with '[t]he anniversary of the birth of Robert Burns, the Ayrshire poet, was celebrated **here for the sixth time**' (emphasis added), which appears to show that the Greenock Club at that time counted its foundation as this evening's separation from the Greenock Ayrshire Society. That adds to the controversy over who is the older club.[78] At some point before 1844, Greenock Burns Club returned to numbering its meetings from the time of the Burns Suppers under the Greenock Ayrshire umbrella, but it is important to reflect that the 1806 club members had valued and celebrated their independent celebration of Robert Burns which occurred on exactly the same day as the Paisley Burns Anniversary Society had its inaugural meeting.

The Burns Supper celebration was now seen as an annual calendar custom each January in Ayr/Alloway, Sunderland, Paisley and Greenock. Although due to weather and the age of the men of Burns's own generation, Alloway (from 1805 to 1808) and Greenock (in 1807 and 1808) reverted to summer dinners around the date of the anniversary of Burns's death in July. It is incorrect to assume that the early Burns Suppers 'shifted between winter and summer, but eventually, due to pressure of work in the farming community during the summer months, it was decided that January was the most suitable time' as the change in season was a simple practical case of older gentlemen finding an unheated cottage uncongenial in January.[79] Interestingly, Paisley and Greenock kept to 29 January as the anniversary for many years, which seems to indicate a lack of correspondence with the Alloway grouping who had corrected that error as early as 1803.[80]

The phenomenon at this point was firmly, but not exclusively, rooted in the western Lowlands of Scotland – with new clubs being established in Kilbarchan (at least by 1806 and possibly even the year before) and Kilmarnock (in 1808).[81] While in Paisley, the Literary and Convivial Association (known as 'the LCA') started holding their own Burns Dinner from 1808. Dinners were also arranged by at least three Scots militia units notably the Argyllshire Militia during their postings around Scotland between 1807 and 1810.

The Renfrewshire Militia also convened a Burns Supper while encamped at Reigate in 1809.[82] In 1814, the Royal Ayrshire Militia formed a 'Burnsonian Society' which met in the Hammerman's Inn, Perth on 25 January and probably in Cavan, Ireland the following year (which is true, would be the first dining celebration of Burns in Ireland).[83] The popularity of Burns within the Scottish military tradition will be discussed in detail below.

Paisley was indirectly involved in the first Burns Supper in the South of England which was held at Oxford University in 1806. The prime mover behind this event was John Wilson (1785–1854), then a student at Magdalen College, but a Paisley man by birth. This was the first speech in a long career of Burns oratory for the writer who would become best-known through his *alter ego* in *Blackwood's Magazine*: Christopher North of the *Noctes Ambrosianæ*. The Oxford dinner was an expatriate affair: 'the meeting, though not numerous, was select and respectable and afforded ample scope for the indulgence of those feelings which the occasion was calculated to inspire'.[84] Samuel McCormick, of Balliol, performed the Ode which is likely to have been written by Wilson, as his poetical talents secured him the first award of the Newdigate Prize later that year, although that ability is not reflected in this particular anniversary ode. Wilson took his degree in 1807, so may have had one further Burns dinner at Oxford.[85]

The use of a Burns theme as an expatriate celebration developed from this with the first recorded Burns Supper in London held at the Queen's Head, Great Titchfield Street in January 1809, where 'many… Members were dressed in the Highland costume, which had a very grand effect'. The musical entertainment was provided by a 'celebrated Highland piper', and by Burns's son Robert on the German flute.[86] Further afield, there are allusions to a dinner held by the Royal Scots when stationed in Bombay, India in either 1810 or 1812, and specific reports on fund raising dinners in Bombay in 1810 and again in 1822 where the Scottish merchant community raised a contribution towards a fitting national monument to the poet.[87]

These convivial evenings could all be characterised as club dinners of between 20 and 100 diners, associations of men more or less intimately linked and where attendance was by invitation or selection. The clubs ranged from the constitutionally formal (typified by Paisley both in the Burns Club and its friendly rival 'The LCA') through to the informal (Alloway/ The Allowa' Club) and were seen as an annual cycle (albeit circumstances might cause an occasional cancellation).[88]

This format seemed incapable of taking root in Scotland's capital, for setting aside the celebrations by militia units stationed in the city, which have been previously mentioned, the nearest celebrations would have been from Dalkeith in 1811 and 1812 which were organised by a local draper, Peter Forbes, one of the small army of men in those days who had published a volume entitled *Poems, Chiefly in the Scottish Dialect*.[89] He invited his friends to dine and commemorate his poetic hero over haggis, verse and an 'oration' through this *Circular Letter* in the form of a Scots Standard Habbie:

YE sons of Scotia, 'tis your turn,
Wi' brimfu' e'e to weep an' mourn;
An deck wi' cypress boughs the yrn,   [urn
Where ye may read,

Your friend an' fav'rite bard, Rob Burns,
   Has lang laid dead.
On Friday next, at seven o' clock,
Some canty, decent, honest folk;   [merry
That aye admir'd what Robin spoke,
   In verse or prose,
Intend to meet to crack an' joke
   O'er Scots kail brose.

It is important to notice the influence of Tannahill here, too: Dalkeith follows Paisley's approach with only the verse invitation, but the entertainment including both a prose 'oration' as well as 'blads o' rhyme'.[90] This club met continuously until at least 1825.

The first meeting of the Dunfermline Haggis Club was in the New Inn '[o]n 25th January, 1812, the members met, and did justice to their "chieftain of the Pudding race," and to Scotland's chieftain in song'.[91] Some of that club's celebratory verse can be found in the published poems of James Aikman.[92] This club dissolved in 1820, re-constituting itself as the Dunfermline Burns Club, while a splinter group, calling themselves the Junior Haggis Club, also held an annual Burns Supper. A third society, The Dunfermline Thistle Burns Club, was also in existence around that time. In 1847 the rival parties concluded that it would 'add more to the hilarity of their meetings if they could with propriety be united into one', which they were, calling themselves The Dunfermline United Burns Club, which celebrated its 200th Burns Supper in 2016.[93]

Glasgow also saw its first Burns Suppers in 1812, with the annual dinner of the Glasgow Ayrshire Society and the Coul Club's January meeting each taking the form of a Burnsian celebration.[94] The Glasgow Ayrshiremen met for many subsequent years to celebrate Burns's birthday at the Black Bull Inn (where the poet had stayed on his visits to their city) and the indefatigable Hamilton Paul provided them with several odes over the years.[95] The Coul Club was founded in 1796 to celebrate the legendary King Cole (traditionally associated with Ayr's Kyle district – apostrophised as 'Coila' in Burns's poetry). Their poet laureate William Glen records a further Burns dinner in 1815, but there is no record of what happened in the Januaries between, or thereafter.[96]

Now the trend gains momentum, with another Burns Club arising in the village of Broughton after Paul's translation to that Parish in 1813 (he would still send an ode to Alloway for the next few years, and he occasionally attended the Glasgow Ayrshire meeting).[97] There are three odes in an anonymous collection of poems based around Lanark published in 1816, but it has not yet been possible to align them with a particular celebration, but this would indicate the existence of another club from 1813.[98]

In 1814, a group of Ayrshire students at Edinburgh University took the bull by the horns and arranged the first Burns Supper by residents of the capital city: on the 'Anniversary of Burns's birth, a number of Airshire Gentlemen, principally Students at the university, partook of an elegant entertainment in St. Andrew's Tavern, Edinburgh in honour of the day'.[99] This club of Ayrshiremen were to meet annually for several decades. Whether inspired by these students, or the wider adoption across Scotland, James Hogg seems to have been the first mover in correcting the absence of a major Burns Supper in the capital city for the indigenous Enlightenment crowd. Hogg wrote to George Thomson in November 1814 that 'I have had it long in contemplation to establish an anniversary dinner to the Memory of Burns in Edinburgh'.[100] Consequently, the following January Burns's friend, Robert 'Bob' Ainslie took the chair with Gilbert Burns acting as croupier (and director of the punch bowl) supported by John Wilson. James Hogg was the main speaker, having chosen Edinburgh over a rival Burns Supper in Dunbar, composing his poem *Robin's Awa* to follow his toast to Burns's Memory.[101]

The evening's entertainments included professional singers performing other songs by Hogg and by Alexander Boswell along with a recitation of William Roscoe's *Elegy*.[102] The arrival of the Burns's marble punch bowl kept them busy 'until the approach of morning admonished the joyous company, that (in a phrase sometimes used by Burns himself), *"There was sic a thing as ga'en to bed."*' There may well have been a third Edinburgh supper held that year by Willison Glass (later a part of the *Noctes* coterie). This minor poet 'kept a small public house in Edinburgh, where he composed punch and poetry – of which the former was by far the best'.[103] His collection of poetry, *The Caledonian Parnassus,* has a rhymed toast to both Burns's memory and his portrait which seems certain to be an occasional ode performed at an 1815 dinner in his own tavern.[104] Certainly, by 1816 the *Scots Magazine* was able to report that 'the birth-day of Burns is celebrated on the same day in most of the towns of Scotland, and also in several places of England'.[105]

The commemoration of Robert Burns in the town where he died started through the project to build a suitable monument in Dumfries by old friends were active in securing subscriptions from Scots and Burnsians across the globe. They were in a position to lay its foundation stone on 5 June 1815. That day's ceremonies commenced with a Masonic procession and concluded with a commemorative Burns dinner where Burns was toasted following a new ode written and recited by one of the guests.[106] In 1816, the Committee's attentions were occupied by the fundraising dinner at Freemason's Hall in London (which will be discussed below) and in 1817, in addition to their fundraising, they resolved to have a dinner too:

> the birthday of Burns should be celebrated by the friends and admirers of the poet in Dumfries as it has been done in other places, it is proposed that the Committee and such friends and admirers of the

> bard as may incline to join them should dine together
> in the King's Arms Inn in honour of the day.[107]

The Mausoleum Committee did not meet to dine in January 1818 but did agree to do so once again on 25 January 1819. It was at this dinner in the Globe Inn, that a group of 34 subscribers agreed to commission a punch bowl from Spode.[108] The bowl (along with ladles, glasses and sundry implements) arrived in Dumfries 12 months later, and received such great approbation at a meeting of the subscribers on 18 January 1820, that the gentlemen present resolved to form the Dumfries Burns Club whose first formal Burns Supper was in the Kings Arms Inn one week later.[109] The Dumfries Burns Club continues to meet to this day and members often say it was 'baptised in the punch bowl'.[110]

Edinburgh's first major Burns Supper in 1815 passed off well, but the attendees decided not to form a club but rather to commemorate the Bard by instituting a triennial public dinner in a grand form. The Ayrshireman and minor poet, Sir Alexander Boswell of Auchinleck (James Boswell's son) was elected chairman of the organising committee with John Wilson again being one of the stewards tasked with arranging the inaugural dinner on 25 January 1816.

> A meeting of the friends and admirers of Burns
> was held in this city last year [sc: 1815], which
> was attended by a number of most respectable
> individuals; but it was not until the present com-
> memoration of the Poet that his memory was cel-
> ebrated in a manner which could be considered
> as the indication of a general national feeling.[111]

The evening heard toasts from Walter Scott and Burns's collaborator, George Thomson. Hogg was slated to appear, but he failed to turn up due to a snow-storm in the headlands. Despite his absence, the arrangers were highly satisfied – even if they were dismissive of the range of dinners across the western counties – and the triennial plan for Edinburgh was forthwith agreed. Accordingly the stewards committee delivered its second event in 1819 in the Burns Supper recorded by John Gibson Lockhart in *Peter's Letters to His Kinsfolk*.[112] While the grandiose claim of Edinburgh being the first national celebration in 1816 has been accepted as a fact by James MacKay and other, more recent commentators, it is an unfairly Edino-centric belief given that there were at least 13 other recorded suppers that year, with a range of over 120 dinner commemorations held over the previous 15 years in other villages, towns and cities. As the *Caledonian Mercury* described it: '[m]eetings are announced in many of the country towns, some of them in England, to celebrate the anniversary of his birth on 25th of this month', while the *Scots Magazine* concluded its article on the Edinburgh dinner: '[t]he birth-day of Burns is celebrated on the same day in most of the towns of Scotland, and also in several places of England' so it is an error to see this particular dinner as a cultural, national turning point.[113]

In many ways, the importance of 1816 was that a large public dinner happened in both Edinburgh and London in the same year. The London Mausoleum Burns Supper was the first major 'fundraiser' dinner for a physical monument or memorial to the poet. The wealthy Scots merchant J Forbes Mitchell had returned from Bombay, heading a committee of fellow Scots in London. Accordingly, 200 men met at the Freemasons' Tavern, London to the noise of bagpipes and the odour of haggis with the Earl of Aberdeen in the chair and proposing the toast to the Bard's Memory. The toast to Burns was combined with the health of Robert Junior who was present as one of the top table guests.[114] Gilbert wrote to Robert's mother about his nephew's speech: 'You would see in the newspapers that your Robert made a good speech and an interesting exhibition at the late commemoration of his father in London'.[115] The highlight of the festivities was the celebratory ode, this time of some real poetic quality having been composed by Thomas Campbell which includes the first enunciation of the trope of a global view of the Scot carrying Burns (or of Burns carrying the Scot) throughout the wide world and meeting in 'delicious revelry' to honour their Bard:

> And see the Scottish exile tann'd
> By many a far and foreign clime,
> Bend, o'er his home-born verse, and weep,
> In memory of his native land,
> With love that scorns the lapse of time,
> And ties that stretch beyond the deep.
>
> Encamp'd by Indian rivers wild,
> The soldier, resting on his arms,
> In BURNS'S carol sweet recalls
> The scenes that blest him when a child,
> And glows and gladdens at the charms
> Of Scotia's woods and waterfalls.[116]

The final toast of the evening was 'The City of Edinburgh and the Society of Burns, established for the triennial commemoration' showing that both London and Edinburgh seemed to have more of a dinner committee than a club or society with Walter Scott, James Hogg and George Thomson being prime movers in Edinburgh and the novelist and adventurer John Galt adopting the title of president of the London committee.[117]

London's next meeting was in the Freemasons' Tavern in 1819 with a recognisably Hamilton Paul-ine format including haggis on the menu (albeit there is no record of the haggis being addressed) with added tartan tokens.[118] HRH the Duke of Sussex took the Chair and Thomas Moore, the Irish poet, was one of the most energetic of the stewards. Moore recorded his observations on the poet's eldest son who again gave the reply to one of the toasts: 'Burns's son was brought forward, and spoke sensibly... too manly and free, poor fellow, for his advancement as a placeman.'[119]

By this time the generation that knew Burns personally, or who read his poems fresh off the press, was dying out thus bringing the Charismatic period of the Burns Supper to its close. At Dumfries Burns Club in 1825, John Syme gave his valedictory speech for his friend, who had been dead for nearly 30 years, calling him 'the most extraordinary man I have ever known'.[120] The last genuinely 'Charismatic' Burns Supper was held in January 1827, following the foundation of Irvine Burns Club by a dozen locals, including two good friends of Burns: David Sillar and Dr John Mackenzie. Their group sought to establish 'a Club, or Society for Commemorating the birth of Robert Burns the Ayrshire poet' with Sillar providing the club's first Immortal Memory, part in verse, part in prose, paying his due honour in this fashion to his friend.[121]

The Burns Supper by now had become a recognised annual festival throughout the United Kingdom through the enthusiasm of the 'Charismatic' clubs. Now it was a well-founded tradition and so the next chapter will look at the second phase of the development of the Burns Supper: the Traditional Period.

CHAPTER FOUR

The Traditional Period

For Scotchmen of this description [sc: the diaspora] more particularly, Burns seems to have written his song beginning, *Their
groves o' sweet myrtle,* a beautiful strain, which it may be confidently predicted, will be sung with equal or superior interest,
on the banks of Ganges or of the Mississippi, as on those of the
Tay or the Tweed.[122]

International Scope

EVEN BY THIS stage, the Burns Supper was neither the sole preserve
of the old Burns Clubs nor, indeed, of the Scots themselves: as
Bueltmann *et al* describe it, 'perhaps [nothing] matches the Burns
Supper as an outward sign of the Scottish diaspora', so within a
few decades, the Burns Supper was not to be found in enclaves
of Scots, but wider in the world they were colonising.[123] To show
how this came about, this chapter will look at this period of
development geographically, as the breadth of early adoption
across the English-speaking world has not truly been focussed
on before. Gathering the ephemeral reports and records of these
far-flung Burns Suppers has been simultaneously enjoyable and
deeply frustrating as research success is driven by the haphazard
extent to which yesterday's newspapers were not used by
previous generations of guests at Burns Suppers as wrappings for
fish suppers the day after. To achieve any form of completeness

will take a 'big data' project where many myriad sources can be combined to show a fuller picture.

The Burns Supper followed in the train of different patterns of Scots diaspora generation: in 'single M' diasporas (constituting migration for life) compared to 'triple M' diasporas (being military, merchant and missionary sojourners) which means a great breadth of potential source material, yet not all of it is equally accessible. As one example, there are relatively few accessible resources in the Caribbean and, given the very high percentage of Scots (and the fact that Burns made plans to emigrate to Jamaica to share the life of those expats), it seems highly likely that there was a pattern of celebrating the Bard's birth beyond 1819 fundraising when £70 from was remitted by Scots in the West Indies towards the Edinburgh Burns Monument.[124] The chairman of the 1820 Burns Supper in Paterson, NJ recalled that 'a friend of mine, who has resided for upwards of 14 years in the West Indies, and who has repeatedly attended the anniversary of our poet's birth in Jamaica, informs me that his works are very common and much admired all over those islands'.[125] Another key diaspora location, Africa, has yielded no early records of Burns Suppers and while 'the clubs and societies celebrating Burns, St Andrew and the Highlands were in evidence from the second half of the [19th] century' it would seem wrong to assume that there was no convivial celebration of the poet on the African continent until the 1859 centenary.[126] On the other hand, the USA, Canada and Australasia all have deeper reportage which allows more concrete analysis.

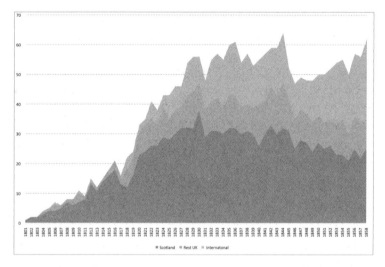

Number of Burns Suppers Held Each Year from 1801 to 1858.

The national and international growth trend can be seen in the table above which captures the total number of references to the holding of Burns Suppers in newspapers, biographies, and other literary works from 1801 to 1858, showing a total of 2,221 in that period. Given the resource data, it is highly likely that this number captured is a significant understatement: but the powerful fact is that this number disproves the theory that the Burns Supper was a Scottish niche affair until the 1859 centenary.

Although the aggregate number of Burns Suppers globally looks to have grown fairly consistently over the period, there were some reverses. There is a dip in the number of newspaper reports in January 1845, which was the first birthday anniversary after the June 1844 Festival; whether the reportage was low because the editors were fatigued with Burns as a newspaper report or indeed the audiences sought a rest in participation is a point of conjecture. Additionally, some venerable clubs in Scotland fell into desuetude for quite long periods, notably Paisley which neither met nor dined between 1837 and 1884 (being unable to reconvene even in 1859 for the Burns Centenary celebrations in the town) and this shows that the desire to remember Burns in a dinner was wider than the number of formal clubs, and moreover, having an established club was no guarantee of permanence. Just as there was a discernible trend of social and ethnic widening of the constituency, there were political angles in how and when the Bard was remembered as the generation who knew Burns personally or shared the introduction of his poetry through his lifetime and early editions died.

So, from around 1826, the Burns Supper was increasingly the preserve of groups of people who saw it as a true tradition – of relatively recent foundation, to be sure – but both as a core part of what it meant to be Scottish (or to share the values seen as characteristically Scottish) and also as a defining character trait of frontier success in a geographical and cultural context wider than the borders of Scotland This chapter addresses the Traditional period of the development of the Burns Supper, first by looking at each of the major international loci up to 1885 (being the foundation of the Burns Federation, which is the start of the Bureaucratic Period) , then will return to the three nations of the United Kingdom over the same timeframe.

The United States of America[127]

Ambrose Bierce's *Devil's Dictionary* includes this iconoclastic definition: 'KILT, n. A costume sometimes worn by Scotchmen in America and Americans in Scotland' and there is a significant danger in any analysis of Scottish diaspora culture within the USA of falling into a general dismissal of their activities as being 'more Scottish than the Scots' and in any case, considering their rituals as probably slightly risible.[128] That is to display carelessness over a US tradition of holding Burns Suppers which is around 200 years old, with dinners had held in the poet's memory in the USA for some years even before venerable clubs like Dumfries and Irvine held their inaugural meetings.

That American readers took to Burns early is already well known.[129] Burns had an established contemporary readership through the new USA which appears as strong in some respects as in his home market. [130] With that installed audience in place, his works began to become part of the performative element of the social life of the diasporan Scots. These Caledonian migrants had founded St Andrew's Societies initially as charities for the relief of fellow Scots who had, by mischance, fallen on fallen on hard times. The first of these, the Scots Charitable Society of Boston, was created in 1657 in the image of the 'Scots Box' of London and sister societies arose through the American colonies through the next century including New York (1756) – which formalised a further obligation within its constitution, equal to its mission of good works, of 'promoting social intercourse amongst Scots'.[131] Their annual cycle culminated in the grand anniversary feast to 'the pious memory of Saint Andrew' on 30 November (which is an interesting example of the difference in 'Scottishness' between the new generation diasporans and those 'at home' where the Kirk would still frown on 'popish' observations of saint's days). Looking back on these festival dinners, they have a great similarity to the format of a modern Burns Supper with haggis and toasts and tartan.

At these particular dinners, Burns's poems are recorded as recitation pieces relatively shortly after his works were pirated and published. At the St Andrew's Night dinner in Pittsburgh in 1790, for example, after the company 'sat down to a haggis and a sing'd sheep's head, and grace being said by gude auld man Mester Scott, the gully was put i' the haggis reeking hot, and ilka ane had his share in his ane trencher' the entertainments and toasts included 'a part of Robert Burns, the Ayrshire plooman, [which] was chanted by Sawney Shaw' and his works feature in regular quotation and song at many of these occasions over the next years.[132]

Wider than that, Scots immigrants appeared hungry for news of a man who was gaining recognition as Scotland's national bard. Across the gamut of newspapers was a consistent run of his poems, anecdotes of his life and wit, and advertisements for new editions of his works such that when he died there was a huge coverage of his obituary and biography in the American papers and journals throughout the remainder of that year.[133]

Commemorating Burns in the 20-year old independent USA really took off after his death when the extant American Scottish societies uniformly added Burns's memory to their already extensive toast lists. Thus, they effectively adopted him as one of the defining attributes of being Scottish: alongside 'hamely fare', fraternal bonding, a lot of whisky and conspicuous tartan. By 1804, newspaper reports of the St Andrew's feasts commonly included a toast – admittedly one of maybe two or three dozen of an evening – along the lines of 'The Memory of Robert Burns, The Ayrshire Poet'.[134]

There was a desire to retain a Scottish flavour particularly around festal dining, as Annette Hope describes it: 'distinctly national forms of feasting have more significance for exiles than for those who remain in the home country'. In this case, the potential cultural clash between the Scot at home and the Scot 'furth of Scotland' (still not an uncommon event) was rarely far away allegiance, mixing broadly Highland and some Lowland concepts within an American context. This sometimes created jarring tones, particularly around the identity and cause for celebration of the poetic icon Robert Burns. One of the earliest Scots travellers to record his reaction to an American toast to Burns at a St Andrew's Night was John Duncan of Glasgow when visiting New York in 1818. Duncan's rather ungracious diary note complained of the absence of the haggis, and at the end of his litany of complaint, he picked on the local customs and accent set against familiar cultural effects:

> We had however a laughable proof of the danger
> of any but Scotsmen meddling with our *Doric* dia-
> lect. A young American... volunteered a recitation;
> – and to evince his partiality for the national bard

> he announced his choice to be Tam o'Shanter. The
> young gentleman however soon betrayed his igno-
> rance of Tam's mother tongue and tortured our
> ears with the most terrific imitation of the Scottish
> dialect that ever I heard... He thought probably
> that if he made very bad English, he could not
> miss making very excellent Scots, and bad enough
> English he certainly did make. Happily he stuck
> fast about half way through, and we silenced him
> with a very equivocal thunder of applause.

Duncan's bitter reflection the following morning was that he 'was sadly mortified last night; – a miserably insipid mixture of Yankeeism and Land-of-Cakeism; neither one nor other, but both spoiled'.[135] That relatively ungracious criticism aside, it should be remembered that these St Andrew's and Caledonian societies are thriving today on essentially the same programme so they evidently still cater to a particular need. However, there was a consideration that, as was happening throughout the British Isles, a free-standing commemoration of Burns and his life and works was called for. At one level, the exclusive membership requirements of the St Andrew's Societies with regard to Scottish birth or ancestry cut off the wider American population from mainstream participation in the act of celebrating Burns, so a more open forum developed, albeit one which unconsciously absorbed some of the traditional tartan baggage from the older clubs. There was a need for a more open venue to enjoy and to praise Burns the Bard and it was the Burns Supper that could meet that need.

The holding of Burns Suppers in Alloway had been reported in the American press in some detail. These reports seem to have been cross posted through various states and territories, opening the concept of dining in memory of Burns around his birthday to the American market.[136] Following peace with Britain after the War of 1812 and the downfall of Napoleon in 1815, we find the formal memorialisation of Burns through the medium of dining expand through the USA leaving the local Scottish charitable associations and communities to dine in November while the newer, wider congregation of Burnsians feasted in January. At the London fundraising Burns Supper in 1818 'the American Admirers of Burns', were toasted with Richard Rush (1780–1859), the US ambassador responding heartily:

> The Strains of Burns were alike intelligible to the people of all nations; and the representative of another nation might therefore, with perfect propriety, participate in the honours shewn to the memory of Burns. In the nation which he represented, his works were universally circulated; and, in the name of the nation, he drank success to the object of the Meeting.[137]

And not just empty compliments either, as the secretary reported that 'several subscriptions were received from [American] gentlemen'.[138] Expatriate Americans were also continuing to sign up to the phenomenon, with a joint Supper being held to commemorate the births of Washington and Burns in Edinburgh on 22 February 1819.[139]

In this reception through a community of 'admirers' we can see clear influence of Hamilton Paul's approach alongside the genre poetry of Scots immigrants, notably Paisley's radical ornithologist Alexander Wilson (1766–1813, who emigrated to the US in 1794) and Ayrshire's Hew Ainslie (1792–1878, emigrated 1822).[140] In those early years, the concept of the Burns Supper was far from alien to the Americans and a combination of Freemasonic brotherhood and blood-brotherhood saw the adoption of the new Burns Supper format as part of the annual social cycle.

There are secondary references to a Burns Supper being held in Baltimore in 1812, as an edition of Burns's *Works* was published in that city that year included a page with Hamilton Paul's 1803 Ode, so it could be that reference was of interest to readers because an event had been held that January, or that it confused memory into thinking that one had been held.[141] There is another case, being an edition of Burns, published in Salem, NY in 1815 which contains an 'Anniversary Ode'[142] which seems to indicate a trend of some momentum.

The earliest newspaper report discovered to date points to the Philadelphia Burns Club's first annual dinner in January 1817.[143] While the duration of the speeches would be impossible for the 21st century posterior, with its 21 toasts, it could only be a Burns Supper as we know it.

We see, through the extensive cross referencing within the toasts and sentiments of the praiseworthy elements of Scots life in America with the works of Burns, the appeal to traditional virtues and values from the 'old life' in Scotland, engrafted onto a burgeoning new US polity. This is very similar to every reported St Andrew's dinner, however, Burns – the real man – has supplanted the nebulous Saint.

The Philadelphia Burns Club held its third Supper in 1819 toasting its brethren in Dumfries who were instituting their new club that same night. This shows an interesting transatlantic correspondence in matters Burnsian: the Philadelphians exhibiting the brotherly loved that their name implies, although definitively positioned as the elder brothers to the Dumfriesians.[144] The Philadelphians, and who better than they to sing about being 'brithers be, for a' that', continued to meet annually and by 1822 had established themselves at the Burns Tavern, Bank Street kept by one Muirhead, under a portrait of the bard by a local artist named Borthwick.[145] Thereafter, there are regular if not annual reports of Burns Suppers in the city from then through to 1859 and beyond.

The chairman of the Burns Supper held in Paterson, NJ in January 1820 was 'proud to remark, that the people of the United States with their wonted liberality, have not been the last to recognise and to do justice to [Burns's] merits... This evening thousands of his admirers are toasting his memory with enthusiasm in various parts of the world, from the Banks of the Ayr to the Banks of the Ganges. Let us join them with equal enthusiasm on the Banks of the Passaic'.[146] The Burnsonian Club of New Jersey subsequently flourished for many years. Its success probably influenced the first Burns Supper to be held in New York City in 1822 where the anniversary odes were written and published by the radical New Jersey lawyer James B Sheys (1798–1857). He was a resident of Paterson, NJ so it is not unlikely that he attended the 1820 and 1821 dinners there and was then moved to create a similar festival across the Hudson where he was to provide a regular supply of Immortal Memory odes. His first work ends with a rousing call to fill and empty the toasting glass:

> Oh Scots' wha' in this westlin clime   [western
> Far frae your native heather,
> Gie honor till the son o' rhyme
> Wha was fair virtue's brither,
> Come – toom the glass again – again   [empty
> To him the Bard an a' that,
> Whase proud heart pour'd the noble strain –
> 'A man's a man for a' that!'

Again, the sentiments of equality (through 'a man's a man') and universality (with a toast to 'Scotchmen all over the globe') are key underpinnings of the tone of the evening.[147] These dinners in New York City were continued year-on-year by differing groups, such that in the late 1820s and 1830s there were at least four independent Burns Suppers in the city and its environs including, from 1825, Shey's group now calling itself the New-York Burns Club (this excludes 'upstate' events such as Albany from 1828). Each of these New York societies happily toasted each other's efforts from the comfortable surroundings of The Blue Bonnet Inn or the Rob Roy Tavern, in Greenwich Village.[148]

These Scots hostelries would be joined later by others, catering to the immigrant, the expatriate and the new generation of 'Scotto-Americans'. Robert Ernst cites a total of nine hotels or inns that were used as Scottish rendezvous in the 1830s: their welcome was emphasised by the daily presence of whisky, haggis and sheep's-head and, no doubt, shared through the celebration of the Bard's Birthday each January.[149] This is a significant concentration given that most Scots towns had a single event with only Ayr/Alloway (holding three or four on average), Edinburgh (three) and Perth (three or four) having a consistent record of multiple annual suppers 'back home'. By 1828, the practice of holding Burns Suppers appears so prevalent that a poem was published in the *National Advocate of New York* 'Addressed to Those Intending to Celebrate the Anniversary of Burns' Birthday', asking that, while the whisky would be used up in the evening, the various poems in celebration of their Bard be kept for posterity so as to 'gie [one's] poor heart mair content/Than chappin' stoups o' whiskey'.[150]

Other US cities had runs of suppers from the 1820s: notable examples being Baltimore, MD (at least from 1825 then running for over a decade as a formal club from 1828 and in Connecticut, at Greenwich (from 1826 for at least three years) and also Tarriffville and New Haven (both from 1833).[151] In 1832, the trend for holding elaborate suppers in honour of Burns in the USA gained the ironic admiration of London's *Athenaeum* magazine a few weeks' later who exclaimed that 'they manage things better everywhere... our American friends did honour to the memory of Burns and the meeting seems only to have been right social and becoming'. No doubt the journalist was contrasting that approach to the controversy over the London 'Fiasco' dinner that year.[152] By the 1840s there were regularly around a dozen Burns Suppers reported in the USA compared to around 30 in Scotland and another dozen across England.[153] By this stage in the development of the Burns Supper, one could transpose the reportage and be unable to tell which side of the Atlantic the celebration had been held.

This extended to the menu, too. The earliest records of a formalised haggis ceremony in a US Burnsian context come from around this time: in Philadelphia (1824) and Baltimore (in 1830) which will be reviewed later.[154]

As the USA occupied its new territories, pioneers carried the poems and celebration of Burns ever westward. Louisville, KY's first celebration was held in 1838 and St Louis, MO and Cincinnati, OH both followed in 1843.[155] Celebrations in Milwaukee started around 1845 through the Robert Burns Society aiming 'to honor both Scotland and the United States'.[156] The Burns dinner first held in California was in January 1846 with repeated events in Ohio's other cities (Columbus and Cleveland) from 1849. A few years later, a Scot wrote to the *Glasgow Herald* to extol Cincinnati Burns Club where membership embraced 'every gentleman who gives literature any study, for no American of literary pretentions in unacquainted with Burns'.[157]

By the 1850s there were many, many events some large public banquets, others more circumspect such as the Sacramento 'Sons of Scotia' who were reported to have 'got tight privately' in a quiet corner in 1856.[158] This effectively proves the point that differing groups could canonically celebrate Burns in different (sometimes opposing) ways. As the Burns Literary and Social Club of Boston inaccurately described their perception of the historical position of Burns celebrations on the continent:

> Prior to 1850, when the Club was first organised, parties had frequently met to celebrate the birthday of Burns; but these celebrations were the results of impulses begotten on occasion, and gratified, to be revivified or not as errant chance might suggest. We know of no associated Burns Club or society before our own had its origins.[159]

This is a statement was challenged by Albany Burns Club who asserted that 'as far as we can find out, our club is the oldest in the country' and (with merit) based their claim on a series of celebrations which began in 1828.[160] The following year 'the anniversary of the birth day of the Scottish poet Burns [on 25 January 1829 which], was celebrated in Albany by a splendid gala at the Knickerbocker Hall. Nearly 400 ladies and gentlemen were present' (this being of note as one of the earliest Burns Suppers which records admitting women and men as equal participants).[161] From the reportage above, of course, Philadelphia, New York or Baltimore had stronger credentials to be the oldest association.[162] Leaving aside controversy over who is the oldest Burns Club (a traditional pursuit common on this side of the Atlantic, too) the analysis shows that, despite the lack of robust and perennial club structures, the annual number of commemorations held across North America grew towards the 1859 centenary of the poet's birth not solely through the expanding Scots immigration, but due to the resonance of themes of the poet's life and works with both the pioneering era in the USA and its increasing debate on democracy and human rights including the tendentious topic of slavery. The anti-slavery movement used set-piece dinners such as at the Burns Club of Rochester in 1849 where the leading abolitionist, Frederick Douglass, pointedly used Burns's poetics in the context of Burns Supper fellowship as a direct reproach to segregation:

> [T]hough I am not a Scotchman, and have a colored skin, I am proud to be among you this evening. And if any think me out of my place on this occasion (pointing at the picture of Burns), I beg that the blame may be laid at the door of him who taught me that 'a man's a man for a' that'.[163]

This was well received by his audience, and subsequent readership. Yet their opponents had no difficulty in commemorating Robert Burns unselfconsciously while being waited on at dinner by chattel slaves, such as in Birmingham, AL in 1857. One of leaders of the South, James Orr of South Carolina, who served as Speaker of the House of Representatives between 1857 and 1859, was famed for his party piece of singing *Auld Lang Syne*.[164]

The expansion in participation was such that the 1859 centenary year saw a total of 61 US Burns Suppers recorded in Ballantine's *Chronicle*, with celebrations in 18 of the 33 admitted States (plus Washington DC) which is, probably, an understatement of the extent of the phenomenon as it was claimed by one Burnsian that '[t]here is a Burns Club in every city and town of the Union'. There are a further ten newspaper reports beyond Ballantine's list. The oldest clubs each organised its annual festival, joined by eight younger clubs but, as in Britain, the Burns Supper was no longer the preserve of the formal Burns Club. Three-quarters of the dinners were events held in a wider community constituency. Of equal importance, only nine of those 70 were composed exclusively of 'Scotchmen' – as the gathering at St Louis, MO heard: 'It was not left to Scotchmen alone to commemorate the man. Burns belongs to no nation. Humanity claims and loves him'.[165]

This echoed the preamble to the Boston Burns Club's booklet on its 1859 gala dinner, which stressed that 'never been any national, sectional, or other bar to membership'. This was further emphasised by the co-opting of many of the great living US authors to the 1859 festivals: in Boston, Ralph Waldo Emerson sat with James Russell Lowell and Oliver Wendell Holmes while New York was entertained by Revd Henry Beecher Ward, William Cullen Bryant, Fitz-Greene Halleck and Horace Greeley.[166] Abraham Lincoln gave the Immortal Memory speech in Springfield, which, alas, was not recorded.[167] The enthusiasm which drew contributions from many of the greatest American poets, rhetoricians and litterateurs of the time can be better understood in the context of a tradition of Burns Suppers stretching back for over 40 years across the States. While those decades had seen some lapses into Brigadoonism, such as the chairman's reported closing remarks in Newark in 1837:

> The night drave on wi' sangs and clatter, till
> the wee short hand ayond the twal; pointed
> to discretionary men, and ejaculated, time is

wearing awa! – so up got the Chairman, and
said, Gentlemen, you have spent a canty night
together, your kytes hae been weel stowed wi'
haggis, and plenty other dainties, – your thrap-
ples have been weel anointed wi the mountain
dew of Glenlivit, – your een hae witnessed laugh-
ing jollity, flitting and playing on ilka cheek, like
the Aurora Borealis aboon your head; – your lugs
hae drank in the simple, but sublime melodies of
the immortal Burns; – in fact, your whole senses,
hae been steeped in the gushing fountain of love
and tenderness, and least ye tint the impression
of this cheering night, you had better depart, in
peace, and love and joy, be wi' you a'.[168]

The adoption of the Burns Supper was typically not 'being more
Scots than the Scots', but rather a positive embrace of Robert
Burns as a poet who spoke to American life and American
interests too.

This breadth of commemoration was to continue even
through the horrors of the American Civil War (1861–1865)
when Burns Suppers remained a regular occurrence in towns
and cities of both the Union and of the Confederacy throughout
the struggle, although often depleted of participants on active
service, such as the Burns Club No 1 of Schuylkill County, PA
several of whose members were 'serving their adopted country
in the army of the Union'.[169] It is a fair assumption that this was
not a unique occurrence: a member of the Cincinnati Burns Club
(Lieutenant-Colonel Patrick of the 5th Ohio Volunteer Infantry)
telegraphed his club fellows while he was in the field and they
at Burns's table, and the Union's 79th New York Volunteer
Highlanders celebrated 'the anniversary of Burnes [sic] birth day'
at least once, at Fredericksburg in 1863.[170] Given that three other
regiments had participated in 1859 celebrations, the 12th Illinois
Volunteer Regiment ('The First Scotch') for the Union and the
Confederate's Union Light Infantry and 1st South Carolina ('the

Highland Guard') may well have had Burns Suppers, too.[171] One of the final set-pieces of that war also had a Burns reference. After General Lee (in full uniform) had signed the terms of surrender over to General Grant, as the former mounted his horse, Traveler, the latter instructed the Union Band to play *Auld Lang Syne*.[172]

After the death of Lincoln, in the complex reconstruction of the federal US, the Burns Supper maintained its growth over the next three decades until the foundation of the Burns Federation, which gained little traction in America, despite Colin Rae Brown's brother who had emigrated to Tennessee, being an Executive Committee member. A mere three clubs joined in its first 20 years.[173] However, that period saw an explosion of associational activities in the Scots (and Scotch-Irish) communities across the USA, through clubs and highland games societies, each of whom would have celebrated Burns Night as part of their annual syllabus.[174] So, by the beginning of the Bureaucratic Perion, and onwards, the Burns Supper was a recognisable calendar festival in every state of the Union.

The tradition of the Burns Supper is effectively as old in America as it is in Scotland and England, nd Murray Pittock describes the USA as one of 'three distinct dominant spheres of geographical operation' of the Burns cult (beside the British Empire and Continental Europe) with a 'framework of memory [around] Burns, the democrat, evidence that Europe was not wholly abandoned to tyranny, absolutism and obscurantism'.[175] To cement that US context, he was, and still is, seen in some ways as an 'honorary American'. Oliver Wendell Holmes accepted a Burns Supper invitation intimating that 'it would give me great pleasure to enjoy the hospitalities of your association on a day which makes half of us poets and all of us Scotchmen'.[176] This judgement was endorsed by Colonel Burns speaking in Dumfries marking his father's centenary in 1859, saying that 'even Americans, wherever we have met them, have exhibited almost as much enthusiasm in responding to the names of the sons of Burns as our own countrymen. (Loud cheers)'.[177]

This sentimental and sympathetic reception of Burns throughout America is summed up by Susan Manning who believes that American 'readers felt that in reading and appropriating Burns' poetry that they had absorbed Burns's character into their own imaginative identities'. Certainly, Americans actively embraced the celebration of the birthday of Burns (in addition to, and over time, ahead of St Andrew's Night) with several towns and clubs holding anniversaries before even Scots towns directly linked to the poet's life. In addition, as will be discussed below, while Hamilton Paul and many early UK adopters made the haggis central to their evenings, the increased theatricality and ritual around the Haggis Ceremony came directly from Burns's US admirers. That appropriation can be shown not only in the tropes of the frontier farmer, the self-educated striver, the honest soldier or the would-be emigrant, but importantly and for decade after decade that appropriation recognised the conviviality and fellowship of the Burns Supper which is as strong a tradition in the US today as in Scotland.[178]

Canada

The assimilation of the Burns Supper followed a similar fashion in Canada, having their own, albeit more secondary, history of access to Burns's works in print ranging from a possible subscription edition in Quebec in 1789 through to a steady stream of imports over the following decades.[179] In another similarity, the oldest charitable institutions in the Canadian provinces were typically founded by Scots emigrants and traders. The first of these was the North British Society (known as 'the Scots Club') in Halifax, Nova Scotia, founded 1768 and followed by the St Andrew's Societies in New Brunswick, Quebec, and Ontario between 1798 and 1840. Unlike their sister associations in the USA, there seems to have been less of an emphasis on keeping up the festival for St Andrew until around 1822–1827 (perhaps to some extent due to the inclement weather prevalent in November) and the earliest dinners of a truly Scots flavour were those of the Beaver Club where the hard-living fur traders met in Montreal from 1785 in 'a blend in highland and fur trading culture. Meals were piped in and plenty of whisky, along with other alcoholic beverages, was consumed' however toasting seems not to have been as important as song at those parties.[180] As St Andrew's night dinners gained momentum in Canadian society they, too, added Burns as a subsidiary toast. Montreal first records 'The Memory of Robert Burns, our Rustic Bard' and the singing of *Auld Lang Syne* in 1820 and both the toast and the song featured regularly thereafter.[181] It is interesting to speculate how the Ayrshire author John Galt may have celebrated Burns in Canada while acting as secretary to the Canada Company between 1824 and 1829, as he makes no mention of this in his *Autobiography,* but given his enthusiastic involvement in London, some form of celebration might well have been undertaken on his watch while he was resident in Ontario.

Tracing the expansion of the Burns Supper as a Canadian tradition is impeded by the relative paucity of newspaper materiel when compared to its southern neighbour and perhaps a suggestion, that they were the kinds of occasion which might well be kept out of the newspapers. During this period, the word 'respectable' was often journalistically applied to reports of other Burns Suppers in other countries, Michael Vance looks back at this period in Canada's history seeing Scottish affinity as more than conviviality, but rather as 'elite all-male drinking clubs that met [on St Andrew's Day or for Burns] for a bacchanalian dinner... marked by heavy drinking and speeches from invited and local worthies'.[182] Certainly, the temptation to have such an evening to break the monotony of the long Canadian winter could easily be forgiven, as Elizabeth Waterstone says, the 'Burns Night Supper... pulled rural communities together in coldest January [... providing] much-needed warmth'.[183]

There are suggestions of a Burns Dinner being held in Toronto in January 1834 with a Burns Supper in Newfoundland shortly after.[184] The first printed record is a meeting of the Ramsey Library Society (of Kingston) who met to celebrate Robert Burns's birthday in 1836 on the day of their Annual General Meeting.[185] The toast list shares a great deal with the dinners that were happening that year in the USA although featuring a mere 14 toasts.

Four years later there was a dinner arranged by the gentlemen of the Montreal St Andrew's Society who purchased Highland Mary's bible in 1840 and subsequently donated it to the Trustees of the Burns Monument in Alloway. The emigrant poet, Revd William Wye Smith, who was a fanatical Burnsian and a Highland 'mariolater', founded a Burns Society to commemorate the anniversary in the appropriately named Dumfries Township in 1846.[186] In 1851 the first free-standing Burns Supper was held in Montreal, arranged by the local Curling Club (by its own tradition, the oldest organised Scots society in British North America, dating from 1807).[187] By the first centenary year of 1859, this handful of dinners had expanded to 37 recorded celebrations across the Canadian provinces which, interestingly, included a relatively high involvement of women with nine dinners where ladies ate with gentlemen and three others where they observed the speeches.

This tradition was more than maintained over the second half of the 19th century and, despite there being but a single Canadian club joining the Burns Federation (number 25, Winnipeg St Andrew's Society – 1886) prior to 1900, Canadians celebrated Burns as widely as anyone by the beginning of the Bureaucratic period.[188]

India

The Burns Supper was evident in the Eastern Hemisphere too at least in the parts under the control of Great Britain in the 19th century.[189] Under the flag of the Honourable East India Company, local societies sprang up as the Scots landed in new colonies, entrepôts and encampments throughout the growing Indian Empire. On the civilian side, the (mainly Scots) merchants of Bombay (now Mumbai) in 1810 had at least one dinner which met to contribute to the appeals for cash to support Burns's widow and children and the officers of the Royal Scots reportedly had an early Supper in 1810 or 1812 while on Indian service. The mercantile interests in Bombay later gathered in support of the monumental projects in Edinburgh and Alloway, raising some £300, and were accordingly recognised in a particular toast at the gala fundraiser in London in June 1819'.[190] The other two Presidencies, Madras (now Chennai) saw 'The Memory of Burns' toasted by its Highland Society in March 1814 while Calcutta (now Kolkata) saw a Scots festivity based on Burns's birthday in 1822.[191]

As in the Americas, St Andrew's Societies in the three principal cities of provided the social highlight of the expatriate Scots year in November, albeit the society's energies were less effective than its North American equivalents, as the run of dinners appears to have been regular but not annual.[192] The enthusiasm reportedly was as strong when they did occur on the sub-continent: 'There is no mistaking the national attachment that is so strong in the Scottish character.... Scottish festivals are kept with Scottish feeling on... India's coral strand'.[193] As elsewhere, after his death, the toast to the memory of Burns joined the haggis, kilts, pipes and endless toast lists as part of a wider Caledonianism.[194]

Some of the colonial dinners had the additional boost of having a Burns descendent in tow with the younger Burns sons, William Nicol Burns and James Glencairn Burns holding commissions with the Honourable East India Company before ultimately retiring as Colonels to Cheltenham. The combination of early patronage of the Governor-General (a leading Freemason) and his wife (an Ayrshire heiress) added the sons of Burns to the high percentage of well-educated Scots officers and civil servants.

They were likely to see their father's name regularly honoured at dinner as in this recollection from 1818: 'I should like to have seen Elphinstone on that occasion rise to propose "the immortal memory of Burns," and hear him add the words, "success to his offspring", for a son of Burns was there and sung one of his father's blythest lays'.[195] James's love of his father's memory and songs at this period must have been well-known, he wrote to congratulate the Dumfries club on its foundation, requesting 'that a quart stone bottle might be filled with punch out of the new bowl and despatched to him at Calcutta.'[196]

Sir John Malcolm (1769–1833), the Scots soldier and administrator 'never left home, even for a few days, without carrying with him Burns's Poems, Burke's Maxims and the Book of Common Prayer'.[197] He first met Lieutenant JG Burns that same year, describing him as a 'fine young man' making him sing his father's songs for his supper 'which quite delighted' him. They were to meet again when he chaired the 'Fiasco Supper' in London in 1832.[198] The army officer turned educator, Professor David Lester Richardson recorded his feelings on hearing Burns's youngest surviving son sing his father's songs to an audience in India. In this aisling-like poem, 'the past' is equally Burns and Scotland which have ventured out to meet the 'wanderer' and 'exiles' on their own land, but the dream becomes embodied through the literal son of Burns, now himself a wanderer, and uplifting the other wanderers in the singing of the exiles' favourite songs.

The *Calcutta Journal* carried reports of the 1819 London Burns Dinner which shows a level of local interest, unfortunately, records about Scottish activities in the Indian subcontinent during this period are limited, although *Blackwood's*, in its customary voice of Edinbourgeois authority, reported in March 1820 that '[t]he anniversary of Burns's birth is fondly commemorated by his countrymen in India' and given the regular references to India and the Ganges in the multiplicity of odes at Scottish Burns Suppers during this period, it seems certain that the tradition was carried on across the sub-continent.[199] One historian of the colonial poetry of the period captures this atmosphere; '[t]o imagine the "sound" of English in Calcutta [at the turn of the 19th century] is to imagine the language not of Oxbridge but of Burns'.[200] And as with other diasporan communities, *The Calcutta Journal* through the 1830s records a toast to Burns at the city's St Andrew's Night dinner while there are numerous chance references to his memory being honoured at Masonic dinners and festivals.[201]

Certainly, there is a poem published in 1823 entitled *Lines: Written for The Anniversary of Burns's Birth-day 1823*, which indicates some commemorative activity in the city that year.[202] The number of military and mercantile Scots present on the sub-continent during and after the periods of service of the Burns sons would certainly add a likelihood of celebration. Colonel George Vetch (1785–1873) was an old comrade of JG Burns who acknowledged him as 'the author of many a Burns birth-day ode'. His (pre-1844) *Lines Written for The Anniversary of Burns's Birth-Day in Bengal,* uses the Standard Habbie, although in standard English:

> Afar, where Scottish exiles pine,
> 'Neath polar night, or tropic shine,
> Genius of Burns! O then 'tis thine
>   To hover o'er,
> And with the songs of auld langsyne,
>   Their homes restore.[203]

India in 1859 was recovering from the trauma of the Indian Mutiny, so it is not totally surprising that there was only one single report of a civilian Burns Supper in India in Ballantine's *Chronicle*, the Masonic Supper and Ball in Bombay which did proceed in a 'the scene seemed one of enchantment rather than reality'.[204] It is fair to assume, that it is unlikely that this was the only event on the sub-continent, particularly with the level of troop activity.

Certainly, Surgeon General Don recalled many years later, while speaking at Burns night after his retirement in England, that he and fellow officers held a mess Burns Supper that year:

> in Central India... engaged in stamping out the embers of the great Mutiny; yet under such circumstances, they did not overlook the celebration, for a few kindred souls met together, toasted the lad that was born in Kyle, and sang 'Auld Lang Syne' in the very jungle's depths.[205]

So it would appear that smaller groups of Scots would dine on the day as the established custom earlier recorded in *Blackwood's*.[206] A number of orators at Scottish dinners in 1859 directly mentioned the activities of Scots soldiers in the Indian campaign, calling imperial imprecations like 'Scotchmen, worthy of the country of Wallace, and of Bruce, avenging 'neath India's burning sun, their murdered and outraged kindred'.[207]

The formality of Burns Clubs appears to have been a late adopted phenomenon in this region, with the Cawnpore Burns Club being briefly affiliated to the Burns Federation (as number 87) in 1896.[208] In later years, there were formal suppers in Calcutta from the late 1920s at least, with a Calcutta Burns Club being formally inaugurated in 1926, affiliating to the Burns Federation that same year as number 355, but records are scattered.[209] Elizabeth Buettner, looking back at family archives in her 2002 paper says that 'Burns Night never attracted the same public attention [as St Andrew's Night] and tended to be smaller and more private affairs' but that seems to be more from the perspective of the wives and daughters of colonialists, where the men may have adopted a more masculinist approach to Burns Suppers contrasted with a greater female participation in the balls and dinners of St Andrew's tide.[210]

Fragmentary as these references are, it points to a consistent and mainly masculine culture of celebrating Burns in smaller gatherings across India throughout the 19th century.

Australia

There is a greater selection of contemporary newspaper reports from Australia which allow a more nuanced look at the way in which the phenomenon was received and propagated in the early British colonies of the Antipodes. Scots emigration to New South Wales was initially very light, only gaining momentum following the governorships of two Scots: Lachlan Macquarie (served 1810–1821) and Thomas Brisbane (1821–1825).[211] Scots were very much a minority in the convict class, with immigrants drawn to farming in New South Wales (and subsequently Victoria) and by the fisheries in Van Diemen's Land. The concept of the Burns Supper came into Australia mainly through Scots famers, fishermen and freemasons.

The first commemoration of Burns which is recorded is in Van Diemen's Land (now Tasmania) in 1825, where an absolutely typical evening was spent in White's Inn, Launceston as over whisky and haggis the immortal memory was pledged to the sound of Burns's songs.[212] The people of Launceston were to carry on celebrating Burns in suppers and also in picnics (January, of course being in the Australasian summer season) for at least the next 50 years.[213]

Widespread toasting of Burns again appears to have gathered momentum through the colonies' St Andrew's societies, with the toast to Burns growing in importance from 1820, sharing the international tradition of including the 'Memory of Burns' at St Andrew's feasts as a form of public celebration of the Bard.[214] Again, Freemasonry provided another vector of transmission. There are several newspaper reports of the 'memory of Brother Robert Burns' being given at Masonic dinners in the late 1820s and carrying on through the 1830s.[215] By November 1835 in Sydney (at the Burns' Head Tavern) after the principal toast to 'the pious memory' of the Patron Saint: 'the immortal memory of Robert Burns, was drank in solemn silence'.[216] It was through this tradition that the first convivial dining commemoration of

Burns on the Australian mainland occurred in January 1840. The Freemasons of Sydney resolved to establish a freestanding celebration 'to commemorate the birth of our late brother Burns', and the event appears passed off well for it was held again in January 1841 this time 'with a private band in attendance'.[217]

There are ghost references to a Sydney 'Burns Festival' in 1835 and there was a lecture (with undefined refreshments) on Burns's works which was held on his birthday in Melbourne in 1839 by the Reverend James Foster with a similar talk by James Rae in Sydney to co-celebrate the day of the Doon Festival in 1844.[218] The combination of these events and the Mason's well-known tradition meant that from 1845, independent Burns Suppers were arranged in local communities by organising committees rather than formal clubs, as Burns activist and scholar Gordon Ashley described it, 'all without a single kilt or sporran to show for it'.[219] The London press commented favourably on the concept: 'A Burns Festival in New South Wales – it is interesting to find the name of the Scottish poet thus honoured in the most distant quarters of the globe'.[220] Melbourne/Port Philip joined Launceston and Sydney with a virtually annual series of Burns Suppers from 1845 (and possibly earlier, given that the first Port Philip settlers came from Launceston).[221] Around 300 men dined (on 'cock-a-leekie, hotch-potch, sheep's head broth and haggis') and toasted Burns at the Queen's Theatre in 1846 drawing the press comment that '[the Burns] festival appears to have been got up with great splendour [this year]'.[222] It was seen as important to be able to put on a good show, the following year's festivities being described in the newspapers as 'excellent, the only falling off being in the haggis, which was not of very first rate quality'.[223]

Merri Creek started its own celebrations at least in 1847[224] and Geelong followed from 1848.[225] As these events became more frequent, a unique concern in the colonisation of Australia (and in New Zealand as well) was to avoid destructive nationalistic competition between the three home kingdoms, as reported in the Australian press in 1845, where confining the Burns dinner to Scots resulted in 'an unhappy division of feeling created on a subject otherwise claiming and receiving sympathy from all.'[226] The Scottish community in Melbourne responded promptly to the concerns by broadening the invitation list to all comers, and they continued to hold Suppers in increasing numbers, peaking at 'between 400 and 500' in 1848, with an inclusive 'colonial' message in their celebration albeit garbed in the trappings of Scotland. Burns was both a Scot but an exemplar for dealing with the hard colonial life: what might be thought of as 'The Colonial's Saturday Night'.[227] This directional change mirrored the London dinner and some of the US suppers in particular and is an important step in moving away from a limited or 'clannish' use of the Burns Supper, or perhaps even, escaping a Scottish *nostalgia-fest* to find a global conception of the celebration. Again, from contemporary newspaper reports: 'the festival being no longer exclusively Scotch, the attendance will consequently embrace many representatives of the admirers of Burns from other lands.[228] Of course, while the guests were increasingly heterogeneous, the fare and festival remained as fully Scottish as could be managed with increasing incidence of tartan and bagpipes as the tradition extended. So the evening could at times remain almost parodically 'Scotch' to the non-Caledonian attending. As Tyrell describes the trend, '[w]ith the passing of the years, Highlandism and the Burns cult were often fused to produce hybrid rituals of nationality'.[229] In Queensland, the challenge over inclusion or seclusion led to the creation of two Scottish societies with differing aims and attitudes in the 1850s. The Scottish Society which 'had a philanthropic focus... its funds for needy Scots being limited... it tended to be ethnically exclusive' and the Brisbane Burns Club which 'was renowned for its welcoming attitude to all comers, Scots and non-Scots alike'.[230] Burns thus became the patron not solely of a national diaspora, but of a colonial, venturing class.

This tradition set within the context of colonial growth set the stage for Australia's participation in the 1859 Birth Centenary celebrations, the *Melbourne Argus*, which consistently reports local Burns Suppers over the years, looked forward to the anniversary around the corner: 'Festivals like these, if wisely celebrated, are the secular Sabbaths of our Calendar. Men of all creeds and all classes can associate in an act of "hero-worship" without impiety and without diversity of sentiment'.[231] The centennial kicked off on Ne'erday with the Geelong Highland Society's annual highland games (including, not only the traditional pursuits, but a silver medal for the calculation of simple and compound interest and commissions), followed in the evening by a 'Nicht wi' Burns'.[232] The anniversary day itself was marked officially when the Legislative Council of Victoria adjourned early as a 'graceful tribute to the memory of Burns'.[233] Unofficially, the diasporan community celebrated broadly with fellow colonists in the traditional form such that 'in every city and town and hamlet, the name and fame of the poet have been proclaimed'. There were three separate dinners in Sydney ('notwithstanding the Cricketers' dinner and other counter attractions' which might have been expected to lure attendees away), and with suppers reported by Ballantine in each of Geelong, Melbourne, Tarrangower and Yaas, and with around a further dozen also recorded in various newspapers.[234] Of course, 'down under' sees the seasons reversed, so Burns Night was part of a summer season starting at Hallowe'en, to St Andrew's, Hogmanay and Highland Games in January. This saw a boom in Caledonian clubs and other Scots associations in the 1880s each of whom included the remembrance of Scotland's poet.[235] That associational network assured an albeit limited Australian participation in the Bureaucratic period of Burns Suppers, with Sydney Burns Club (founded 1880) and Adelaide South Australian Caledonian Society (1881) being early affiliates, the 16th and 23rd, to the Burns Federation in 1886.[236]

New Zealand

As with India, the Antipodes had direct links to the Burns family's story. One of the leaders of New Zealand's Scots immigration being Gilbert's son, the Reverend Thomas Burns (1796–1871) who helped found Dunedin in 1848.[237] Although his strict moral leadership was not conducive to an increase in convivial celebration of his uncle's fame, he was supportive of the celebration through the singing of his uncle Robert's songs, if not the reflection on his life or promotion of his habits.[238] The local Burns historian, James MacIndoe, confidently reported that: 'from the first year of the settlement [1848], when the poet's birthday came round there was a regular recognition thereof, whether publicly notified or not'.[239]

The sister colonial towns and cities of New Zealand had been created under less watchful eyes and fraternal societies had already emerged by the era of the Reverend Thomas's ministry, with the first such dinner being in Wellington for St Andrew's Night in 1840.[240] By 1850 the newspapers in Auckland reported that 'the memory of Burns' was a major toast for both the town's Masons in June, and also for the St Andrew's Society in their November feast.[241] Certainly, by 1855 the papers were reporting formal Burns Suppers in Dunedin which cemented an annual tradition of 'paying a Tribute of Respect to the memory of the departed poet, whose manly integrity and love for his country has endeared him to every true and generous hearted Briton'.[242] This tradition at first was carried not by formal Burns Clubs, but by informal associational groups whose sole aim was the holding of an annual convivial festival for Burns. Occasionally there were other forms of remembrance, including public lectures on the poetry of Burns complimenting the tone of the dinners.[243] A key influencer of this trend appears to have been James Barr (1818–1889), a Paisley born poet and a likely member of either Paisley's LCA.[244] He emigrated in 1852, became a farmer and more importantly in his eyes, a founder and the laureate of both the Burns Club of Otago (in 1861) and the Caledonian Society of Otago (in 1862). As Patterson *et al* summarise it '[d]esignated Burns clubs were latecomers in the overall development of New Zealand's Scottish associations' but 'as a result of Burns's wide appeal, anniversaries in his name saw a cosmopolitan group of settlers from all backgrounds partaking of haggis and whisky... which underscores not only the inclusiveness of Burns's anniversaries, but also of the Burns clubs who organised them'.[245] In this fashion within New Zealand society as Tanja Bueltmann summarises it: 'it was Robert Burns whose birth became the national-day proxy most commonly celebrated'.[246]

It is interesting to observe that, as seen in the earlier development of the Burns Supper across the Tasman Sea, the Burns Clubs in New Zealand 'maintained an outward orientation' and did not see their role as exclusively serving the Scots diasporic community, but sought a wider audience of hard working colonists who found resonance in the message of Burns's poetry and solace in a convivial evening.[247]

Ballantine has no reports at all from New Zealand, perhaps the package of newspaper clippings and reports was lost on the long route to the motherland. James McIndoe confirmed that there was a banquet in Dunedin's Commercial Hotel in 1859.[248] Local press also captured wider activity: the inhabitants of Canterbury, Christchurch and Lyttleton agreed to amalgamate their individual plans for dinners into one grand anniversary event 'in doing honour to the memory of Scotland's National Bard, the poet Burns'.[249] One further event in Wellington, which sounds entirely traditional is captured in a classic newspaper advertisement guaranteeing guests 'Real Scotch Haggis' and 'Genuine Mountain Dew'.[250] [251]

So, while New Zealand's adoption of the Burns Supper appears to have occurred relatively close to 1859, after that and in all likelihood because of the level of local press coverage of the many events globally its popularity grew significantly. Certainly by 1874 the Scottish vocalist David Kennedy described his season in

Dunedin as an extended Daft Days, stretching from 'Boxing-Day to Burns's Birth-Day' describing his concert of Scots songs as 'like "taking coals to Newcastle" to bring Scottish Sentiment and song and story into a community where nationality was so pronounced'.[252] That national sentiment, and possibly the sheer distance between New Zealand and Scotland, drove the strongest associationalism amongst the Scots community, with Bueltmann reporting over 100 Scottish societies operative in 1900, with a further 50 by 1930.[253] Interestingly, however, despite that intensity, there was no greater interest in the nascent Burns Federation when compared with the other dominions, neither Otago Burns Club nor Thames Auckland Burns Club (founded 1877) chose to affiliate with only Auckland Burns Club & Literary Society (founded 1884) joining as number 19 in 1886, with Dunedin Burns Club following later as number 69 in 1894 and which alone remains a federated member in 2018.[254] In contrast, the local press have consistent reports over the years of many Burns Suppers held across both the North and the South Islands.

Hong Kong and the Far East

It is hard to imagine an absence of Burnsian celebration in the early history of Hong Kong given its dynamic Scots founders. We know from reports of the London Monument committee that the Scots in nearby Penang raised £60 towards that project in 1819 and it could be that a dinner and associated toasting the poet's memory was involved in encouraging donations, but no records have yet been found.[255] There are, however, records of St Andrew's Dinners arranged by the powerful Matheson trading family on board one of their ships in 1832 and with annual dinners at the family residence in Canton in subsequent years.[256] Over time these dinners moved from Matheson's HQ to the Hong Kong Club, then falling under the aegis of the Hong Kong St Andrew's Society at its 1882 foundation. They added a Burns Supper a few years later possibly when the noted Burnsian Dr James Cantlie arrived there in 1886 to teach medicine in.[257] These dinners remain highlights of the Special Administrative Region's social year even years after the Union Flag was hauled down by the Black Watch as the Empire closed to the strains of *Auld Lang Syne*.

The Scots of Singapore held their first St Andrew's feast and ball in November 1835 and events followed fairly regularly thereafter, although the only reference yet to hand of a toast to Robert Burns was in 1836.[258] As in other colonial settings, the Freemasons remembered Brother Burns of Tarbolton and Dumfries such as the freemasons of Lodge Zetland in the East using his songs at their harmony in the late 1840s in Singapore.[259] However, none of these groups seem to have stimulated an independent Burns Supper.

Ballantine records no reports of events held in the Far East during the 1859 celebrations although there are many references to Scots to be found out there, in speeches made at Scottish dinners, who were assumed to be celebrating Robert Burns as conscientiously as their home-based cousins.

Interestingly, Mackay in his history of the Burns Federation records no affiliates from this region, with the Hong Kong St Andrew's Society only affiliating after a century, as number 1048 in 1984 and its Java sister, the year before as number 1033. This seems to corroborate the view that, as a primarily sojourner class, the Scots of Hong Kong and the Far East had less of a requirement or desire to create wider community activities and gatherings preferring as Graeme Morton describes it, 'smaller and more private affairs for the cultivation of business and personal links'.[260] Burns Suppers were evidently held, but by being focussed on intra-company (or regimental) occasions effectively amongst closed groups, it was only really from the 1880s that the celebration seems as common as elsewhere, leading to a parody review of the Scots Community celebrating Burns in January 1913:

Scots wha hae on haggis fed,
Scots wha Burns hae seldom read,

Welcome to a muckle spread
   An' a michty spree.
Wha wad scorn the Mountain Dew?
Wha wad swither tae get fou?   [drunk
Wha wad daur be sober noo?   [dare
Let him turn and flee![261]

Scots, anecdotally and almost archetypally thrived in the imperial network of the Far East. There are simply few direct references to formal Burns Suppers, but given that Bueltmann records the following Scottish communities or associations extant in 1910, it is almost certain that there are many Burns Suppers yet to be discovered: Singapore; in China: Hong Kong, Tientsin (now Tianjin), Shanghai, and Weihaiwei (Weihai); in Indonesia: Batavia (Jakarta); in Malaysia: Kuala Lumpur, Ipoh, Penang, and Malacca; in Japan: Kobe, and Yokohama; in Myanmar: Rangoon (Yangong); in Thailand: Bangkok and in the Philippines: Manila.[262]

Africa

The history of the celebration of Robert Burns in Africa is harder to determine but it appears to have taken root later than in other colonial spheres, only flowering in the 1880s. This could partly be attributed to the early spread of Scots emigration to South Africa being much smaller than to other colonies with no sustained mass immigration until the 1870s.[263] Another factor is the scarcity of primary source materials particularly newspapers which are only held in local archives and need visiting.

That smaller emigration pattern has led several commentators to make the point that 'it has been conventional to say that Scots in the Cape and other territories constituted mainly a professional elite' who would have less of a need perhaps of the wider social need for bonding and mutual support than a more heterogeneous and less socially and economically secure

community.[264] That being said, there was a St Andrew's Friendly
Society founded in Cape Town in 1820, which was still holding
quarterly meetings in 1828.[265] Records are sparse, but it would
not be too much of an assumption that these Scots gentlemen
such as Hogg's friend Thomas Pringle, a poet and abolitionist
who lived at the Cape in the 1820s, could easily have toasted
Burns during the extensive toasting on the patron's day (and
maybe on the bard's day, too).[266]

The first definitive record of a St Andrew's Dinner on the
continent is one held at Port Elizabeth in the Eastern Cape in
November 1851 and marked the inauguration of a local St
Andrew's Society which would hold an annual dinner before
mutating into the still extant Port Elizabeth Scottish Association
in 1882.[267] There was a Burns Centenary Dinner in Durban,
Natal in 1859, which is missed in Ballantine's *Chronicle*, but
it does record reciprocal greeting to South African dinners,
along the lines of the invitation to '[c]all in at the Cape of
Good Hope, and our emigrant brothers and sisters will be seen
commemorating [the birthday of Burns]'.[268]

At the 1859 St Andrew's Day celebration in Durban 50
Scots men formed a 'Scotch Volunteer Rifle Corps' with a
'special uniform of green doublet, tartan trousers and a forage
cap with a band of Rob Roy tartan round it. The new corps was
led by its piper in January, 1860 for martial duties on the parade
ground and in field exercises after which 'on the 25th the Scotch
Company, C[ape] R[oyal] R[ifles] met at a dinner to celebrate
the birth of Robert Burns'.[269]

Tanja Bueltmann has found an early reference to a
Caledonian Society in Durban in 1862 which could have
sprung up in the aftermath of the 1859 Burns Centenary and
the volunteer's enthusiasm, and then two other clubs back in
the Cape Province: The Kaffrarian Caledonian Society of King
William's Town (founded 1870) and the East London Caledonian
Society (1876).[270] Prompted by these early societies, there was
a period of significant growth in associational activity with the

various Port Elizabeth societies combining at a Burns Supper in 1882 to form the Scottish Association. During the tensions of the Boer Wars, these societies would appear to have suspended all meetings, and it seems to have taken until January 1900 for first formally named freestanding Burns Club to meet in which was in Natal, rather than the Cape, in Johannesburg, and which joined the Burns Federation (as number 154) in 1906.[271] Other Burns Suppers were held in Nairobi (Kenya), Bulawayo (now Zimbabwe) and in Mafeking (Mahikeng), South Africa around the turn of the 20th century.[272]

Once again, these few recorded Burns Suppers probably understate the popularity of the celebration given the growth of Scottish associations across Africa. Bueltmann records a boom in the formation of Caledonian Societies across the Anglophone communities of sub-Saharan Africa but also other in colonial cities beyond the bounds of the British Empire with significant merchant and mining cadres of Scots, such as at Delagoa Bay (latterly Lourenço Marques and now Maputo) in Angola.[273, 274]

Decades later, just as Burns was used by the abolitionist movement, so his view of 'a man's a man' found resonance with the supporters of the African National Congress in its long walk as supporters held fundraising Burns Suppers during the 1970 and '80s. These efforts were recognised by a gala Burns Supper which was held in South Africa House, London in 2002 with Oliver Tambo as the principal guest speaker.[275]

Back to the United Kingdom

It is, therefore, necessary to re-evaluate academic perceptions such as Leith Davis's statement that '[a]part from two dinners in Edinburgh and London in 1816 that James Mackay suggests hinted at a "Burns celebration on a national scale," it was not until 6 August 1844 that there was a wider celebration of Burns'.[276] Burns Suppers were already well entrenched by 1819 and so both Edinburgh, 1816 and Alloway, 1844 should be seen in that wider context.

There appears to have been a widely held belief that the Burns Supper was not just about conviviality, there had to be a valuable commemorative point to it as well. Looking back at 1816, 'several admirers of the sweet carols of the Scottish Bard' in Newcastle-upon-Tyne had entertained an unnamed friend from Haddington to dinner on Burns's anniversary, joining their brethren in Sunderland in dining on the Bard's birthday. Thus, they started a tradition in that city which would run for over 50 consecutive years as part of a vibrant annual culture across north-east England. The Novocastrians published the first collection of Burns homage poetry in a pretty booklet in 1817 after their second dinner:[277]

> Bless'd be NEWCASTLE Birkies then,   [chaps
> Who yearly mind Poet Robin's pen,
> And meet, with cordial treats to spen'
>   Some honest pence:
> This action shows how to be rich
>   O' common sense.[278]

The celebration of Burns by 'the Geordies' seems to have commenced through the efforts of John Mitchell (1772–1819) who was the founder and editor of the *Tyne Mercury* newspaper, an Ayrshireman who had learnt the trade of typesetting at John Wilson's press in Kilmarnock, including (it is claimed) laying the press for the Kilmarnock Edition.[279] It is in this cross-border context, that when Cadell and Davies were corresponding with Gilbert Burns over the enlarged edition in 1819, they sought 'an account of the annual commemoration of his birthday in Scotland and in England'.[280]

It is important to stress the inclusion of both Scotland *and* England, for following the series at each of Sunderland and Newcastle-upon-Tyne and with the single example in

Oxford, then Bristol and Carlisle (from 1819) and Sheffield (from 1820) each had multi-year dinners. These typify the modes of generation, with Bristol arising derivatively through the local Caledonian Society, Carlisle from its proximity and trade with Scotland, and Sheffield came about through heartfelt poetical admirers of Burns. In Sheffield, inspired by the news of the Dumfries Burns Club, local Scots founded the Burns Commemoration Society and, overcoming his religious scruples, they successfully co-opted the abilities of James Montgomery (1771–1851) as Chairman.[281] He was an Irvine born poet and hymnist, as well as a noted radical polemicist and newspaper publisher who founded the *Sheffield Iris* in 1794 where his reportage, having been deemed seditious, found him fined and gaoled in both 1795 and 1796.[282] This Burns Society first met to dine in Sheffield in 1820 where the toast to Burns was accompanied by the Montgomery poem beginning: 'What bird in beauty, flight or song/ Can with the bard compare?' Its strong conceit – aligning the aviary with the modes of Burns's songs, effectively embedding him in a pastoral trope without defining him as 'plowman' – is hardly hampered by Montgomery's required (but relatively understated) religious caveat on his 'failings' capped by a final stanza of Christian forgiveness. The poem was quickly copied in newspapers across the UK and US as the most anthologised paean to Burns:[283]

> What bird in beauty, flight, or song,
> Can with the Bard compare,
> Who sang as sweet, and soar'd as strong,
> As any child of air?
> ...
> Peace to the dead! — In Scotia's choir
> Of Minstrels great and small.
> He sprang from his spontaneous fire,
> The Phœnix of them all.

At its subsequent dinner in January 1821, the Sheffield Burns Club members voted to present Jean Armour Burns with a set of silver candlesticks, atop a tray bearing a new verse of Montgomery's that caught the public imagination and which would be quoted in many Burns Suppers in the period:

> He passed through life's tempestuous night,
> A brilliant, trembling *Northern Light* –
> Through years to come he shines from far,
> Fixed, unsetting polar star.[284]

That 'star quality' allowed the increasingly ubiquitous John Wilson/Christopher North in *Blackwood's* in 1819 that the Scots 'rightly hold the anniversary of his birth to be a day sacred in the calendar of genius'.[285] But it can be seen that through the 1820s, Burns Suppers could be found as a repeating tradition through the four corners and the capital of England as well as Scotland. The format now often included pipes and tartan as natural Scots tropes, often along with a sentimental Jacobitism, adding to the bardology, for example at Shields in 1822: 'the Duchess of Northumberland's Pipers... animated performances added a special character to the day.'[286]

Certainly, the 1820s saw all sorts of suppers springing up, including the founding of several major Burns clubs of subsequent longevity in 1826. Irvine's – the last Charismatic foundation – met in June to arrange its first dinner the following January while Dalry, was founded and dined that year by Hugh Morris a weaver and great friend of Tannahill and RA Smith.[287] Peterhead, Leith and Ardrossan Burns Clubs being each, like Irvine, constituted in 1826 and dining first in January 1827, each representing a Traditional foundation. Interestingly, by this time, some towns had more than one party celebrating Burns on 25 January 1826: Ayr/Alloway, Dunfermline, Paisley and Perth each had three dinners with two held in Edinburgh. In Ireland there is less evidence of activity, with only records of dinners in Belfast around this period (at the Edinburgh Tavern in both 1828 and 1829) and apparently taking until 1840 to reach the social life of Dublin.[288]

The Dalry Burns Club asked one of its founders, Andrew Crawford (born 1772, emigrated to USA in 1843, last heard of in 1851) to capture the spirit of the occasion and his introductory precepts captured Hamilton Paul's original format:

> Dalry eighteen hundred and twenty-six,
> Assembled a few friends of Burns
> To make regulations and yearly to fix,
> What's to be done when his birthday returns.
>
> This year in Montgomerie's, it first shall take place,
> Where drink of the best, will be got
> With a haggis and bannocks the table to grace
> And a slice from the hip of a stot.   [beef
>
> Political questions – all banished shall be
> The song it shall circle in turns
> Each shall have a glass of the barley bree
> To drink to the memory of Burns.
>
> No insulting language our lips shall defile
> Let no man's good humour be crossed,
> But let every face be bright with a smile
> When round goes the song and the toast.[289]

This remains a recognisable description of a modern Burns Supper and was obviously a powerful and effective encapsulation of the concept as the Dalry Club holds the palm for having the longest continuous unbroken annual run of Burns Suppers from its foundation to today.

It is interesting to pause and reflect on one of Crawford's precepts: 'Political questions – all banished shall be'. The arrangers and participants of the early Burns Suppers were truly varied: the gentry (as at Alloway or Glasgow Ayrshire); weavers and artisans (Greenock, Paisley, Kilbarchan, or Dalry); townsfolk and shopkeepers (Sunderland, Dunfermline, Dalkeith); students (Oxford and Edinburgh); Military NCOs and private soldiers (the various Militia parties); or Scots expatriates (London, the US and Bombay). The assumption made by some commentators that the genesis of the tradition of celebrating Burns was shaped by Scots aristocrats and landowners is plainly false. (It can be seen to be true in part when considering monumental commemorations, but not at all in terms of the dining tradition).[290] There is another thread to that assumption being that the prime movers were Scots Tory aristocrats and landowners who to some extent looked to mould the Burns movement into a buttress for the social, political and economic status quo that they sought conservatively to maintain. That, too, is not a tenable argument.

The spontaneous geographical and social spread of private or club/lodge Burns Suppers could not by definition be organised by any central political force. In fact, the evidence at the early public dinners (in Edinburgh and London) on the contrary, shows a desire from the organisers to be even-handed politically. The Edinburgh Burns Dinner in 1816 saw Alexander Boswell in the chair, supported by William Maule MP. Boswell was later described by his biographer as 'pre-eminently a Tory of the Tories', while Maule was an arch Foxite (to such an extent that he named his son 'Fox'). They were both ebullient, social men who found no need to allow party politics to interrupt a companionable evening of gentlemen celebrating Burns's anniversary.[291] Similarly, the London 1816 Burns Dinner had the Earl of Aberdeen, a relatively moderate Tory, in the chair for the first part of the event, with Thomas Campbell the famous poet and Whig, following him later in the evening.[292] The same case stood for the London 1818 fundraiser for the Burns Monument in Alloway where Sir Alexander supported HRH the Duke of York in the Chair.[293]

1819 saw the promised triennial dinners in Edinburgh and in London. The London Burns Dinner, held in June, was again to raise another round of subscriptions for the Edinburgh Monument. Here, however, the Chairman (HRH the Duke of Sussex) and the two croupiers (Sir James Mackenzie MP and Sir Francis Burdett MP) were all known as radicals. Looking at the stewards list, of the four other peers two were Whig and two supported the Ministry and of the six MPs on the list, they too were equally split. Despite the well-known opinions of the top table that night, none of the press reports, however, sought to characterise the event as party political in any regard. This was a national, literary meeting without political animus.[294]

On the other hand, the Edinburgh dinner was famously 'hijacked' by the Whig interest. This was the first time that public and literary dinner had been used to place a 'slate' of speakers from one side of the political divide to the exclusion of the other. As Lord Cockburn recalled: 'This was long remembered as the first public dinner... that showed [the Whigs] the use to which such meetings could be turned, and was the immediate cause of the political dinners that soon after made such an impression'.[295]

Lockhart, in *Peter's Letters to His Kinfolk,* made a more detailed critique of the offense given in the management of the toast list, but it is interesting to note that, despite the Whiggish hegemony which prevailed, an original song of Sir Alexander Boswell's was performed, which does make a small reach across the bitter political divide.[296] Certainly the Tories felt 'dished' and consequently aggrieved. John Wilson, one of the more junior stewards that evening would remember the tactic and attempt to use it on behalf of conservatism at the peak of his career, albeit without effective success in 1832 and in 1844.

The appeal of Burns extended across the political spectrum. While individuals may interpret Burns's poems or his politics in a right-wing or a left-wing way, the cross-party admiration was undoubted. So, by-and-large, orators (unless preaching to their own party choir) avoided giving specific offense. Beyond the unusual machinations at Edinburgh in 1819, there are a few cases where within a given community there was a sharp disagreement. Here the way to avoid open conflict was to form a new Burns Club (or dinner) where only likeminded men would attend. One classic example is in the village of Kilbarchan where the weavers in Kilbarchan New Club compared their more radical political views and agenda against those held by the largely older cadre of weavers in Kilbarchan 'Old' Club in 1820. The Kilbarchan New Club sought to strike at the fiscal sinews of Lord Liverpool's administration through constructive self-denial as 'they only partook of bread and cheese and cold water... they did not take anything that was taxed, their object being to starve the Government and cause them to submit to the views of the inhabitants.'[297]

Similar stories could be told nearby, too, and the development of Burns Clubs within the town of Ayr and its Alloway suburb at in the Radical times is illustrative. By 1830 there were three principal clubs who met on 25 January: the 'Original Burns Club', who saw themselves as the heirs of the Allowa' Club and who met in the Cottage from 1821; the 'Air Burns Club', founded in 1820, which met at the Crown Inn and a third group called 'The Ayrshire Burns Club' dining at the Inn at the Monument. Furthermore, there were an unnamed number of less formal parties held in the other inns in the burgh on each Anniversary night.[298] A fourth formal club had had less success, as it tried to operate over the political party lines through the radical controversies in Ayrshire but riven by 'party spiritit 'completely blew up.'[299]

But the evening the groups were celebrating was on the same evening. There was no need for there to be one political or social colour of Burns Supper. It was not until the politically boisterous year of 1832 that there was a Burns Supper with a specifically planned political agenda under the arch-Tory hand of John Wilson. The plan was to hold it again in Freemasons Hall, London and to cement its conservative, anti-Reform message by the presence of Robert Burns Junior and his brother James Glencairn Burns.[300] As in Edinburgh and the earlier grand London dinners, there was to be a heavy literary bent to the event with guest appearances from Hogg, Galt and Lockhart. This dinner had a difference, of course, as 1832 was a pivotal year in the debate over parliamentary reform in Britain and this Burns Supper was conceived as an appeal to the *status quo* with all of the key speakers and stewards attending on the night being supporters of the Tories or at least the anti-Reform movement. The 'draw' was planned to be around the first visit of 'The Ettrick Shepherd' to the capital. This introduction of *rus in urbe* was planned to stimulate nostalgic thoughts about the dead ploughman but with the more amenable shepherd as the malleable focus. To achieve that there was considerable publicity around 'the fact' that the two poets shared the same birthday which was the day of the dinner itself. As Hogg rather Pooter-ishly described the plan to his wife: 'you will see that a great literary dinner is to be given to me on Wednesday, my birth-day, for though the name of Burns is necessarily coupled with mine, the dinner has been set on foot solely to bring me forward'.[301]

The publicity patently succeeded, for twice as many arrived to dine as places had been set, meaning that the evening started with the competing wails of the bagpipes on the one hand and of the famished guests on the other. As has happened to many an organiser of Burns Suppers since then, the plan and its execution drifted apart as the guests arrived. One contemporary (liberal and hence unfriendly) journalist waspishly described it as:

> A public dinner at a public-house... provided by Scotch booksellers, presided at by a Scotch baronet, accompanied by Scotch bagpipes, and prepared for two hundred Scotch appetites, there being four hundred of the said appetites admitted to partake of it... The most ill-conceived, ill-concocted,

> ill-managed and ill-attended affair of its kind that
> ever flung disgrace and ridicule on the public.[302]

After the chaotic repast, Sir John Malcom's Immortal
Memory fell flat and the last half dozen toasts were squashed
together. In the tumult the toastmaster misheard how he should
introduce Hogg, 'The Ettrick Shepherd' as guest-of-honour
and his announcement, 'Pray silence for Mr Shepherd', was an
unintentional highpoint of the evening.[303]

The 'Fiasco' Burns Dinner subsequently drew columns of
debate both in attack by the Liberal/Reform papers and in defence
from the establishment presses. The former uniformly and
vociferously condemned 'a Tory trap designed to commandeer
"the high name of Burns, the noblest of Scotland's reformers"',
to be prostituted to the purposes of Anti-reform!'[304]

Jerdan used his own columns to decry his critics: 'to us
it appeared distinctly, that the old advice of Tullochgorum
was strictly observed, and that 'Whig and Tory did agree/ To
spend the night in mirth and glee'.[305] This dinner generated
more controversy than any Burns Supper before, or since, and
there are relatively few occasions after this where a literary or
civic dinner in honour of Burns's memory became a contested
political battlefield.

There would be one further serious attempt to arrogate Burns
to a conservative political message, once again concerted by the
indefatigable Professor John Wilson, this time in June 1844. To
be fair to Wilson, his love of Burns was deep and longstanding (he
once walked 70 miles in a single day to attend a Burns festival in
the evening).[306] His conservative view of Burns as an archetype
of the lower link in the old order of feudal Tory Scotland was
put more positively by supporters who called on the memory of
the late Sir Alexander Boswell whose 'favourite project' was to
have bolstered that view through 'an annual national meeting
for this day, on an extended scale, with a surplus fund for the
encouragement of Scottish literature and arts'.[307] This would be
the thesis, which had been hinted at in Edinburgh in 1816 and

to a greater extent there in 1819, but which now underpinned Wilson's project to manage the development of the nascent Burns Cult into a buttress of traditional anti-radical values, or as Pittock and Whatley describe it, an 'elite manipulation' which would have one final throw of the dice at capturing the legacy of Burns.[308] There was to be no confusion over the standard bearer as happened in 1832, this time the immortal Burns was being conjured on the banks of the Doon to vouchsafe good Tory order. In retrospect, one is uncertain if Wilson were playing King Saul, or the Witch of Endor.

This desire to create effective 'elite manipulation' had not worked in London in 1832 partly through the press controversy, which left no-one the undisputed victor on the field, and partly because the tool used was a single metropolitan dinner in a year when a far greater number of people had attended more successful and apolitical Burns Suppers throughout the three kingdoms (let alone abroad in the already reformed republican USA and some of the British colonies). The next decade saw different groups – right wing, liberal, radical, apolitical – continue to organise their own dinners with their own friends. Beyond the occasional political sniping as a part of the speeches and the occasional heavy artillery fire between *Blackwoods* and the *Quarterly*, the attempted seizure of the Burns heritage was apparently ineffectual in the face of an existing tradition of arranging Burns Suppers which was not defined by a particular class, region or party. The elite (or, in fact, any group) could no more influence the working men of Dalry or the burgess cadre in Ayr than they could alter the editorial position of *Blackwood's*. The manipulation was more in trying to perfect, as Tyrrell says, 'a prelapsarian view of Scotland as an arcadia, a clannish society where inherent loyalty was the political spring rather than democracy, reform or progress'.[309] The manipulation might be seen in a stronger, or more successful, mode by looking at how Scott and his novels were used (as in set-pieces like the Eglinton Tournament of 1839 or 1845's Waverly Ball, or yet

more controversially in Mark Twain's severely negative view of
the use of Scott's 'chivalry') to underpin the decadence of the
antebellum Confederate States of America, but the use of the
traditional Burns Supper or Dinner was not strikingly effectual
in converting opinions in a wholesale fashion.

Wilson's proposal was to have a grand festival on the banks
of the Doon in 1844 when William Nicol Burns was planning
to return home to retire from India and proposed to visit to
join his younger brother James Glencairn Burns in visiting their
aunt Isabel at Alloway. January 1844 saw, for the first time,
over 50 Burns Suppers held across the country but Wilson
sought to make a bigger impact than that: creating a monster-
meeting in the style, pageantry and traditional appeal of the
Daniel O'Connell meetings which were highly effective political
tableaux then current in Ireland to promote separation. There,
parades featured prominent O'Connell 'branding' through the
use of tropes of 'Irish-ness' ranging from the wearing of the
green and of shamrocks, carrying harps and even walking with
Irish wolfhounds. These rallies saw large numbers of people
assemble surrounded by national icons as totemic support for
'the Liberator' and his politics. As Wilson was to sum up his
vision of an equivalent Scottish meeting:

> Before the epoch of agitation approached, we
> were a peaceful and a happy people. The peerage,
> the gentry, the yeomen, and the peasantry — all
> classes were bound together with the links of
> respect and of affection... It seemed as if all classes
> had spontaneously assembled to join hands above
> the grave of Robert Burns, and there to renew the
> vow of enduring reconciliation and love.[310]

The day was planned in two parts: a grand opening
parade from the railway station at Ayr out to Burns Cottage
where an extensive marquee had been built to accommodate
a formal dinner for over 1000 ticketholders. Despite the poor

weather (which seemed to dog poor Lord Eglinton's dramatic endeavours) estimates of over 80,000 people arrived to join in the festival, with the more exclusive dinner being sold out.[311]

How effective was this grand manipulation? The parade was a great success, featuring myriad magistrates and masons, marching bands, Oddfellows in Lincoln green, working men in big blue bonnets, banners and a majestic, monster thistle.[312] However, the practicalities of arranging the dinner made it significantly less successful. The atmosphere was not helped by a poorly chosen and sloppily served menu which called forth the ridicule of *Punch*: 'fifteen shillings per mouth for a piece of cold tongue, a plate of gooseberries almost ripe and a pint of some mystery, calling itself Sherry'. While another reporter was served 'a fowl that might have been fed by Robert Burns himself in its younger days'.[313] Wilson's abilities as a litterateur were unquestioned, but he was a consistently poor traiteur. On this day, even his literary ear deserted him: the real cause of its failure was Wilson's interminable speech. In fact, it was not interminable, because adverse audience reaction forced him to cut it short. Wilson's substantive error was that his thesis of the great chain of social being, the Tory message which was supposed to be underpinning the whole event, required him to explain why the lad o'pairts kicked against the hierarchical pricks. He, therefore, dwelt *in extenso* with the hero of the day's 'frailties' which, in the presence of the hero poet's close family and friends let alone the multitude of 'fans' was not well received – thrusting the keynote speaker into an early peroration. James Glencairn Burns said afterwards that the speech 'gave greater pain than pleasure'.[314]

In retaliation, Wilson vowed to 'shame the fools and print it' not as the speech was actually received but as it had been conceived. corresponding with a number of newspaper editors, such as Paterson of the *Ayr Observer,* whose first published transcript was marked up immediately by Wilson and returned for emendation in his next edition, being told that the Professor 'intended to have it published... according to my recollection of it, in the next edition of Blackwood's *Magazine*'.[315] He could not overcome the disappointed comments such as Captain Vetch (had served with the younger Burns in Nepal) who channelled his anger at the manipulation (or the inefficiency of the attempt to manipulate) by publishing his thoughts in an anonymous pamphlet broadly enjoying the occasion, but deprecating Wilson's 'lecture on moral philosophy' during the dinner:

> With more of [Burns's] melodies and recitations from the Poet's best pieces by such an eloquence as Professor Wilson's, the ceremonies of the pavilion would have truly been – A FESTIVAL OF BURNS.[316]

One of the reasons that so many came to the Alloway Festival from Glasgow was the involvement of a young newspaper man called Colin Rae Brown (1821–1897). There is possibly no more important figure in the history of the popularisation of the cult of Burns. This Greenock-born Freemason was then serving as president of Greenock Burns Club and had written the club's anniversary Ode in 1842 (involving an extraordinary 42 stanzas) and was personally involved in finalising the first memorial to 'Highland Mary' in his home town. He was now drafted in *ex-officio* to help the Glasgow committee supporting Wilson's Doon Festival.[317] Rae Brown held a significantly different and populist view of what was required for a successful festival: in addition to the exclusive dinner, and the choreographed march, Rae Brown was behind concept of a day-trip from Glasgow to Alloway so that anyone to join in as a spectator for the day. As a result of his approach, tens of thousands descended on Ayr by train or steam boat. As *Tait's Magazine* described the effect of Rae Brown's intervention:

> ...this Festival was first talked of [as] a sort of monster pic-nic party at best, where a few dozens of doubtful sherry, with a hamper of sandwiches,

some half dozen or so of bad speeches, and the
usual quantity of rain, were expected to complete
the entertainment. Somehow or other, the thing
expanded, till the cloud that was no bigger than
a man's hand covered the face of the heavens.[318]

Rae Brown's philosophy (which saw him found the wide
circulation penny-paper, Glasgow's *Daily Bulletin* in 1856)
aligned with the failure of the Tory attempt to corral the
phenomenon, ensured that the annual celebration of Burns
was already too widespread to permit any single group to
dominate or enforce a 'house view' politically, religiously
or culturally. That scale and breadth of participation and
spectators underpinned the parade's social success, while the
narrower political plan of Wilson's for the dinner engineered its
own failure. As Christopher Whately wisely sums up Wilson's
failed master plan: 'despite their best efforts, conservatives in
Scotland were unable to corral Burns's legacy in the service
of the political and social status quo against... the dangers of
unbridled "democratic ambition"'.[319] In future years there was
no concerted attempt to create a monolithic, controlled arena
for the celebration of Burns.

The Burns Supper was now a defined tradition of over
five decades and one neither bound by central governance nor
exclusively for Scots, the *Aberdeen Journal* in the preceding
January had called it 'the anniversary... so hallowed in the
affections of every Scotsman' and so Wilson's essentially
unsuccessful 'manipulation' must be disentangled from the by
then already common celebration by way of a convivial dinner
or Burns Supper.[320]

This theory is proven by the totally different approach used
in arranging the 1859 Birth Centenary which from the outset,
was conceived as a global social participation in the celebration
of Burns's life and works. Colin Rae Brown looked back at the
lessons of 1832 and 1844 and chose a polycentric concept for
1859, 'to celebrate the approaching centenary by meetings in

every town throughout the kingdom'.[321] While the invitation
also makes a respectful reference to the Doon Festival, this
concept is radically different. Rae Brown asked every town in
the country and abroad, every Scots association, every group
interested in Burns to make its own arrangements. He followed
up his initial idea of the 'Universal Centenary Celebration'
with a circular letter sent to every conceivable society, club or
interested individual suggested his new many-headed approach,
ending with the exhortation:

> To Scotsmen and Scotswomen everywhere – and
> to their posterity in the generations to come – this
> Centenary Celebration will, if universal, prove
> not only a source of the greatest delight but a
> lasting bond of union between the inhabitants of
> Caledonia and those of every country and clime
> who sincerely adopt as their creed – 'A man's a
> man for a' that'.[322]

The success of the Burns Centenary was almost entirely due
to this inclusive (but devolved) vision, with the additional and
startlingly modern proposition from the New York Burns Club
(a society which had celebrated Burns Suppers for well over 30
years at that point) that all the various dinners across the world
toast the Bard simultaneously and if possible send greetings to
other clubs and dinners by telegraph (this was less successful
than might have been hoped as the cable link across the Atlantic
was inoperative due to a cable fault and as the New Yorkers,
solipsistically, chose 10pm New York time for the toast, which
was 3am in Britain). The concept was relished, however, as
the chairman at the Royal Hotel Glasgow saw it: 'the Atlantic
Cable is mute; but this night the eastern and western worlds
are united by the golden chain of fellow-feeling'.[323] Leith Davis
characterises this suggestion as Burns being a core part of the
'technology of communication [resulting in] a celebration of
global connection with Burns reconceived as the message and

the medium of that connection' (while Ann Rigney cleverly calls this a 'Twitter-fest *avant la lettre*').[324]

The vast majority of these celebrations took the form of a Burns Supper and the desire for participation outweighed Rae Brown's thoughts of a single focal point – with Ayr, Dumfries, Glasgow, Edinburgh and London all expecting, and competing for, the leading role within the celebrations. The matter was further compounded by the elder Colonel Burns feeling that he and his brother had both committed to be present in Dumfries on the anniversary. Despite a grand ticketed festival arranged as a commercial venture by the proprietors of the Crystal Palace in London, therefore, the focal point was not geographic, but was the actual toast to the Immortal Memory of Robert Burns being performed in hundreds of venues internationally, in events which would be recognised by both Hamilton Paul and the modern observer as Burns Suppers.

James Ballantine's compendium *Chronicle* tallies 872 varied celebrations in its opening page: however, his arithmetic skills are suspect, there being 1,039 actual records.[325] Additionally, an anonymous volume *The Burns Centenary* has 16 Scottish suppers not recorded in Ballantine, and the four scrap-books of James Gould, held in The Mitchell Library, along with other newspaper searches add yet more, making a grand total of 1,226 – almost 40 per cent more than Ballantine's own summary. Three-quarters of these were in Scotland, with 147 in England/Ireland; 71 in the USA; and 68 in the 'colonies'. There were even 5 recorded in Europe. With over 1000 parties, it is small wonder that Ballantine's compendium captures a happily innocent but triumphalist mood: 'The celebration of the 100th birthday of Robert Burns, on the 25th day of January, in the year 1859, presented a spectacle unprecedented in the history of the world'.[326]

Some recent commentators have seen the 1859 Burns Centenary in Ballantine's 'unprecedented' terms, but it would be wrong to take this out of the context of the already strong tradition throughout the English-speaking world of holding Burns Suppers. Certainly, the Burns Centenary publicity drove (as was seen in 2009) a heightened awareness which generated incremental participation, but its success is firmly rooted in the preceding 58 years of Burns Supper celebration.

The publicity and 'hype' was not universally accepted as a good thing by some conservative followers of Burns, who were beginning to exhibit cult-like concerns. The successor to Paul's Allowa' Club was divided in its opinion of the wider centenary, voting 'by a majority of one to "dine in the Hall of the 'Cottage' as usual"; a considerable number of the members being of the opinion that, having celebrated the poet's anniversary for so many years at the place of his birth, it would have been a violation of their sense of honour and duty to have deserted it on the 25th January, 1859'.[327] So, in addition to the major civic dinners in London, Ayr, Dumfries, Edinburgh and Glasgow, and the festival of Crystal Palace (with its national poetry competition), each of those cities saw other different audiences group around smaller venues to mark the Burns Centenary in their own suppers. For example, in Ayr, the County Hall saw the gathered great-and-good, with a broader social group in the Assembly Rooms; the several Freemasonic Lodges met in the Corn Exchange, the 'Original' Burns Club held out on their own at the Cottage, and the Ayr Working Men's Reform Association met on temperance terms.[328] And unrecorded, in Ayr and elsewhere, were smaller suppers were held in halls, inns and workplaces: as one speaker described it, 'whenever any half-dozen Scotchmen are assembled, then this night must be a Burns festival', and of course, it was not confined to the Scots.[329]

The success of the 1859 centenary, both in terms of wide participation, and perhaps more importantly widespread international publicity, encouraged many diners to either to formalise their activity under the aegis of a Burns Club, or at least to continue to meet informally in subsequent years to celebrate the anniversary with a dinner. To that extent, the tone is captured by Carol McGuirk's observation that '1859 [was] the point at which the transformation of Burns from controversial literary celebrity into "immortal memory" seems to have been completed'.[330] However as we have followed the progress of the Burns Supper from 1801, 1859 should really be seen as the culmination of a period of momentum. With 2,221 recorded Burns Suppers from 1801 to 1858 and then 1,226 held in 1859 the Burns Supper was a truly widespread tradition.

For the next 25 years, there was to be a steady growth of celebrations, now all broadly following the accepted traditional format. Colin Rae Brown's direct involvement with the Burns movement continued after his move to London a few years later, being founder and president for 12 years at the London Robert Burns Club, promoting the Westminster Abbey bust and the Embankment Statue fundraising. He was instrumental in founding the Burns Federation, served as Honorary President of the 1886 Kilmarnock Edition Centenary, was the pioneer of *the Burns Chronicle* and, in his dying days, remained the moving force behind the Highland Mary monument at her putative birthplace of Dunoon. In speeches, poems and pamphlets, Rae Brown consistently called on the philosophy of 'a man's a man' and it was the concept of brotherhood through the works of Burns reaching the widest possible audience, regardless of nationality, gender or age, that would result in his championing a wider formal bond between the lovers of Burns and the international network of Burns Clubs, which was to result in the institution of the Burns Federation in 1885. This development heralds the advent of the Bureaucratic period of the Burns Supper which will be analysed in the next chapter.

CHAPTER FIVE

The Bureaucratic Period

Whenever a year is 'five and twenty days begun', a great mob assembles all over Scotland, to drink whisky, and eat haggis, and make speeches in the Idol's praise.[331]

ABSENT A FEW VERY large parades in 1859 and 1896, Wilson's experiment in creating the single-venue monster-meeting with an identified political purpose was not to be repeated. The trend was clearly polycentric and localised. But that raised a question, if the love and celebration of Burns was universal, why was there no communication between the myriad local groups?

Colin Rae Brown concluded his toast at the Glasgow City Hall in 1859 by expressing his 'hope that this great festival may not terminate in a mere ovation to the memory of the mighty dead' but that their feelings might be 'embod[ied] in some monumental edifice' reminding his auditors that the Burns Supper was not the sole method of commemorating Robert Burns.[332] Leaving aside the obvious ways to do so (through the enjoyment of his songs and poems), or the religious possibilities (primarily the laying of wreaths on his mausoleum) and the commercial opportunities (such as the Mauchline-ware industry of wooden commemorative artefacts) considerable efforts were made by groups in various towns and cities to honour Burns through the medium of statuary. These were projects which by necessity took several, even many, years to complete and so required a formal infrastructure to raise funds, select designs, execute the construction and, finally, organise a ceremony of unveiling and dedication although as James Coleman accurately sums it: 'none of the myriad statues to Robert Burns in Scotland is in any way as effective in communicating the poet's significance as are the annual Burns Night celebrations with their whisky, haggis and Immortal Memories'.[333]

It was after the bust unveiling at Westminster Abbey that the representatives of Kilmarnock Burns Club were walking along the banks of the Thames with Colin Rae Brown, who suggested the idea of an overarching federation to provide a formal fraternity of Burns Clubs to create, in line with the Masonic experience of those five gentlemen, a grand lodge of the Burns cult worldwide.[334] The circular letter sent around the world, and which was to form the objects clause in the new Burns Federation constitution bears the clear mark of Rae Brown's rhetoric: 'the object of the Federation shall be to strengthen and consolidate the bond of fellowship presently existing amongst the members of Burns Clubs, by universal affiliation: its motto being – "A man's a man for a' that"'. Colin Rae Brown embodied that combination of conviviality and earnestness that was to mark the Bureaucratic period of the Burns Supper: the first 17 Burns Suppers of the London Burns Club were staged in his own home with him as orator and host to a party of both genders and many nations.

As with the Burns Supper, the Federation's birth was suitably marked by Freemasonic indicators such as the agreement that London should stand as number one on the federation roll to acknowledge Rae Brown's suggestion of the concept in London but with Kilmarnock arrogating 'number zero' to itself in a conscious recollection of Lodge Mother Kilwinning's mythic status. Not all Burnsians enthusiastically accepted the new structure and several of the older clubs resisted falling in line with the new body. The overall history of the Federation is tangential, however, to the analysis of the Burns Supper with the only tangible change to the running order of the Supper being the addition of the exchange of 'fraternal greetings' between affiliated clubs, which had not been an uncommon occurrence in any case. To some extent, the growth of the Federation was partly propelled by more progressive Burns Clubs who wanted to build a year-round programme to augment the annual anniversary festival dinner, so not only was it broadly unnecessary to outline the requirements for holding a 'canonical' Burns Supper but, other than the reports from clubs describing their evenings, the *Burns Chronicle's* efforts were focussed beyond the dining table as they could trust their fellows in the dining rooms. It was around this time that the nomenclature of 'Burns Supper' started to be commonplace. Prior to this, events had been called Anniversary Dinners or Birthday Dinners. The first recorded use of the phrase 'Burns Supper' was in a widely syndicated press article called 'Burns and Scotchmen in the Back Settlements of America' which appeared across Scotland and England in 1851.[335] There are few other uses of this allocution but from the 1880s this American phrase begins to attract common concurrence.

The Burns Supper was not, however, immune from criticism. One running question was whether the attendees were celebrating Burns, or Whisky? One of the first acts undertaken by the Trustees of Burns Monument when they bought Burns Cottage in 1880 was 'to meet the general public desire that the sale of intoxicating drink should be banished from the premises'. While that exhibited great respect for the fabric of the building, it did squash the merry tradition of holding a Burns Supper in the room of Burns's birth which had survived for some 78 years.[336]

The second part of the Bureaucratic period, from 1896 to 1996 was one of limited development in terms of the format Burns Supper but a significant growth in penetration. The number of events continued to grow as many non-Burns clubs and societies, particularly but not exclusively in Scotland, now held a Burns Supper as a part of their social syllabus, with a general and maintained interest through United States and the English-speaking Empire (latterly the Commonwealth) alongside military and expatriate celebrations in other foreign posts. Burns

Night became the open event. Over that period, New Zealand had a wider range of Scottish associations so that '[b]y the late 19th century, Scottish associations formed part of civic life all over New Zealand, comprising around 100 Caledonian societies and at least 20 other societies, such as Burns clubs and the Gaelic Society and its branches', and most of those societies (with the exception of the Gaels) held an annual Burns Night.[337] The same could be said of Australia, where conviviality was renowned, which permitted the occasional side-swipe as reported by the Editor of the *Northern Argus* who attended Burns Night in Clare, South Australia in the late 1880s.

> What I did on Burns's Anniversary. —Dressed myself in Scotch Tweed. Attended a Burns dinner. Partook of Scotch cockie leekie. Ate Scotch haggis. Sang Scotch songs. Heard Scotch speeches laudatory of Scotland and Scotsmen. Drank Scotch whisky. Listened to Scotch music. Drank more Scotch whisky. Took Scotch snuff out of a Scotch snuff mull. Some more Scotch whisky. Indulged in Scotch bannocks and Scotch cheese. Scotch whisky made into toddy. Told some broad Scotch stories. A little more toddy. Sang 'Here's a health, my trusty frien'. 'Took a ' richt gude willie wacht' for the sake of auld lang syne. Had a rare ' doch-an-dorris' as a wind up. Took a drink from the landlord's 'stirrup cup'. Was induced to — no, as far as I remember, I think that was all. (And quite enough, too).[338]

While in North America, Burns Nights and Burns Suppers burgeoned with the growth in Scottish associational culture which was also exhibited in the holding of Highland Games and the building of statues. In 1889 a US commentator suggested that 'in the USA and Canada, every January, there are some 200 meetings in honor of the Poet.'[339]

Although he went on to suggest that the Scottish diaspora should find more constructive ways to commemorate and preserve their heritage than 'this system of useless celebration'. That was evidently not an assessment shared by the many, as Michael Vance has estimated that '[b]y the turn of the century most Scottish societies put on a Burns Supper'.[340] Reviewing the movement east of Suez, Graeme Morton points to a different structure, being

> less a story of settlement as sojourning. India and Hong Kong were worker outposts where Burns Suppers never attracted the same community involvement as they did in North America, instead tending to be smaller and more private affairs for the cultivation of business and personal links.[341]

It would seem in keeping that groups of fellow Scots would congregate on the day to commemorate their poet. It is important to stress that while the geography was diverse, the following of ritual was not. As the Bureaucratic period developed, the Burns Supper ritual (and to a large extent the oratory) became universal and commonplace.

1896 had seen a great centennial event to mark the death of Burns – midwifed by the indefatigable Lord Rosebery who famously gave the Immortal Memory both at lunch in Dumfries and a few hours later at dinner in Glasgow – but there was a feeling in many quarters that a local celebration by means of a Supper was preferable to a distant Crystal Palace-like extravaganza.[342] As there was no Ballantine that year to establish a compendium critical attention has focussed on the outdoor events – such as the massive wreath of antipodean flora embedded in a monumental block of ice sent as a tribute to be laid at the mausoleum in Dumfries from the association of Burns Clubs in Australia (which, unfortunately, arrived several days late). It also would appear that there was no centennial cult around the 1909 birth sesquicentennial, primarily due to the now engrained traditions in most towns of holding a Burns Supper. As Mackay, the historian of the federation, puts it: 'it was a relatively quiet affair. To be sure, the custom of holding anniversary dinners was by then so well established that perhaps it did not call for the same degree of comment that the demonstrations of 1859 had provoked'.[343]

Around this time, some groups took an enthusiasm for formal rite to an extreme level. The Library of Congress has in its collection a ritual manual for 'The Robert Burns Society of America: Tam o'Shanter Cavern' where a mix of faux Masonic ritual and tartan trumpery achieve a near-parodic summit. With the 'Mighty Chief' in the chair, his lieutenants, the 'Captain of the Sporran', the 'Captain of the Kilt' and the 'Captain of the Bagpipes' each ritually catechised blindfolded candidates under the tutelage of the 'Sergeant of the Cutty Sark', before subjecting them to a hazing based on Tam's famed midnight ride. If the catechumen responded wisely he received the secret signs and had the honour of being capped by Tam's guid blue bonnet. Fortunately, this extreme Burns Supper format seems not to have caught on.[344]

The 60 years between the founding of the Burns Federation in 1885 and the end of the Second World War saw a growing number of Burns Clubs being created and joining the federation, each with its Burns Supper, or Anniversary Festival Dinner, as they were increasingly called.[345] Simultaneously, an increasing number of Scottish clubs and societies across the world adopted Burns Night as a secondary feast to St Andrew. Over time, with the exception of the St Andrew's Societies themselves, January, not November, came to represent the highlight of the social year.

In general the trend was as that 'Burns-worship, whatever the superfine critics may say, is no dwindling cult', but this 100-year period would also appear to be a time of near stultifying orthodoxy.[346] The formula and ritual of the event became important in and of itself, and even after 1946's changes in political landscape which saw a more left-leaning post-demobilisation group of voters returned to the UK and quickly absorb the poet into the iconography of Labour politics (which had espoused Burns two decades before through Keir Hardie's fervent and personal avocation of the poet as the fount of his understanding of socialist principles, 'I owe more to Robert Burns than any man alive or dead!') however, this political lurch brought little additional informality.[347] Some Burns Nights would be accoutred in black tie or increasingly tartan wear in hotels or restaurants, and in contrast some were held in the working-man's Sunday best or casual dress in village halls and union rooms. Regardless of that seemingly contradictory approach to social formality, the internal formula of the Burns Supper appeared cast in stone.

The Death Sesquicentenary in July 1946 was naturally eclipsed by the end of the Second World War although, as discussed below, while formal centennial undertakings were few – notably a sober wreath laying at Dumfries by the former lion tamer, Labour MP and Burns Federation President John S Clarke (1885–1959) in the months of January 1946 and 1947 had seen a rise in the number of Burns Suppers as many had been forsworn for the duration of the war and so an early opportunity of celebration was grasped as life returned, even under rationing, to some level of normality.[348] The Burns Federation were active in this, successfully campaigning against government restrictions that no more than 100 people could be seated at dinner ('even of haggis and potatoes') while clarifying that the traditional Burns Supper did not fall within the purview of the Entertainment Tax regime.[349]

Again, it is important to stress that while every Burns Club would hold an anniversary dinner, many other groups of people arranged their Burns Suppers, too. Overall, the trend was towards a growing formality both in social customs ('black tie' and all-male) and in setting the order of proceedings. Over this period, the running order that is seen as 'traditional' was substantially established, in a formalised etiquette to look like this:

Grace (now almost always the *Selkirk Grace*)
Dinner
    First (typically Soup) Course
Ceremony of Piping in and Addressing the Haggis
    Haggis Course (sometimes this would be an intermediate
    course, sometimes the only main course)
    Main course
    Pudding, Dessert and/or Cheese
Short Break
Toasts (interspersed with songs and/or recitations)
    The Loyal Toast(s)
    The Immortal Memory
    Subsidiary Toasts (the Club, the Town, etc)
    The Ladies/Lassies (and latterly a Reply)
    Vote(s) of Thanks
Communal Singing of *Auld Lang Syne*

As the phenomenon deepened and spread, many wanted to enforce traditional uniformity. As the Federation trumpeted in 1975, seeking to maintain its standards in a changing era: 'it is clear that some guidelines are necessary for hard-working but innocent secretaries of Women's Guilds and bowling clubs, and in some instances, for Burns Club committees'.[350] While that breadth was a fact, this displays the perception that the core Burns Supper had become hallowed, prescribed and, unalterable:

> Apart from questionable aberrations... to 'modernise', there is a formula for holding Burns Suppers which is recognisable from Alloway to Adelaide... Burns Suppers often fall short of their avowed aims..., The intentions may be good, and the organisers work with the best will in the world, but perhaps something was lacking, or inattention to some detail may have marred the evening.[351]

This fear of change, embodying a near obsessive/compulsive belief that a failure to fulfil any of the step-by-step rituals ruined the evening is a significant issue and as such, it gained a significant critic, Hugh MacDiarmid who challenged the status quo with the broadside: 'Mair nonsense has been uttered in his name/ Than ony's barrin' liberty and Christ'.[352]

The excoriation of the Burns Supper was but one strand in MacDiarmid's wider attack seeking the regeneration of Scotland within his highly particular political and linguistic world-view, but it was a key issue (as one MacDiarmid scholar bluntly describes it, the principle of 'The Burns Supper as the epitome of Philistine stupidity').[353] His outspoken (perhaps over spoken) criticism defined academic views of Burns for a considerable length of time, and still has some adherents. This book is neither the place to review MacDiarmid's obvious talent as a poet, nor his extreme political views (which ranged in his life from supporting the Nazis through to an advocacy of Stalinism) except where they colour his critique of the Burns Supper and the attendant 'Burns Cult, forsooth! [which] has denied his spirit to honour his name [in] stupid and stereotyped sentiments it belches out annually'.[354] There are three particular fights being picked by MacDiarmid that need to be reviewed critically and measured for justice.

The first denunciation is over his perception of the identity of the 'cult', and in particular the participants at Burns Suppers in general ('the ordinary illiterate Burnsians' as he called them).[355] At one level, his communist distrust of the 'bourgeoisie' makes him attack the round of club suppers (be they Burns Clubs or golf clubs), which he characterises as fundamentally exclusive, the haunt of the middle classes and not for working folk. Essentially, he believed that 'Burns, in fact, has fallen into the hands of the Philistines, who exalt his name, but deny his practice, if not in precept, all the values he stood for'.[356] In an attempted proof that the Burns Supper had squeezed out the ordinary Scot, the Drunk Man complains that:

You canna gang to a Burns Supper even
Wi'oot some wizened scrunt o' a knock-knee
Chinee turns roon to say, 'Him Haggis – velly goot!'
And ten to wan the piper is a Cockney.[357]

Whether this, or other *ad hominem* attacks are supposedly the maunderings of the Drunk Man, the bile spills into an outright and unacceptable racial slur. MacDiarmid scholars have spent many words supporting, glossing or brushing over this intemperate racist attack, which would hardly go unchallenged if made by a right-wing English writer.

His second complaint revolves around the propriety of reciting and debating anyone's poetry (let alone Burns's) in the milieu of a formal dinner. Spleen is one of the few viscera of the sheep not to feature in the production of haggis, but it was in evidence in MacDiarmid's poetic contribution for the 1959 bicentennial. *Your Immortal Memory, Burns!* addresses 'the poet intestinal' and his votaries in a poetic series of eructations.[358] As Boutelle glosses the poem: 'It presents a Rabelaisian view of the Scottish Philistine who is willing to honour Burns if he can fill his stomach at the same time'.[359]

This is a particularly pregnant description. Again, this is an assumption open to challenge. At the simplest level, Burns (all too often) honoured Burns while 'fill[ing] his stomach at the same time'. As explored above, the concept of literary conviviality was a defining characteristic of society at Burns's time, and therefore was intrinsic to the way in which he casts his performative verse. It is that key element which sits behind the format of the Burns Supper, as audiences choose to enjoy a dinner rather than a lecture (or even worse, a harangue) to accompany their speeches, poetry and songs. That form of conviviality was (and is) as available to the lads and lasses as much as to the lairds and ladies, as the *Montreal Pilot* newspaper stated back in 1861: 'The memory of Burns can be honoured by the lowliest in their lowly manner, with quite as much sincerity as by the lordly, ostentatious, wealthy few'. And, of course, vice versa.[360]

His third level of complaint is that the success and format of the Burns Supper in focusing on Burns does not admit of inclusion of other poets (one assumes, particularly MacDiarmid). In effect, his contention is that the Burns Supper arrested poetic thought and development as of the date of the death of Burns, as he said, '[t]he fault of the Burns cult has been to conceive poetry as a static thing, established by Burns once and for all, and no more admitting change than the laws of the Medes and the Persians'. [361] While it has been shown that there was a 'mainstream' resistance to change within the core Burns clubs and federationists, this statement patently ignores a tradition of recognising other poetical talents on the Burns Supper programme, and there certainly was no bar to new bards, although Burns was naturally very much the focus of the entire entertainment. Again, as there is no necessary prescription, it would be possible to conceive of other poets being added to today's entertainments as they often were in the early Burns Suppers as still happens in Paisley Burns Club and in some other Suppers (depending on the time constraints, attention span and taste of the audience).

Like all criticism, there are foundations to MacDiarmid's points many of which were addressed in the transition from the Bureaucratic period to the Global period, which happened mainly beyond the milieu of the traditional Burns Clubs but was seen much more in the wider participation in Burns Suppers. Just as MacDiarmid could be prevailed upon to speak if the audience were interested in his particular position, so too 'the punctual stomach of thy people turn[ed]' to any of the several hundred Burns Suppers he attended in his career. The ultimate irony of his position was that outside his published writings, his venue for criticising Burns Suppers was by speaking at Burns Suppers – whether in communist Bowhill (where he gave seven Immortal Memories between 1954 and 1974) or elsewhere.

MacDiarmid by his actions, if not his words, recognised that the Burns Supper need not be based on the formality or politics he despised. In focussing on one group, albeit a large one at the time (the classic federation anniversary festival dinner), MacDiarmid misses the key, protean nature of the Burns Supper. He and his communist friends are as free to hold a supper in their way as his enemies and targets are free to participate according to their lights. Neither need attend the other's but each is valid. At the end of the day, MacDiarmid's primary gripe with the Burns Supper is the same as the old Tories like John Wilson, each frustrated by their inability to dominate and manipulate the tradition of celebrating Burns for their own party-political agenda.

While the format seemed perhaps to become stuck in a traditional groove, the geographical spread continued to expand. One proxy for measuring that is to look at affiliations to the Burns Federation. It has been shown above how entrenched the Burns Supper was in the USA, Canada, Australia and New Zealand. It is interesting to see further flung clubs joining: in the 1930s from Iraq; in the 1940s/50s, from Denmark, Norway, Nigeria, Palestine and Pakistan; in the 1960s/70s, from Sierra Leone, Bahrain, Thailand, and in the 1980s, Kuwait and Java, the Netherlands, Switzerland and Spain. It might be guessed that these clubs flourished as Scots engineers, workers and businessmen found expat employment. Certainly, none of these locations maintained their affiliation for more than a few years, which could suggest that transience of expat community lifestyle. The important evidence is that there was a desire to add a Burns commemoration to a local calendar in these locations.

MacDiarmid's bluster and its broad acceptance at face value in Scottish universities in between the 1960s and 1980s, was surely one of the key reasons for the Pittock paradox in the run up to the 1996 bicentenary of the poet's death, the journalist Ian Jack described the state of debate as: 'The Burns cult now is to attack the Burns cult'.[362] Yet the paradox is while Burns clubs on the one hand and the establishment of poetry and education

on the other glowered at each other wi' gilpey glowrin' e'en, the
Burns Supper continued to thrive. The bicentenary of the poet's
death in 1996 saw fewer press reports of formal Burns Suppers
held by Burns clubs, but saw that compensated by an increasing
number of suppers having a shorter, lighter and more thoughtful
Immortal Memory, a trend which was conspicuous in the run up
to 2009 and the 250th Birthday Anniversary.

The Burns Supper is essentially amateur, and so the speeches
range from the banal to the brilliant, from gifted literary
critique to cliché and schmaltz just as the range of singers and
speakers, or the quality of the food, varies. It is precisely that
variability that a MacDiarmid communist fears, the absence of
control is what terrifies him in his attack and it is that absence
of control that is the fundamental driver of the growth of the
concept in the last two decades. Edwin Muir was not uncritical
of the Burns cult, but he recognised the different motivations
that MacDiarmid could not see and shared a similar perception
to Hamilton Paul: 'When we consider Burns we must therefore
include the Burns nights with him... if we sneer at them we
sneer at Burns'.[363]

To some extent the attacks by MacDiarmid shocked the
Burns 'Cult' establishment into its trenches however, the reverent
status quo was challenged constructively by forward thinking
supporters, such as the journalist Ian Nimmo, who counselled
to keep the event as living entertainment in honour of the poet,
warning the traditionalists that:

> Although the Burns Supper today follows a defi-
> nite pattern of set pieces and toasts, it does not
> mean that the events and speakers should be so
> similar each year that the final result is boredom.[364]

This is how the battlelines were drawn between the
federationists and a mix of edgy journalists who, when looking
to fill press columns or air-time in slow Januaries, posited that
the Burns Supper like the televised Hogmanay show, had seen its

day. This Supper cringe was a primarily Scottish phenomenon with the Burns Supper being seen in the diaspora and others abroad as a cornerstone tradition admittedly perhaps overgrown by the weight of traditional expectation in some areas, but still a core exemplar of convivial celebration.

Regardless of the controversies, the suppers continued annually, outside as well as inside the Federation and within and without Scotland and the Scots folk. Before turning to the changes in attitude that saw a move from the Bureaucratic to the Global period, let us look at what happened to the Burns Supper during the upheavals of the World Wars in the 20th century.

CHAPTER SIX

The Burns Supper at War

Tonight there will be few of the ordinary Burns celebrations. The blasts of Januar' win' will not this year [1915] be fragrant with haggis and cock-a-leekie and the national beverage. Most of those who used to foregather with us are now doing more for their country than toasting the immortal memory of a poet: and some of the best have drunk the darker cup and learned the secret which no poet, however gifted, has discovered. But, ladies and gentlemen, a time of national crisis is the very time to turn to poetry.

John Buchan, London Robert Burns Club, 1915[365]

THE MANNER OF HOW Burns was commemorated in wartime shows another example of how the Burns Supper could be adapted by various constituencies while conscious of a wider social and political message. Contemporary analysis of Burns's poems and philosophy commonly tends to assume the poet held a broadly left-wing outlook and by implication he was at least anti-war, if not a true pacifist. As in most Burns study, is too simplistic as there have been competing interpretations from some of the earliest Burns Suppers.

In the 19th century, the traditional toasts to the Army and the Navy were accompanied by other references to the Napoleonic Wars. For example, Greenock passed resolutions of sympathy in 1806 to a member whose son had fallen at Trafalgar; and the 1807 Paisley dinner revolved around a poetic and musical patriotic extravaganza.[366] These sentiments typically characterised Scotland's people as standing united against the continental might of Bonaparte inspired by a bardic recollection of historical resistance to external (or internal) tyranny. Thus, Tannahill captured that sentiment and anchored it to a key Burns quote from *The Cotter's Saturday Night:*

> Yes, Caledonians! to our country true,
> Which Romans nor Danes never could subdue,
> Firmly resolved our native rights to guard,
> Let's toast — 'The Patriot and the Patriot Bard'.[367]

The common and repeated trope of taking arms against Imperial Bonaparte in the same fashion as resisting Imperial Rome uses Napoleon's imagery as a weapon against himself and the consistent theme at Alloway, Greenock and Paisley is that the men present seek inspiration through Burns's invocation of the myth of Bruce and particularly Wallace to fight when provoked, but always with honour, to the death, in a just war.

From the early days the Burns Supper was an active festival for serving men. The first recorded military Burns Suppers we have are attributable to two friends of Robert Tannahill's: James Clarke who was the bandmaster of the Argyleshire Fencibles and James King who served with the Renfrewshire Militia. Tannahill's wrote to King in June 1809 about an ode for a Burns Supper in January 1810 while King was stationed in Reigate in Surrey.[368] Bandmaster Clark throws up more evidence of a regular annual festival as his regiment was billeted around Scotland. He arranged Burns Suppers in Edinburgh in 1807, in Aberdeen in both 1808 and 1809 and was the instigator of this Alloway/Ayr event in 1810 when the soldiers visited the cottage where Burns was born, attended by the band of the Regiment, who played a number of appropriate airs' before returning to a celebratory dinner in Ayr.[369]

As mentioned above, the Royal Ayrshire Militia around this period also had a formal 'Burnsonian Society' which held at least one, and probably two, birthday festivals in Perth in 1814 and potentially in Cavan in 1815. So the celebration seems relatively widespread across the militia.

1815 saw Napoleon's final defeat at Waterloo. We know from contemporary records that the Scots regiments used Burns's songs as part of their life on campaign with an evocative reminiscence of sabres being sharpened to the sound of the men singing *Scots Wha Hae* on the morning of the battle. That day, Alexander Armour (Jean's nephew) was wing man to Sergeant Ewart of the Scots Greys when he captured the Eagle of the 45th.[370] The popularity of Burns amongst the troops led one of the army's official printers to bring out a special edition the following year in 'a convenient size and shape for the Soldier's pocket', showing the level of literacy in the Scots regiments.[371]

Young Armour was not the only Burns relative engaged in combat that year. Ensign James Glencairn Burns was serving with his battalion in the British war against Nepal. It was here he met his longstanding friend Vetch on the front line. Just as Armour's kinship to the poet appears to have been a touchstone for his colleagues, the presence of a son of Burns, so far from home, seems electric.

Vetch composed the first of his Burnsian poems to commemorate that meeting and its effect of the troopsand it would not seem too great a leap to imagine verses like this and others being recited and toasted in the Officers' Mess in the presence of the young Burns upon his father's birthday. [372]

Through the 1859 centenary, the feats of Scottish arms, in the Crimea, Afghanistan and India (through the Indian Mutiny) are regularly cited – with more regularity than 'radical' attributions across the varied reports, however, by and large, the wars of Empire rarely intruded upon the evenings subsequent to 1859, although some clubs cancelled their 1900 dinner in the wake of the 'Black Week' defeats at the hands of the Boer forces, no military incident caused widespread cancellations such as happened in January 1901 out of respect for the death of Queen Victoria (or to a lesser extent in January 1936 for her grandson, George V).[373] The half century following the close of the Queen-Empress's reign, however, would see two world conflicts, with conscription and total war bringing the military reality closer to home.

The first months of the Great War were traumatic and Burns featured in many aspects of that drama. David Goldie has made a strong reassessment of the propaganda use of Burns. As a national icon and inspiration he shows that Burns's memory could be shifted along a national to a patriotic to a propaganda continuum whose apogee was the famous 'Take His Tip' recruiting poster.[374] In January 1915 it was patently obvious that the war was not 'over by Christmas', let alone in time for the traditional Burns Night conviviality, however, even with the recognition that the combat would be a much harder task, very few Burns Clubs appear formally to have suspended their anniversary celebrations at that point in time. Paisley and Dumfries were some of the first to do so – until 1919 and 1920 respectively. Abroad too, some clubs suspended their dinners.[375] As the *Scotsman* reported in January 1915: 'owing to the war, few of the customary dinners... were held last night, but in some cases concerts and lectures were substituted'.[376] This move was not because Burns was seen as anti-war or in any way pacifist, it was more a reaction against holding a formal, convivial dinner at a time when so many families were suffering through bereavement or hardship. Most clubs transmuted their energies into Scottish charities – either through formal fund raisings, or by sending comfort packages to the front, or in holding entertainments (usually with a Scottish theme and often an 'Immortal Memory' speech) for troops on home leave. A good example was at Elgin where 'to honour the immortal memory of Private Robert Burns of the Dumfries Loyal Volunteers, a smoking concert was held'.[377] Across the UK this trend increased with more clubs cancelling in January 1916 and then in each subsequent year of war.

Notwithstanding that laudable trend, a significant number of groups held firm to the custom of meeting to dine. Dalry carried on unabated, but reflected the harsh times by adding an extra toast in 1915 to follow that of 'The Imperial Forces' when they toasted 'Our Local Forces' (and then in the peace of 1919, after the toast to the 'Imperial Forces' the company sang a song of thanksgiving entitled *God Sent Ye Back To Me*).[378] In Edinburgh the Scottish Arts Club became a focal point for celebrations outwith the few private dinners (such as Canongate Kilwinning Lodge's annual dinner) being held and in London, the London Burns Club (Scots) carried on dining as before at the Venetian Salon of the Holborn Restaurant. These continuing dinners appear less grand in form and menu, but retain the characteristics of the Burns Supper, typically with an Immortal Memory which carried a positive war message. However, beyond the combatant nations within the British Empire, the traditional banquets were routinely held, with a few exceptions.[379] In the United States enthusiasm for the Burns Supper remain unchanged even at the point of the country becoming a belligerent nation. In 1916, the Immortal Memory speaker in New York invoked the recent news of the early death of the poet Rupert Brooke as an apologue to the short life and works of Burns citing both poets as brief lives spent breathing exhortations of freedom and democracy.[380] That same day, the *Trenton Evening Times* opined that 'Scotchmen in the blood-soaked trenches of France and Flanders will fight all the more furiously because of their remembrance that they are the defenders of the land of Burns'.[381]

This confirms a heroic view of the fighting Scot and his motivation, so it is unsurprising that, amongst the troops in the war zones, Burns Suppers, albeit in an attenuated format, could regularly be found as celebrations in or beside the theatre of war. CM Grieve wrote home from Salonika in February 1918 describing 'a champion Burns Night' and later indicated that he had been a participant on the toast list at several earlier Burns

Suppers in Greece, Italy and France during his period of service.[382] So, while at home, the dinner had to be sacrificed for the greater good, it retained an important role in supporting military morale on or near the battlefields. [383] However, often the basic ingredients were missing when these privations were recognised at home, the civilian population decided to make a difference:

> Burns day was duly celebrated yesterday by a large number of Scotsmen at the front, and in some cases at least, the delicacies appropriate to the festival were not lacking. A few days ago Provost Malcolm Smith of Leith, received a letter from Sergeant McDonald of that town, saying that many Scots were with him resting after a trip to the trenches, and that they would greatly appreciate gifts of haggis &c., which they could not buy at the front, to enable them to celebrate Burns night in real Scottish fashion. A firm of fishcurers gave two firkins of herrings, and these, with haggis sufficient for 100 men, were sent off by Provost Smith to the front. [384]

It was this kind of thoughtful support which prompted the Scots/ Canadian poet Robert W Service (1874–1958), who claimed kinship with Burns, to write one of his verse monologues, *The Haggis of Private McPhee*, imagining the joy two Scots privates have at the prospect of a haggis supper on January 25 after their stint in the trenches, and finding that the latest food parcel from home included

> 'The brawest big haggis I ever did see.
> And think! it's the morn when fond memory turns
> Tae haggis and whuskey--the Birthday o' Burns.
> We maun find a dram; then we'll ca' in the rest
> O' the lads, and we'll hae a Burns' Nicht wi' the best'.[385]

Within what might be thought of as Service's characteristic mix of Burns and Kipling, albeit with the realistic and numb view of the horrors of the Front, this poem reminds us that celebrating Burns in the middle of war was a Godsend and regularly celebrated in the mess.[386] The *Scotsman* carried uplifting stories telling readers that 'The 25th of January does not pass unheeded even amidst the spasmodic roaring of the great guns' while the poet's songs retained a diurnal importance.[387]

> We were in a large town, and were going up the line. Before we separated to get to our billets and have our impedimenta strapped up, we got to our feet, and sang [*Auld Lang Syne*], as many before us had done in similar circumstances. Then we heard from all over the town, from the various messes, that wonderful, though-moving refrain floating across the night. Many who sang it there never met together on earth again. And we knew it was to be so. It was thus we learned how it gets in behind the heart to the deepest fountains of emotion.[388]

Auld Lang Syne also featured in an impromptu sing-along on Christmas day 1914 during the famous 'football' truce. Sir Edward Hulse (1889–1915) of the Scots Guards recalled that

> Scots and Huns were fraternising in the most genuine possible manner.... so we went on, singing everything... and ended up with 'Auld Lang Syne', which we all, English, Scots, Irish, Prussian, Württembergers, etc., joined in. It was absolutely astonishing.[389]

The Tommies' use of that nostalgia was multi-faceted however, for at the same time as the Revd Lauchlan Watt's poignant reminiscence above, one of the many soldiers' parody marching songs used the tune of *Auld Lang Syne*. The popular *We're Here*

Because We're Here was an interminable repetition of that one phrase to the favourite tune where, in Graham Seal's words, '[t]he hopelessness of their situation, the futility of it all, was perfectly captured in the repeated absurdity of those lines, throbbing with the musical nostalgia and sentiment of the "Auld Lang Syne" music and lyric'.[390] This shows that the power of Burns's song could be utilised in a number of ways, and not always conventionally which is in and of itself an exhibition of its inherent power.

It was not just amongst combatants, however, that celebrating Burns was a welcome break from the fatigues of war. At the commencement of hostilities around five thousand Allied civilians were interned by the German government at Ruhleben Camp (outside Berlin). As part of the civil infrastructure of the internment, a Scottish Circle and a Burns Club were formed to celebrate 1914's St Andrew's and Hogmanay and 1915's Burns Night respectively (the two societies subsequently merged). The camp committee seems to have gone to great lengths to make their Burns Night as traditional as possible, even to the extent of sending out a 'Fraternal Greeting' to Burns Clubs at home: 'the Members of the Ruhleben Burns Club (composed of Scottish civil prisoners of war) at its inauguration send warmest greetings to sister clubs the world o'er'.[391] There is a contemporary recollection of their celebrations:

> a traditional 'Burns Nicht', comprising Scotch songs, readings from the poet, an address on Burns, orchestral contributions, bagpipe selections, and a sword dance by a Highlander in costume... but the gem of the evening came at the end when the [Kommandant] who was present with his wife, expressed his thanks for the pleasant and instructive programme and concluded with the cry: 'Hoch die Schotten!' (Long live the Scots!)— as though the Scots, forsooth, were an anti-British nationality.[392]

These morale raising events carried on within the camp community for the duration of their internment and here we find the cross over between the desire to celebrate Burns through good works by those in London and traditionally by those incarcerated in Germany. Throughout the war the London Robert Burns Club not only sent food parcels, but petitioned the Government to obtain better conditions for those incarcerated.

As Germany's war position deteriorated and its economy contracted severely through the effects of the allied blockade, conditions inside the camp went into further decline with a concomitant effect on the health of the internees.

With the ending of the conflict in November 1918, people looked forward to a resumption of Burns festivities with the *Southern Reporter* joyously welcoming the Burns Supper back to Selkirkshire, 'after a few years pent up by the emergencies of War, the flow of Burns oratory has come down in a mighty spate. We are glad of it'.[393] As Duncan McNaught wrote in the 1919 *Burns Chronicle*, he and many Burnsians were 'in confident expectation of better things when the clubs resume their wonted activity. When the Boys come home again, joy will lighten sorrow, and Time heals all wounds'.[394] In that sense, it was only fitting that (as an example) the Sunderland Burns Club pipers lead their municipal peace parade in 1919.[395]

Twenty years after that, the events of the Second World War similarly made their mark on how the community celebrated Burns's birthday in January 1940 and for the duration of that war. Most of the large dinners and many small ones went ahead as planned during the 'Phoney War' including events held by the civilian volunteers such as the ARP or the Home Guard.[396] Ayr was conspicuous in immediately abandoning its dinners until peace returned, and instead once again threw its efforts behind a community wreath laying service at Burns Statue Square on the poet's birthday. The home effect – both in terms of attack and rationing was significantly more challenging in the Second World War than in the previous conflict and (again, absent

Dalry) most British clubs and societies closed down large formal dinners, while again, the Australasians and Americans felt no need to cancel.

Most British clubs endeavoured to find a suitable commemoration by an act or event felt to be more suitable to the times of trial. In particular the custom of sending 'Fraternal Greetings' from club to club was maintained, expressing both solidarity and hope. The Annan Burns Club's fraternal greeting for January 1940 was typical:

> From Pole to Pole the God of War
> Summons the Empire from afar.
> For Liberty and Freedom's cause,
> For Motherland and Britain's laws.
> But yet someday the sun will shine,
> And gone will be the gun and mine,
> When this mad world to Peace returns,
> To Brotherhood – and Robert Burns.[397]

In Glasgow in 1942 it was literally 'pole to pole' as the Scottish Polish Society held a Burns Supper to celebrate the cause of freedom and the (unfortunately ultimately vain) hope of fighting for a free Poland.[398] While larger formal arrangements were mainly eschewed, there was also an element of propaganda that Burns Night could bring people closer together, in the spirit of camaraderie or fellowship which underpinned the struggle. Even the trusty haggis was drafted in to help the war effort – with a Socialist MP raising a question in the House of Commons in December 1941, asking His Majesty's Government 'to do anything to increase the supply of this wholesome and economical food?'[399] A perfect example of this propaganda can be seen in 'The Broons', the *Sunday Post's* legendary strip cartoon published on Sunday, 26 January 1941. This sees the Burns Supper as initially odd (or even partisan) to non-Scots eyes, but upon closer convivial reflection, becomes a unifying message of hospitality and shared values in adversity (even sharing and enjoying the haggis!).

Naturally, servicemen were allowed greater latitude over civilians when it came to entertainments. As seen in the Great War Scottish messes, where they were able to, they tried to keep the Burns tradition alive as part of *esprit-de-corps*. Alongside those exhibitions, the songs and poems of Burns featured prominently on the radio programmes on 25 January each year of the war both on the home and the forces programmes and 1941 saw the government print some 20,000 copies of a small edition of Burns's *Works* for distribution to the troops. Newspapers carry reports of various Burns Suppers held by the armed forces particularly in the early part of the war, some of which involved imaginative topicality, such as the RAF Northern Command in 1940 who arranged 'models of German Heinckel, Dornier and Juenker bomber aircrafts which were suspended from the ceiling ... that they appeared to be making a bombing attack on the haggis as it rested on the top table. But behind every Nazi bomber was a model of a Spitfire or Hurricane fighter'.[400]

As with the fictional Private McPhee two decades earlier, the army (or at least its Scots contingent) not only marched on its stomach, but once a year insisted that that march should be based on a diet of haggis. Major AAH Fraser of the Royal Army Medical Corps recounts in his diary the Burns Supper he attended in Palestine in 1943.[401] Operational requirements often frustrated that traditional aim: '[t]he Gordons arrived in Tripoli in time to celebrate Burns Night, but had to put up with bully beef ragout in place of haggis'[402] (although the following year, the quartermasters succeeded in providing haggis for the whole Eighth Army).[403]

Using Burns and the Burns Supper to promote morale often included a lighter, ironic view of the customs and a willingness to 'spoof' non-Scots such as at Dalmore in 1944:

> the Scottish Officers... borrowed the kilts from the
> Pipe Band, as well as some rifles from the Armoury,

and set out in the darkness of the preceding evening to 'shoot the haggis' in the woods, at least in sufficient quantities to provide ample fare for the Supper. Those who were in Dalmore House heard sporadic firing coming from the direction of the adjacent woodland, and it can be assumed that those who were ignorant of Scottish habits accepted that a good job was being done.[404]

Life as a prisoner of war was considerably harder – whether civilian or military – in this conflict, but the celebration of Burns continued, often clandestinely. After being captured in the fall of Singapore, groups of Ayrshire Freemasons maintained Burns Night as part of a cycle of Lodge meetings in the railway death camps and the larger groups of Scots incarcerated in Europe, such as those who created the 'Reel of the 51st Division' in OFLAG VII-C PoW Camp in Laufen, Germany, did their bit too to use the memory of Burns as a beacon of hope and the potential for enhancing prisoners' morale through the Burns Supper was not forgotten.[405] Perhaps the most unusual and cross-cultural exhibition of Burns celebration in the theatre of war is in the memoirs of Andrew Winton of RAF Bomber Command who managed to escape from his POW camp in January 1945. While fleeing eastward he ran into the vanguard of the Russian army, headed for Berlin. The female tank commander who stopped him insisted he bivouac overnight with her and the tank crew as it was January 25th and the Russians wanted the honour of celebrating Burns with a real Scotsman.[406]

One of the oddest recorded Burns Suppers was the one hosted by Sir David Maxwell Fyfe in Nuremburg on 25 January 1946 for the international team of prosecution lawyers at the Nuremberg Trials. Sir David recited both the *Selkirk Grace* and *To A Haggis* supported by two pipers from the Gordon Highlanders, while Konstantine Fedin of the USSR gave the Immortal Memory speech highlighting that 'the works of Robert Burns… were increasing in popularity in Russia'. In one of the last East/West collaborations before the Cold War 'the Russians found the combination of haggis and whisky "wonderful"'. [407] After the festivities, the legal teams returned to their head-snedding tasks.

Following peace in 1946, the community saw a return to normal festivities, albeit under the shadow of rationing and rebuilding: 'The number of Burns dinners and suppers held in Glasgow was estimated to be almost of a par with peace-time celebrations'.[408] In fact, as will be discussed below, the return of servicemen had as profound an impact on the perception of the Burns Supper as it was to have in UK politics.

In both World Wars, we see a common pattern, the adoption of Burns's patriotic poems as war cries, both for recruitment into the forces and also for maintaining morale within them. This is linked to a desire to give up 'fine dining' by many civilians at home perhaps translating their efforts into some charitable or helpful cause for servicemen; while people displaced from home, through military service or imprisoned, saw the Burns Supper as a unifying and linking function, rooted in the essential home values that are, at the propaganda level, the aim of the fight.

These responses to global conflict see participants trying to hold onto cultural and convivial reminders of 'what we are fighting for' and 'home' which are consistent tropes in military life and memoir. There are other important responses to other forms of conflict such as the case of the late Professor Tom Sutherland (1931–2016) who was abducted in June 1985 by terrorists in Lebanon, and not released until November 1991. He has written about how his remembrance of Burns and his poems was a crucial part of his survival of the ordeal. In particular, he describes celebrating Burns Suppers (to the extent possible while chained to the wall of a concrete cell) with fellow captives between 1987 and 1991 when 'on 25th January we had Burns to perk us up', sharing their meagre rations while commemorating Burns through line-by-line recitation of the poems. A fellow prisoner, Father Marcel Caton 'prayed but even he couldn't transform pitta bread into haggis or cold tea into wine let alone whiskey [sic]. But our supper flowed over his praying body and by now the chains no longer counted'.[409] Unbeknown to Sutherland, his wife Jean held a parallel Burns Supper with friends every year.[410]

The history of how people maintained the Burns Supper tradition during the World Wars and indeed through many other conflicts shows the resilience of the concept. Servicemen and women found the lively celebration inherent in the Burns Supper to be a reaffirmation of companionship, a reminiscence of home and a much-needed break from the diurnal realities of life and death. At home, in solidarity with those fighting and those bereaved, there was a voluntary reduction in convivial dining but with energies often channelled into other ways of keeping the calendar custom of Burns's birthday. Interestingly, the widespread suspension of Suppers during the two periods of hostilities did not lead to the tradition falling into desuetude; in fact, the number of Burns Suppers held apparently rebounded as soon as peace was declared.

CHAPTER SEVEN

Innovations and the Global Period

And it is safe to say that a hundred years hence [from 1896] he will be more thought of still. By that time the patronising Philistine, and the bourgeois critic, and the malignant detractor with his croak and leer, will have vanished into congenial obscurity. Burns will be able to speak for himself.[411]

WHEN READING REPORTS of Burns Suppers from the 1880s to the 1920s, and even into the late 1970s, it can be hard to tell which decade the report had been taken from, they all seem so similar. The Bureaucratic period was precisely that, an era of strict conformity to a high set of principles and practices particularly exemplified by the ancient (or claimed to be ancient) Burns Clubs under the aegis of the Burns Federation. But it was hard to keep the concept within absolute bounds. The previous chapter looked at the social effect of World Wars, and added to that a recognition of Burns beyond the confines of the English-speaking and capitalist world saw cross-fertilisation with Communism and then leaps in technology (both in communications and in travel) which proved too much for a Federation of Mrs Partingtons. These trends can now be seen as the precursors of very significant change in attitude if not in essential form.

Communism

While Burns and his works had interested and influenced European writers, the Burns Supper had failed to expand much beyond the

Anglophone sphere until the 20th century. Then Communists in Russia and China recognised Burns as a peasant author of the people whose 'man's a man' lyric prefigured the *Internationale* as a rallying cry for their new political order. One of the earliest direct Communist celebrations was in 1937 when Scots, English and Irish members of the International Brigade ('honest to God British proletarian types', as one diarist recorded) who had volunteered to fight for the Left in Spain, held a ramshackle Burns Supper on 25 January prior to the Battle of the Jarama.

> Typically there is a special meal, a Burns Supper, consisting of haggis, turnips and potatoes. In the absence of these ingredients, the boisterous volunteers ate sardines with their bayonets... Several Scottish brigadiers actually wore kilts, to the consternation of the Spaniards... comrades spoke powerfully on Burns' revolutionary egalitarianism, his support of the French revolution and international outlook... In less than three weeks many of those who attended this most extraordinary of Burns Nights would be lying dead or wounded a few miles away on their first and final battlefield.[412]

The poet and Marxist critic, Christopher Caudwell (the pen name of Christopher Sprigg, 1907–1937) contributed verses for the night's entertainments and, although he claimed it hard to understand Burns's poetry because of the 'lingo', he felt the emotional attachment the Scotsmen in the International Brigade had for Burns. He recognised that these Scots volunteers were clearly inspired by Burns, who, as 'a people's poet till he died, was an apposite choice of icon for all of the men fighting under that banner.[413]

While Burns's poetic influence on Russia is clear, as seen in the war memoir above from 1946, the concept of celebrating the poetry over dinner and toasts is less certain. The inaugural meeting of the communist organised Bowhill People's Burns Club in 1940 entertained two Russian sailors and a Polish interpreter as guests of honour.[414] Anecdotally, given the key Russian tradition of toasting at, after (and even instead of) dining, there is a likelihood that the poet's name did not pass unhonoured on his birthday in the Soviet Union at least at the level of the formal or informal toast list. Russian involvement in the Nuremberg 1946 Burns Supper was noted above and a programme of Burns songs, reset by Soviet composers, was broadcast in 1951 from the Moscow Conservatoire to celebrate a poet 'ringing with hatred of the forces of reaction, with the joy of life, and with the love of his people'.[415]

The poet Edwin Morgan celebrated Burns Night with British and Russian friends while he was on a cultural exchange to Moscow in 1955, however, formal Burns Suppers only seem to have taken root there following the celebrated Soviet poet Samuel Marshak's (1887–1964) visit to Scotland that year for the 'Burns International Festival' and its dinner in Ayr.[416] This was followed in 1959 when Marshak proposed the 'Immortal Memory' at a gala concert in Moscow attended by Emrys Hughes, the MP for South Ayrshire.[417] In parallel, that year, the first secretary of the UK Embassy of the USSR was guest of honour at Ayr Burns Club's Burns Supper. Of course, subsequent research shows that his translations were not true but were ideologically controlled and distorted by the Party, but it still provided a convivial approach of brotherhood.[418] This theme was picked up amongst British Communists, too, with JR Campbell writing in the *Daily Worker* in 1956 warning that communists should be doing more to 'rescue' Burns as was happening in Russia. To fail to politicise Burns, he wrote, would mean 'a bicentenary celebrated merely by banquets of stiffed shirts or of shopkeepers aspiring to be stuffed shirts will be a caricature of the poet who held that "liberty's a glorious feast"'. Once again, a desire to use Burns for political manipulation through the Burns Supper would come to naught.[419]

Beyond the USSR, 1959 saw CM Grieve and other communist-leaning artists touring satellite states such as Hungary and Bulgaria to hold Burns Suppers to mark the bicentenary year of Burns's birth, unaware (or unquestioning) of the concurrent repression of non-Russophone poets throughout the Communist Bloc. This perceived Russian love of Burns, and the propaganda use made of it in the Khrushchev years, was skilfully parodied the following year by Alex Atkinson in his *By Rocking Chair Across Russia* the following year.

> By happy chance I arrived in Moscow on Burns Night... a whole army of people on pleasure bent, drawn to the historic Red Square by their reverence for the humble Ayrshire poet... At a lighted upstairs window in the Kremlin, Khrushchev watched the proceedings with a merry twinkle in his eye... the proceedings took an orgiastic turn. Men, women and children moved in a close-packed mass, wolfing down handfuls of fresh haggis, passing mugs of fiery liquor from hand to hand, forming squads of a hundred and fifty at a time to dance the Gay Gordons, duelling with improvised skean-dhus in the shadow of Lenin's tomb, kissing other people's wives, swirling around in trews and ribboned bonnets. It was an unforgettable sight. [420]

With a rather more straight face, the Scottish Union of Students held a Burns Supper at the Royal College of Technology in Glasgow for 28 visiting Russian undergraduates, and there are mentions of an annual dinner arranged by the 'Robert Burns and Alexander Pushkin Friendship Society' in Moscow from 1959, who invited John Grey of Ayr Burns Club to be their guest speaker in 1964 thus starting a tradition of recognisable traditional Burns Suppers in Russia.[421]

From 1975 there were even package holidays from the UK to Russia for Burns Night and, from 1984, people travelled in the other direction too. The *Glasgow Herald* reported: 'Russian Customs officials will turn a blind eye to 30 cases of whisky, 2 cwt of haggis, and the same weight of neeps which will accompany

300 enthusiasts for a Burns anniversary dinner in Moscow [and Leningrad] next month'.[422] The following year a film crew from the commercial Scottish elevision station STV joined the tour visiting Moscow to celebrate its tenth anniversary with a programme called *To Russia with Rabbie* which established a wide perception of the linkage between Burns and Russia which continues today. In the more open society prevailing in Russia, these formal dinners were joined by a new ex-pat St Andrew's Society from 1993 and several smaller Burns events not just in Moscow, but in other cities as well.[423] In Ukraine, the Kyiv Lions Club has been running consecutive annual Burns Nights since 1995 in Kiev.[424]

In China, the history of Scots culture is seen firstly through the remaining influential diasporic societies of Hong Kong. As discussed above, within the commercial history of that entrepôt, St Andrew's dinners organised by Scots 'hongs' such as Jardine Matheson were important relationship building events in Hong Kong and mainland Canton from the 1830s. There were occasional crossovers in London too, Dr Sun Yat Sen's medical tutor and lifelong friend was Sir James Cantlie (1851–1926), a prominent Burnsian and president of the Burns Club of London. Cantlie famously saved his friend's life in an abduction attempt by the Chinese government in London. Amongst the Chinese friends Cantlie brought to the London Burns Club's annual supper was Sir Chih Chen Lo-feng-luh (1850–1903) whose Immortal Memory speech to the Club in declared that 'Burns was as well understood… by a Chinaman as by a Scot'.[425]

As in Russia, Burns is claimed to be the most read of the Western poets in China, through the translations made into Mandarin prior to the Cultural Revolution. This interest was emphasised by Mao's choice of a version of *My Heart's in the Highlands* as the marching song for his cadre of communists while they were struggling against Japanese occupation, playing on the dual connotation of a peasant poet and the chairman's own birthplace in the mountain regions. In 1943 Mao Zedong and Chiang Kai-shek sent a 'Chinese Parliamentary Goodwill

Mission' to the UK. During its tour of Scotland in January 1944, 'Dr Wen Yuan-ning surprised his guides with his knowledge of the works of Robert Burns; frequently during the tour he quoted some lines from Scotland's national poet suitable to the occasion'.[426] This visit culminated in Dr Wen giving a broadcast of an Immortal Memory on the BBC which was described by the *Glasgow Herald* as not 'merely courteous gesture to the representative of a visiting ally... but a man speaking, not for effect on a special occasion, but what he genuinely thought and felt to be true about Scotland's national poet'.[427]

However, in mainland China, while there is no record until relatively recently of Burns in a banquet context. While a concert under the auspices of the local St Andrew's Society is recorded in 1907, the first formal Burns Supper appears to have been held in 1981 and 1982 where Professor Wang Zouliang (of the Beijing Foreign Language Institute) gave the Immortal Memories. In 1982, the whisky for the toasts was donated by Jardine Matheson. Burns Suppers can be found today not only around the vestiges of Scots culture in Hong Kong but in the mainland cities of Beijing and Shanghai too.[428] For many years the Burns Supper has been a way of displaying hospitality and tradition which are core Chinese traditions, in a Scottish frame.

The wider Chinese community also shares this appreciation and, since 1993, each year in Vancouver, Chinese New Year and Burns Night have fused under a banner called 'Gung Haggis Fat Choy'. This is a performance concept created and curated by Todd Wong, whose blog carries the strap line: 'Toddish McWong's Misadventures in Multiculturalism: through arts, culture, food, dragon boats, travel + more...'.[429] A cultural and culinary fusion sees kilted men and lion dancers, haggis won tons and poetry and song from the two cultural groups. British Columbia has had a strong tradition of celebrating Robert Burns, both in suppers and in the prominent statues in Vancouver and Victoria, and it would seem that the multi-cultural ethic that is a highly regarded feature of BC culture extended to Chinese/Scots crossover in another guise in 'the 1930s [Burns] fervour was particularly marked. Even the Chinatown Lions' Club organised an annual Burns dinner, complete with haggis served with a sweet and sour sauce'.[430]

By the 250th anniversary, in Russia, Ukraine and China, there were significant formal celebrations of the Burns Supper where the theme and message were recognisably locally inspired and geopolitically motivated but they were all held within the formal traditional structure.

Broadcasting

The other great societal change in the 20th century was the technology of broadcasting, first by radio, then by television and now, in the 21st century, by internet and social media. Broadcasting interest in the Burns Supper was an extension of the enthusiastic coverage in the *Illustrated London News* for both the Festival on the Doon and the 1859 centenary.

The second ever outside radio broadcast by the BBC was a relay of the Immortal Memory given to the Burns Club of London on 25 January. The choice of this as the second event was probably linked to the past president of the Burns Club, Sir William Noble (1861–1943), who had served as engineer-in-chief of the General Post Office and had chaired the 'Broadcasting Committee' which created the BBC in 1922.[431] The Burns Club chairman introduced Chesterton's ten-minute speech in which 'there were no fulsome eulogies either of the poet or the nation... just the plain truth, clothed in that Chestertonian idiom which is sometimes as baffling as it is always delightful'.[432] The toast was followed by an hour of Scottish songs and dance tunes transmitted from the studio in Glasgow. Despite GKC's idiosyncratic approach (which was to rile Hugh MacDiarmid into an *ad hominem* attack in his *Drunk Man*), the broadcast was well received both as entertainment and innovation:

To listen, for example, to the speeches made at the
Burns' anniversary dinner, was absolutely uncan-
ny, for here the mere fact that the speaker was not
in the artificial surroundings of the broadcasting
room, produced a naturalness which, combined
with the general noises of the assembled diners as
a background, was quite extraordinary.[433]

The following year saw the first live radio broadcast of a
whole Burns Supper by the BBC from Mauchline for that club's
inaugural Burns Supper held within Poosie Nancy's Inn. There
were also live transmissions of the principal speeches from
the Newcastle-upon-Tyne Burns Clubs and the Burns Dinner of
the Cardiff Caledonian Society along with a studio reconstruction
of the after-dinner entertainments from Glasgow and Aberdeen,
the latter by members of Peterhead Burns Club. Mauchline
gathered the greatest press, given the atmospheric venue and its
direct connection with Burns. The *Kilmarnock Standard* carried a
glowing report and photographs of this historic event in wonder
that 'in thousands of homes the ears would be directed to Poosie
Nansie's', to hear the club members recite and sing.[434]

This innovation would appear to have been well received
by listeners as the experiment was repeated for several years
particularly by the Mauchline Burns Club and the Bournemouth
and Cardiff Caledonian Societies. 1935 saw a programme of
singing from Glasgow's 'Burns Supper for Unemployed Men' but
after that annual Burns Night broadcasts took the form of talks
or concerts, with no outside broadcasts from live Burns Suppers,
absent regional programmes from Dumfries in 1946, Greenock
in 1952, an excerpt from the Ayr Burns Club in 1959 and a
particularly grand occasion from Edinburgh that same year with
Hugh MacDiarmid providing the Immortal Memory.[435] BBC
Radio's 'Scottish Magazine' programme held a regular January
broadcast of an 'abridged' studio-based Burns Supper from
1952 until at least 1959.[436] One inspired programme, produced
by Bill Meikle of the BBC an aired on 24 January 1956 saw

a 'collage' of international recordings that had been collected by the BBC. The programme opened with music by the Massed Pipe Bands of Queensland, the *Address to the Haggis* had two verses performed in each of Montreal, Perth, Johannesburg and New York, the Immortal Memory was collated from speeches in Otago, Winnipeg and Montreal, while the Toast to the Lasses came from Gisbourne, NZ.[437] Subsequently, the radio broadcast Burns Supper fell out of fashion.

Even with this number of radio broadcasts over the years there were relatively few disc recordings: Thomas Keith in his *Discography* only identifies seven (possibly nine) Burns Supper commercial recordings between ca 1948 and 2002.[438] At the other end of the cultural spectrum, one fairly light-hearted book of instruction on how to hold a Burns Supper was created with a 45 rpm vinyl record as an appendix in 1965.[439]

Equally on television, the focus (often with a highly sentimental approach) was on having programmes about Burns's life and works around Burns Night, rather than televising the ongoings at a Burns Supper.[440] The BBC made the first TV broadcast of a Burns Supper in 1955 from the 'Heads of Ayr Hotel, on 19 January as part of a Burns International Festival' (as mentioned above, welcoming Samuel Marshak).[441] It received some level of popular acclaim and the BBC televised Burns Suppers (as well as other Burns themed broadcasts) from 'The BBC Television Burns Club' in both 1957 and 1958 and again in 1961.[442] TV Producers seem to have lost enthusiasm for the concept after that, with the Burns Federation passing a conference motion seeking to 'make representation to the television authorities with a view to improving the coverage of [Burns Anniversary Celebrations]'.[443]

The BBC had made the editorial decision to focus on other kinds of Burns programming, and so there are no films of Burns Suppers (absent a short documentary film which exists of the Irvine Burns Supper in 1971, whose purpose is unknown) for just over a decade.[444] Then, in 1973, STV filmed (for the first time in full colour) a Federation Supper in Glasgow where the Immortal memory was given by Robert Graves, a second Burns Supper was shown in 1975 and then a third and final show in 1977 with the Revd Jimmy Currie (and John Laurie reciting *Tam o'Shanter*).[445] In short, the Burns Supper was not seen as particularly entertaining on television. To that end, producer Donny O'Rourke's programme *Supperman*, set out deliberately to 'challenge some of the more manifest Burns Supper absurdities', contrasting, amongst other aspects, the highly formal Bureaucratic form of the event in the face of the less structured conviviality that Burns displayed in his own social life.[446] Candidly, watching other people (often older men), eating and drinking is no highlight, in fact it is a species of torture that was not even visited upon Tantalus.

Given the thesis of this work, the failure to capture the Burns Supper as an audio or a visual broadcast is unsurprising: as the form of the Burns Supper is inherently performative, being a distant spectator through the medium of broadcasting limits the engagement and misses, in a fundamental way, the point of the event. Looking back, that fundamental point was missed by many traditionalists too. For example, in 1950 the Greenock Burns Club noted a decline in numbers attending their Supper. The *Greenock Telegraph* estimated that there were around 20 Burns Suppers held in the town over ten days. The old club's 'rigidly righteous' response to this increasing demand to celebrate was uninspiring criticising the other events for being 'the kind of party the poet himself would have revelled in. But they could afford to be light-hearted because they did not have any burden of tradition or even of responsibility. It was for the Mother Club to preserve the sense of value'.[447] Truly, the best is the enemy of the good.

The core of Burnsian reactionaries could not, however, stop people having fun anymore than they could delay other technological innovations, which not only included shipping haggis across the world by aeroplane, but even in celebrating the Burns Supper in mid-air.

> On 25th January, 1965, a BOAC Scottish Monarch
> jetliner rose from Prestwick and roared over the

> Atlantic towards New York at 400 miles an hour,
> [from] the tannoy radio, the pipes struck up a
> rousing reel in a disciplined, subdued skirl as the
> highest Burns Supper in the world got under way,
> 35,000 feet above the ocean. I gave the Immortal
> Memory in that bright blueness, a mile above the
> clouds, in a luxurious Boeing 707 and watched the
> kilted stewards dispense haggis to the enthralled
> and delighted transatlantic travellers.[448]

The concept of Burns Night tourism also extended to cruises:
1980 saw travel agents arranging package holidays over
Burns Night in Copenhagen and, rather more luxuriously, 'to
celebrate Burns Night off the beautiful island of Las Palmas'.[449]
The freedom and speed of travel had a widening effect on
the ability to arrange a Burns Supper with traditional food
and drink, which might not be available in countries outside
Scotland. In a 1984 article on the international spread of the
Burns Supper, the *Glasgow Herald* discussed celebrations in
Switzerland, Chicago, Mexico, Thailand and the United Arab
Emirates before informing the readers that 'British Caledonian
Airways is transporting pipers, dancers and haggis to various
destinations in the world, including the Cameroons, Gambia,
Zambia, Ivory Coast, Venezuela and Nigeria'.[450] So through
both modern transport and modern transmission, the Burns
Supper continued to extend its boundaries across the globe.

The Advent of the Global Period

By the time of the 1996 bicentennial of the death of Burns, a mix
of local government inefficiency in Ayrshire and weak leadership
from the Burns Federation meant that there was little in the way of
formal grand celebration either within Scotland or internationally.
Apart from the covers of the 1996 and 1997 editions of the *Burns
Chronicle,* the reader found few mentions of the 200th anniversary
of Burns's death. The ability to capture a monster-meeting had

long passed and modern media seemed unable or unwilling to propagate the traditional Supper, but once again local, national and international groups made great play of the anniversary through their own Burns Suppers. The landscape was coloured by the reaction to the overly traditional approach, or as critics would decry it, the 'White Heather Club', of the cultists on one hand, or the belligerent politics of 'people's suppers' on the other. As in 1832 and 1844, the Burns Supper became a political haggis, but this time with a left-wing agenda that was portrayed as the true approach to the appreciation of Burns. In between these factions, West Sound, the local radio station in Ayr, arranged a mega-supper in Glasgow in 1986 as a tribute to the bicentenary of the *Kilmarnock Edition*. They sold 1000 expensive tickets for a Burns Supper with a high-quality banqueting menu (including haggis as an intermediate course with a plate of beef as the main course), and a 'show business' Immortal Memory given by the actor John Cairney who was then famous for his one-man show, *The Robert Burns Story*. While the choice of artistes shows a certain period taste (Andy Stewart, Jimmy Shand, Moira Anderson and Kenneth McKellar) West Sound had created a new type of Burns Supper repeated annually since – a professional banquet (with quality food in a grand location) with equally professional talent and often a charitable dimension and a use of school or student talent. Another organisation formed then was the Society of Scots Lawyers in London who quickly built a reputation for jolly events from its inaugural Burns Supper in 1987 and onwards. The following year had a particularly memorable toast list with the three major speeches performed by three of the greatest Scottish debaters ever, John Smith, Donald Dewar and Malcolm Rifkind. Inspired by these successes, the Chartered Institute of Bankers in Scotland (London District Centre) modernised its longstanding Grosvenor House offering after 1999, which had become tired and repetitive, revitalising what would be for many years the largest Burns Supper in the world.[451] 1996's bicentenary also saw the Lord Provost of Glasgow create a large charity driven event and these more crafted evenings with professional sound quality, lighting and presentation added a new performative dimension to the existing range of accessibilities and challenging the view captured by Helen Simpson: the 'inevitable Caledonian overkill, all those sporrans and dirks and coy talk of the lassies'.[452] Each of these gala Burns Suppers were continuing as popular events in the January 2009 season and, although the London Bankers Burns Supper fell foul of the global financial crisis, the others remain popular and relevant today.

The Burns Supper grew globally and overcame critics mainly due to its simple and accessible format: virtually all follow a form of the Pauline rite albeit with a number of common refinements introduced over the years. Thus, by the 2009 anniversary year, the Burns Supper was celebrated in many countries, by many different groups of people. The whisky company 'Famous Grouse' sponsored a website as part of the wider 'Year of the Homecoming' festivities which allowed the organisers of Burns Suppers in any country to log on and mark their particular event on an interactive, global map. On 25 January 2009, 'The World-Famous Burns Supper' map identified 3,673 different Burns Suppers with representation on each continent in 80 different countries.[453] So while, as in 1859, the concentration of recorded effort was in Scotland, the rest of the UK, North America and Australia/New Zealand, there were many other countries where not just Scots expatriates or members of the Scottish diaspora wanted to join in the celebration. This typified the Global period of the Burns Supper, where the broad Pauline concept was still followed (a dinner, with an Immortal Memory toast, haggis, and the poems and/or songs of Burns) with as much or little extra in the way of programming as the arrangers desired. Again, as with 1859, the aggregate numbers of Burns Suppers held were higher – perhaps very much higher – than the self-selected grouping captured on Famous Grouse's admirable map.

By the 250th Birthday Anniversary in January 2009, the 'formal' demonstrations, whether wreath layings or the national church services of commemoration, were dwarfed by the worldwide interest in Burns Suppers. The importance of the tradition of celebrating Burns was recognised by the Scottish Government, opening its 'Homecoming' with a Burns Supper in Alloway in the new Burns Birthplace Museum. This programme was described as high on performance and low on speeches but which clearly met the traditional standards of an addressed haggis, a toast to Burns (by the First Minister) and a series of different entertainments around the songs and poems of Burns. The anniversary year was bigger than just Scotland's Homecoming and encompassed around 80 countries, such that only a third of Burns Suppers took place in Scotland. But each event can be seen to be sharing a commonly identifiable format. Different people, genders, cultures, attitudes to celebrity, politics and drink: but all recognisable by Hamilton Paul as offshoots of his original concept, all being forms of what Walt Whitman (not wholly appreciatively) called 'the vehement celebrations' of Burns's birth and verse through 'suppers and drinks and speeches'.[454]

Since the successful and happy celebrations in 2009 there has been a noticeable, albeit anecdotal, growth in the celebration of 'Burns Night' in pubs, clubs, wine bars and restaurants, alongside more formal dinner held by Burns Clubs old and new, other societies and associations and groups of friends and families. It has to be admitted that not every pub or restaurant holding a 'Burns Night' sees the sharing of poetry as its primary goal, but the spirit (if you excuse the pun) is present there in a celebratory mood. All of these keeping alive the precepts set by Hamilton Paul. In 2016, in a long-overdue homage to Paul, the Robert Burns Birthplace Museum in Alloway held a Burns Supper in the Cottage itself on 25 January. Twenty-eight men and women met under the famous thatched roof and the chairmanship of Dr David Hopes, the director of BPPM and the watchful eye of the Bard, for in an acknowledgement of that first Supper, the old 'Burns Head' inn sign was exhibited at the atmospheric dinner.[455] The original nine men from July 1801 would have felt at home.

In this journey from that first Alloway dinner to the hundreds of towns and cities in all corners of the continents, the core of the Burns Supper has remained undisturbed. A significant reason for that is the way in which Hamilton Paul chose the essential elements of the format and blended them together in a truly convivial whole enabling a true enjoyment of the power of Burns's works. The next section of this book looks at each of those main elements in turn.

Part Two

The Elements of The Burns Supper

CHAPTER EIGHT

The Immortal Memory

There is a Mexican tradition that states you die three times.
You die once when you cease to breathe. The second death is
experienced when you are buried. And the third death is when
your name is never spoken again. Robert Burns will never
experience the third death.[456]

THE TOAST TO 'the Immortal Memory of Robert Burns' is for
many the highlight of the 'thinking' part of the Burns Supper.
In occupying the prominent role in the evening's festivities, a
speaker is invited to present an appreciation or eulogy (and on
rare occasions, a condemnation) of the Poet concluding with the
formal toast to the Bard. This ritual obtains its power from the
fact identified by Hamilton Paul that the poet clearly expressed
a desire to be famed and remembered. As Burns wrote in the
secrecy of his *First Commonplace Book*: 'Obscure as I am, and
obscure I must be, though no young Poet, nor young Soldier's
heart ever beat more fondly for fame than mine'.[457] To ensure
that, Burns left appropriate poetic markers as part of his
deliberate approach of dramatising his bardship. In effect Burns
guaranteed that, while he might have been obliged to choose
absence through exile, he was not choosing oblivion in life or in
the fullness of time, after death. As he sought of his friends: 'One
round, I ask it with a *tear*,/ To him, *the Bard that's far awa'*.[458]
Robert Burns called on them (as both Brother and Bard) to
honour his memory in future postprandial toasts at the centre
of each evening's harmony after the work of the Lodge. So in

Hamilton Paul's creation the first and primary toast (after the formal nods to the *lares* and *penates*) would be to the Immortal Memory of the man and his talent which brought everyone together on that commemorative night.

The Immortal Memory in Prose

In the early days of the Burns Supper, Hamilton Paul, and many others preceded their toast to Burns with a poem. Today, every Burns Supper will have as the keynote of the evening, a prose speech delivered immediately prior to toasting the 'Immortal Memory'. This started as an innovation introduced by Tannahill at Paisley in 1805. He, as the clerk of the Society, invited his radical friend William McLaren to augment the proceedings (supplementing Tannahill's own ode to the Bard, and other poems and songs) by preceding the principal toast of the evening with a eulogistic speech, which began thus: 'It is with infinite pleasure that I see, at this moment, so many men of taste, so many fond and enthusiastic lovers of Scottish song, met on this evening to celebrate the birth of our immortal bard.'[459] Over the years from McLaren in 1805 Paisley through to 1859, and then on to today, the tradition emerged of an oration as the keynote of the evening where the 'orator' would have a free hand to discourse on a theme connected with Burns or his works, one which resonated with the audience, locale, time or simply with the particular enthusiasms or prejudices of the speaker. While, at the simplest level, the purpose of the toast was and is to honour the birth, genius and works of Burns, the problem has always existed of how to capture the mercurial and chameleon-like complexity of Burns's life and works within this rhetorical confine. The Immortal Memory is like any speech: a combination of the talents and interests of the speaker mediated through his/her oratorical ability to inform, persuade and/or entertain a specific audience. To that extent, it is not correct to see the Immortal Memory speech monolithically: for, as with sermons or lectures, or even conversations, there is a personal input and an individual auditor/collective audience reception which is the nexus of success in any oration. Any of these verbal/oral interactions can be successful, enjoyable, dull or painful, and so it is with an Immortal Memory toast. They range from the banal to the wonderful; from the original to the repetitive.

In the Charismatic period, with some notable exceptions (such as a few speeches with a more radical bent) the theme of memorialising Burns was around a poetic construct of the peasant, whose life was a perceived as a combination of heaven-sent talent and mundane striving, now regretfully and belatedly recognised and garlanded (typically by virgins and Muses) to receive the praise in death he did not fully receive in life as both a great poet and a greater Scot. In the truly Charismatic events which were attended by men who knew the poet or were early readers of his books, there would have been little point in telling Burns's friends and relations the story of his life, instead, the tone of the evening was set by having Gilbert, or Syme, or Sillar being present in person, possibly in a room where the poet himself had had a convivial evening. Here the bardic metaphor, rather than the biographic story, was prevalent within the commemorative verses.

As discussed, Paisley introduced the prose speech as the primary toast but it was not yet necessary to have a long eulogium on every outing. In 1807, for example, Tannahill reports that: 'Mr Blaikie addressed us in a neat [sc: short, exact] speech, concluding with a toast "To the memory of Burns"'.[460] Part of the pleasure of the evening in those early days appears to be wide participation, so rather than having one or two keynote speakers give longer addresses, the president/preses and a range of members each contributed a toast, song or sentiment as a 'party piece' and to allow that wider group of actors, the Immortal Memory had to be quite defined and precise in scope and timing.

The Traditional period saw the beginning of the decline in the presentation of an odes and an increase in the prose contributions based on some level of biographical description.[461] The story of Burns was well-known through Currie's *Life* which was seen as canonical (very much by analogy with Boswell's *Life of Johnson*) and even Gilbert Burns famously shied away from a wholesale re-writing or repudiation of the relatively few parts of Currie which were, in retrospect, over censorious or at least open to rigidly righteous misinterpretation. The publication of Cromek's *Reliques of Robert Burns* in 1808 and its many reprints added a huckster's colour to the poet's life along with new material in the form of more letters, the first myth of Highland Mary and importantly the first general publication of both *The Jolly Beggars* and *Holy Willie's Prayer.* Along with John Gibson Lockhart's *Life of Burns* and Alan Cunningham's writings (and in time, Carlyle's essay on Burns *the Hero as Man of Letters*), the would-be Burns orator now had a set of core volumes from which to draw his inspiration for his Immortal Memory. This could be called the trope of 'dirt and deity' which generated relatively limited number of popular rhetorical *topoi* around Burns's genius transcending the vicissitudes of his poor life.[462] Although the medium of honouring the toast had moved from recited verse to orated prose, the anticipation that this was the high point of the purposeful part of the convivial dinner remained. For, after all, the Burns Supper's purpose is honouring 'him who was far awa".

The detail is explored below in a moment, but as the Traditional period took hold, the Immortal Memory speech crystallised into the form that would be recognisable today: a biographical sketch of all or a part of the poet's life, interspersed with apt quotations from his works, with a particular point, theme or moral adduced by the speaker of personal, party or local interest to the gathered diners. During the controversy over Reform, this move into prose and adoption of a biographical approach allowed attempts by Tories and, to an extent, Whigs and in time Radicals, too, to couple the poet's fame to the changes happening in British polity, however, in the vast range of Immortal Memories which have been discovered in contemporary newspaper accounts, the use of this speech to make an openly avowed party-political statement was less common than imagined. The broadest *topos* can be summarised as Burns (equally in the story of his life as in the genius of his works) being a Scotsman of the Enlightenment, but who represents the universal hope that any ordinary person of talent can succeed was capable of being used by all political parties. Burns was a social man and the format of this supper is one he would happily have joined. Within that universality, there is a particular link with each community dining that night such that within each Burns Supper the participants believed that they were sharing a ritual that Burns himself would recognise and enjoy. Thus, and not just through common enjoyment of his verse, all those present that night would become, in a manner of speaking, partakers of Burns by their participation.

In some respects, the largest differentiator is one of geography, in a local sense of genius and attachment. Just as the seven cities fought over Homer, so 1859 was marked by a tussle between Dumfries, Edinburgh, Glasgow, and Ayr as to who should be the centre point of the festivities. The orators at each of these places focussed on their ownership of their part of the Burns story. In Ayr, they called out his birthplace and the poet's inspirations of Doon and Kirk Alloway; in Dumfries, they honoured the poet's later family life, and his 'state' funeral and Mausoleum. While Edinburgh focussed on the gay life of the literary salon, Scott and the lions of the Enlightenment, the North East recalled the Burness ancestry from the Mearns, and Glasgow stressed that 36/37ths of the Bard's life were spent happily in the west and not the east of Scotland. Beyond Scotland, the message was typically the great myth of the peasant lad o' pairts, using 'a man's a man' as a universal trope.

The 1859 Burns Centenary saw an explosion of oratory and most of the speeches recorded in the *Chronicle* would be recognised and received at a Burns Supper today (although using more sentimental language than humour). In the US in particular, the most prominent public speakers of the day, Emerson (in Boston, MA), Beecher (New York, NY), and Lincoln (Springfield, IL) all proposed the toast which was reported extensively in the local press, in club histories and pamphlets. As Leith Davis has discussed, these orations can be seen in the light of the technological developments such as the electric telegraph, creating a similarity between the poetry of Burns and the invention of Morse code: both of which were seen as bringing humanity closer together.[463] The convivial celebration of Robert Burns had reached a universal scale by building many individual communities, increasingly linked through technology.

There could not be one standard Immortal Memory by 1859, given the diversity of the organisers, audiences and the speakers of the myriad Suppers. Throughout the period, we see new Burns Suppers springing up if old ones no longer met the needs or interests of the locals. It is very interesting to note that some very proud clubs simply did not exist for decades as their particular offering was no longer relevant in their locality. However, proving that this is not the history of Burns Clubs, but of Burns Suppers, there were still non-club meetings in Paisley, Kilmarnock etc during the dark years as interested groups met as the whim took them, but still following what was recognised as the format established by Hamilton Paul. In part, the reason that an overt political propaganda is not a core message is down to the growing number and range of Burns Suppers held. They would either be community based – so as with the Freemasons, politics and religion would be avoided in the sensibilities of common community conviviality, or in the other case, the Burns Supper would be arranged by a specific interest group who already shared a world view and so would expect the orator to cast the toast to the poet in the light of their common opinion.

The growth in Burns Suppers allowed people to choose which kind they would attend, and in time, allow them to hold their own if there were not a specifically welcoming one that they would like to participate in. This balancing act is described by Richard Finlay as a determination to avoid giving 'one ideological camp more rights of possession to a fundamental part of Scottish myth and tradition than the others'.[464] Finlay, however, takes that argument a stage too far in maintaining that '[t]he Burns cult has permitted a safe celebration of Scottish identity which raises no awkward political or cultural questions'. This analysis is true in the limited sense of the approach espoused by the traditional federationists and 'cultists' during the Bureaucratic period of the Burns Supper. However, in the wider awareness that we now have that there were many different approaches to the interpretation of Burns and his 'message' within individual Burns Suppers, the absence of 'awkward questions' was not necessarily a sign of 'depoliticised... Burns Suppers' but more that the ability to create a range of different Burns Suppers resulted in people attending one which already reflected their views, so there was no need to ask 'awkward questions' within what would be relatively homogenous group who could be expected 'to know the answers'.[465] As Rigney summarises, within the celebration of Burns, 'it is difficult to identify a single mnemonic community'.[466]

1859 saw this principle multiplied, and in that centenary year there were around the same number of Burns Suppers arranged as had been held in the previous two decades. The mass oratory of 1859 made several commentators wonder about the kaleidoscopic nature of Burns appreciation: for the message in the 800 odd principal speeches used the same biography and poetry, but often to very different ends. Thus, across Ballantine's compendium one finds all sorts of political, moral and literary themes colouring the different speakers' and audiences' reception of Burns but each relying upon the same source material. This move into prose and adoption of a biographical approach allowed competing attempts by differing groups: those upholding the status quo and radical politicians, temperance campaigners and bacchanalian societies, Scots and non-Scots, and many others commonly seeking to couple the poet's fame to the changes happening in British society and politics. Yet the range of messages was vast. Wilkie Collins, writing for Dickens in *Household Words*, used the conceit of the poet as a hat rack, allowing every speaker a freeform appreciation, but which tells the auditor more about the 'hat' rather than the 'peg' it hangs on.

> To be well aware that the memory of Burns is something to be proud of is only to possess an idea which has been the common property of former generations. But to know that the memory of Burns is likewise something on which the smallest of us can hang up his own individual importance; something which may help the greediest of us to grub up our little handful of money, and the obscurest of us to emit our little speech, is to make one of those rare and remunerative discoveries which we of the present generation may claim as peculiarly our own.[467]

Collins misses the point, though, that one can see Burns's 'universality' and a near-infinite collection of individual receptions of his life and works by individuals. To that extent, the speaker's personal viewpoint, appraisal, or adduced moral is a complement (in both senses) to the richness of the oeuvre and to the many facets of Burns's life (and his complex psychology), as the 20th century poet, Sidney Goodsir Smith, postulated in an Immortal Memory essay for *The Weekly Scotsman*, to describe the problem as how to encapsulate 'all the mony aspects of this mony-heidit hero'.[468] Yet while the Immortal Memory speaker had, in the late Traditional and through the Bureaucratic period of the Burns Supper, an almost limitless length of time to discourse it was – and is – simply impossible to be simple about Burns within the length of either a long speech or a short lecture. This led the modern poet Don Paterson to describe the Immortal Memory as a very complex problem:

> Since the character of Robert Burns is so complicated as effectively not to exist at all – there is barely a human trait which he did not exhibit at one time or another, as if it somehow *defined* him – everyone is free to make their own reading of Burns according to their own personal, critical or neurotic agenda.[469]

Or, as Neil Ascherson colourfully evoked it in 2009, the Immortal Memory speakers could be seen as: 'a procession of biographers dressing their own Burns dolls in their own favourite costumes'.[470] The metaphor is more like the child's toy 'Fuzzy Felt' where every set contains the same rectangular base card and the same collection of apparently random and colourful off-cuts of felt, the object being to create a picture from these unpromising but standardised beginnings. Each of us has the same backboard and the same felt, yet each picture made is different, and each is received by the audience differently. Given the avowed complexity and attendant controversies around Burns's works and life, boiling him down to a communal world view would surely be the worst, and least authentic, outcome?

By the time of the Burns Federation and the Bureaucratic period, an important change occurred in the way speakers approached their subject. In 1859, speakers who had criticised Burns's 'frailties' were openly booed or hissed by the audiences and, in the growth of Burns Clubs and 'the Burns Cult', there was an increasingly limiting trend towards hagiography and an over-compensation to early critiques of the poet's life and habits. For over the next century, in most contexts, it became at least impolite and probably nearly sacrilegious to express critical thought on Burns's moral principles and latterly, to make even a balanced literary critical thought was considered controversial within the circle of Federation dinners.

'The cult wants its oratory thick and slab. Anything quiet and restrained is a disappointment; anything critical is anathema'.[471] So wrote DeLancey Ferguson in 1936 in an essay which reeks of the scholar's pain at sitting through many extravagant eulogies in the increasing formality created by the official network of Burns clubs. The majority of these clubs held very traditional views on the speech and its sanctity, which was emphasised by the growing Federation. In hindsight, on reading the 'official' guidance, it appears that many of these people had lost the plot. From a warm and convivial celebration, a dinner as Paul said that the poet himself would have enjoyed, the Federation's first formal publication on how to arrange a canonical Burns Supper described the keynote speech in these rather depressing terms:

> It lies within [the Chairman's] authority to ensure that the 'Immortal Memory' and its prelude are conducted in a manner suiting the dignity of the occasion... The Immortal Memory... should normally be in a serious vein, paying tribute to the poet. There are circumstances in which a humorous toast could be made but such occasions are so rare and difficult that the 'sermon' type tribute is the rule. The ideal length of the principal toast is 25 minutes – a briefer time is considered sketchy, and only the most gifted of speakers can command the interest of a company beyond a half-hour. [472]

Which was followed up by an unfortunate Freudian slip in 2007, where speakers were abjured 'by all means have a threat of humour' in their speeches.[473]

The laudable aim of the Federationists to encourage common standards created an atmosphere over the century ending in 1996 (or thereabouts) which critics called 'a minor

religion', a 'sanctified illusion and romantic wish fulfilment', or
most vehemently, 'a kailyard level which is beneath intelligent
consideration'.[474] This trend naturally had its concomitant effect
on the form and content of the Immortal Memory. Delancey
Ferguson paraphrased, or parodied, the genre with the following
sample peroration, 'every sentence [of which] was not only
spoken at some Burns celebration but was afterwards committed
to print in official publication':

> When we celebrate the birthday of Robert Burns,
> we celebrate the spirit of America, for America is
> builded on the democracy of the Lord's Prayer,
> and the Sermon on the Mount; and Robert Burns,
> though frail and sin-worn, grasped the vision of
> the infinite and breathed the social and democrat-
> ic gospel of the great prophet of men. He ranks
> next to the Savior in influence for the good of
> humanity. Love is tenderer because of his sing-
> ing of it. Beauty is fairer because of his vision of
> it. Humanity is wiser because of his revelation of
> it. Men have walked with a braver-heartedness
> because of the melody of his marching music,
> which made the poor forget their oppression and
> the rich remember the humane possibilities of
> prosperity. All the world is in his soul: the sordid
> things of it; the hopes and despairs of it; the mel-
> ody of the woodlands; the beauty of the meadow
> flowers; the glamor of earth, and sky, and run-
> ning water, everywhere. Burns has made millions
> happy and has made millions smile, yet his life
> was a tragedy. He was a man of sorrows, and he
> was acquainted with grief. Even the mouse and the
> daisy were not without his tenderness. His very
> sincerity raised him to the catholic and universal
> level. He loved Scotland and everything that God
> had made. He is the Bard of the Beating Heart. All

he has written throbs with brotherhood. Where
liberty was, there was Robert Burns.[475]

Which brings to mind Churchill's description of a speech by
Anthony Eden: 'As far as I can see you have used every cliché
except "God is Love" and "Please adjust your dress before
leaving"'.[476] Ferguson is writing in the period after some great
speakers on Burns such as Andrew Lang, Lord Rosebery, Arthur
Conan Doyle and John Buchan, all of whom made effective and
interesting Immortal Memories worthy of canonical debate.
However, many Burns Clubs held it to be a point of honour
and tradition that only a member of that club could give the
Immortal Memory, and so a great many clubs as the Bureaucratic
period wended its way through its long centenary chose their
'orator' on the grounds of Hobson's choice rather than on any
rhetorical ability or literary insight. Hans Hecht's and Catherine
Carswell's biographies became more popular than those of
Currie and Lockhart around the time that the young men of
the English-speaking world returned from the Second World
War, ready to challenge the *status quo ante bellum* both in the
corridors of power and around the tables of the Burns Clubs.
Therefore, led by a particular representation of the brotherhood
engendered by Burns, there was a growing move towards a
socialist 'man of the people' interpretation of his life and works,
which, particularly in Scotland, became a dominant voice albeit
often with the same eulogistic and mythopoeic approach to the
Immortal Memory, giving rise to a public image of a rigorously
formal and traditional event, which many felt equally removed
from the zone of conviviality as from a genuine appreciation of
the poetry of Burns.

While we will see this change on the Global period when
discussed below, it has to be admitted that it is not too difficult
to find old fashioned hagiography in an Immortal Memory
speech today. That convention of rigorous ritualism represented a
structure almost diametrically opposed to Hamilton Paul's concept
and exemplifies the triumph of narrow form over wider fun.

The Form of the Toast

At any modern Burns Supper, the proposer of the toast will conclude her or his speech with the call to the audience 'to rise and toast the "Immortal Memory of Robert Burns"'. This is a definitive form of words, redolent of tradition. Looking at contemporary sources, however, show that there has been some development over time to reach the current form of words.

Paisley Burns Club calls McLaren's speech the 'first Immortal Memory' which is not strictly accurate and may be seen as another example of the Burns Club mythology. At the simple level, Hamilton Paul gave such a toast for several years in Alloway, and furthermore, Maclaren did not use the actual phrase the 'Immortal Memory', but rather the 'Memory of our Immortal Bard'. As he also referred to 'immortal Thomson' earlier in his speech, at the very least his award of immortality was not exclusively to Burns. The strict formula of the 'Immortal Memory' was first recorded in print for the Philadelphia Burns Club's dinner in 1818. *The Scotsman* of 27 February 1819 reported the first use in Scotland at the Edinburgh dinner (however, the *Caledonian Mercury* of the same date confusingly records the toast as being only to 'The Memory of Burns' so both must be treated with some caution).[477] While Burns's 'immortality' was often cited in poems, songs and speeches, the rubric of the toast seems pretty much to have been 'The Memory' until 1850s with fewer than ten 'Immortal Memory' wordings noted in contemporary reports of these toasts.[478] Using the Dalry Burns Club's comprehensive archives, their principal toast is also 'The Memory' having been the form used in around 90 per cent of the time since the club's 1826 foundation.

Ballantine's *Chronicle* allows us to make a statistical survey of how the principal toast was framed and received throughout the 1859 centenary. There are two competing traditions at work here which overlap: the exact phrase of the toast – and the increasing invocation of immortality on the one hand; and the reception of the toast in silence or with vocal acclaim, on the other.

Taking 'immortality' first, the chart below shows that the majority of toasts in 1859 remained rooted in the 'Memory' tradition, accounting for 58 per cent of all recorded toasts with the exact phrase of the 'Immortal Memory' just under a third of all records. It would take another 40 or 50 years of incremental change (in the Bureaucratic period of increasing formality) before the principal toast became today's effective standard: the Immortal Memory.

Hamilton Paul had been unusual in welcoming the Immortal Memory with three-times-three cheers, and Paisley responded to Maclaren's initial speech with enthusiasm, however most early Burns Suppers followed the silent approach. As Paisley's Ebenezer Picken captured the concept:

> And, where the festive board is spread,
>   Amid the cheerful glee,
> In tender Memr'y of their Friend,
> Shall Mirth the social roar suspend,
>   And heave a sigh for thee.[479]

Greenock only gave up silence after 25 years, in 1826, 'when the president, Neil Robertson, suggested that the toast of the Immortal Memory be drunk with "ringing cheers" instead of the solemn silence that was so frequently the case'.[480] This also happened at the Calcutta St Andrew's Dinner in 1834, with Thomas Babington Macauley in the chair, when the toast to Burns was proposed,

> some of the company here began to cheer, when the Chairman observed that it was usual to drink this toast in solemn silence. Dr Grant [the proposer] said: – Not in silence. I say it is a toast of triumph and we will drink it in cheers. The company accordingly drank it with loud cheers.[481]

That is not to say that the silent toast could not be incredibly moving, which contributed to its longevity as can be gauged from a report by Alan Cunningham's son, Peter, of a dinner at Archibald Hastie's London home, where he entertained two Indian Burns brothers to supper on their father's birthday: 'Then up rose our host with Burns's bowl before him, and gave with due emphasis and reverence, "The Immortal Memory of Robert Burns." This was drunk standing and in silence, each one passing the punch-bowl reverentially to his neighbour on his left'.[482]

While the present-day concept of toasting his 'immortality' appears slower to engage in 1859, the older silent toast tradition was clearly dying out by then, with only 16 per cent of toasts following this convention. Interestingly, there is no difference statistically between 'Immortal' and 'Memory' toasts in terms of silent response, with a constant 15-16 per cent in both categories. This is not to say that the advocates of the silent toasts were any the less enthusiastic in their devotion to the bard, they felt that they were following an older and more valid tradition. 1859 show that increasing numbers followed Paul's route of acclamation, not just calling out Burns's name or repeating the toast out loud, but often with 'honours' to accompany the act of toasting. These ranged from the 'three times three honours' or other more or less elaborate rituals from specific groups: 'highland honours'; 'town council honours' and even 'curling honours' are all mentioned. The most raucous and quaint is probably that conducted in Cawdor who cheered 'Three Times Three (and a Tiger) (and one cheer more for Highland Mary)'.[483] The buoyant mood of the 1859 celebrations – partly because it was celebrating his life, partly due to the inclusion of ladies at many functions, perhaps allowing a greater ebullience in dining habits, saw the balance turn firmly against silence.

Given that performativity and conviviality are twin drivers of the success of the Burns Supper, the act of audience participation at such a key point in the ritual is totally comprehensible and explains the eradication of the older silent tradition.[484]

By the 1896 Death Centenary, the form that we know today, the 'Immortal Memory' with the company repeating the toast (and likely applauding afterwards) was significantly more prevalent, but it is interesting to consider that only 27 per cent of the 1859 toasts followed that convention, so while the toast itself was mandated in 1801, the format we know today came through a more complex evolution.

'Join Me in a Toast'

The very phrase 'Immortal Memory' casts a monumental frame around the oration and the orator ahead of rising at every Burns Supper. While the early ode has morphed into a speech, the honouring of the poet – the hero of the evening – remains a central act of congregation in the format with the proposer building up to the moment when all present rise, apostrophise the Bard and drink a 'right gude willy-waught' to his eternal fame. Its inclusion is mandatory and – however abbreviated – is critical to the structure of every Burns Supper. As discussed, it will typically reflect the attitudes and outlook of a specific audience taking themes from the poet's life and works that resonate geographically, politically, and poetically with the audience.

There is another study to be done on the specific content and rhetoric of these toasts, but as DM Low encapsulated it: 'Burns Supper oratory has its own considerable interest, which is sometimes critical, but unfortunately the Immortal Memory is a sea without limits'.[485] For, however few the tropes and quotations may seem, there is a different Immortal Memory for every gathering. To be balanced, it would not be totally unfair to say that some – perhaps even many – of these orations lack vigour, insight or new perception. And, as with many conventions linked to the Burns Supper, an absence of oratorical originality, an acceptance of biographical myth and lazy literary critique reaches back into the early days of the phenomenon. The *Scots Magazine* ran an April Fool's Day piece parodying the new prose Immortal Memory as early as 1824. It was called 'A speech delivered at the late anniversary of the poet Burns by the president of an obscure club, in the town of Shadow, in Utopia, compassionately published for the benefit of future brain-beating presidents' and is an entertaining farrago of platitude that with a few relatively minor changes in words could be trotted out today.[486]

At one level, Lewis Grassic Gibbon's complaint of 80 years ago, that 'Scotland proceeded to mummify Burns's corpse and set it up in a heathen shrine for the worship of the dull, the base, and the flabbily loquacious' has some historical truth to it.[487] While accepting at the simplest level that not every speech is in and of itself a work of exegesis or of art, this seems a hard judgment on a group of speakers who usually have a proclaimed interest in , or love of, the poetry of Burns albeit delivered in sometimes poorly crafted rhetoric. Yet at one level, the imprecation of 'dull' or 'base' is very sharp indeed. It is relatively easy to find examples of the good, the bad and the ugly in Burnsian oratory over the decades but the same can be said in any study of rhetorical exercises whether epideictic, deliberative or forensic.[488] In 1996, Douglas Dunn wrote: 'In this bicentenary year of Burns's death, the Scottish literati have once again raised their voices in complaint at the spectacle of celebrations deemed false or philistine, and the sound is as disagreeable as that of a dimwit trying to recite Burns after a dram too many (or one too few).[489] Over the last two decades, there has been a considerable rapprochement between the 'Cultist' and the 'Critic' partly through the emergence of people independent of either group who sought to immortalise Burns traditionally but not stultifyingly, and with thoughtful analysis open to all. Every immortal memory speech faces the great problem of encapsulating the hero of the evening in an allotted time span. As Edwin Muir summarised the problem:

> He is more a personage to us than a poet, more a
> figurehead than a personage, and more of a myth

> than a figurehead. To those who have heard of
> Dunbar he is a figure, of course, comparable to
> Dunbar; but he is also a figure comparable to
> Prince Charlie, about whom everyone has heard.
> He is a myth evolved by the popular imagination,
> a communal poetic creation, a Protean figure; we
> can all shape him to our own likeness, for a myth
> is endlessly adaptable.[490]

Modern Burns Suppers will sometimes still feature a long sermon
as an Immortal Memory but it is more typical now to make
fewer points and a shorter speech. This is not a new approach:
the organisers of the 1869 dinner in New York encapsulated
this desire when enjoining the nominated speakers: 'a dull short
speech will give greater satisfaction than the most eloquent
effort can give if it is over ten minutes long'.[491] Or as Murray
Pittock, no mean Immortal Memorialist himself, succinctly
stated: 'Burns Suppers are... parties of good fellowship, where
the speeches are short, the pleasure long, and we may briefly be
'o'er all the ills of life victorious'.[492] That is a good point to end
on, for the Immortal Memory – like the other parts of Hamilton
Paul's formula – has stood the test of time because it should be
as Burns would have wanted it: remembering both man and
work in a convivial setting, respecting the *joie de vivre* of the
man and the genius of the poet in equal measure.

CHAPTER NINE

The Haggis

Haggess: A mass of meat, generally pork chopped, and inclosed in a membrane. In Scotland, it is commonly made in a sheep's maw of the entrails of the same animal, cut small, with suet and spices.

Samuel Johnson, *Dictionary*[493]

KEY TO THE IDENTITY of the Burns Supper is that it is held around the common consumption of food and drink.[494] The choice of dinner and its accompaniments creates the ability to add significant influence over the tone of the evening by being redolent both of Burns but also of the Scottish culinary tradition. As such, the haggis has been a central element of the Burns Supper from the very first recorded occurrence. Hamilton Paul paired it as *chef d'oeuvre* with a dressed sheep's head on the cottage table in Alloway in 1801 while the reverend poet recited Burns's poem *To a Haggis*, simultaneously capturing the feeling of a simple family meal and of a mock-heroic view of Scotland. These represent two important themes in Burns's works and so the choice of menu has an important role to play in the co-option of the Burns myth to establish the tone of the event.

What made Burns use the haggis as his trope and how did it become to occupy such a prominent role in his memorialisation during Burns Night? This chapter will analyse how haggis became 'Scotland's national dish', inspiring Burns and other poets and developing a ritual around the Haggis ceremony at Burns Suppers.

The Haggis for Scotland

In Burns's lifetime, haggis was considered as one of several national dishes of Scotland (certainly not yet exclusively so). Furthermore, it was definitely not a staple food across the people: in fact, it was seen as a rather odd, and perhaps slightly risible, dish both by writers at home (as in Dunbar's poem *Flyting of Dunbar and Kennedy*) and abroad. Rabelais includes a fictitious volume of Scottish cookery in Pantagruel's library called 'Majoris *de modo faciendo boudinos*' (Major, *On the Making of Boudins [Puddings]*) purportedly by the writer's friend, the Reformer John Major. [495] [496] So this dish was accepted as one trope of Scottishness, but Kinsley's logic in his notes to the poem holds good, as sheep's livers and stomach bags being relatively scarce commodities – one each per sheep – the haggis could neither be ubiquitous nor diurnal fare, yet it still held a place in the cultural description of Scotland's cuisine prior to the Reformation. [497]

'Dis-moi ce que tu manges, je te dirai ce que tu es' proclaimed Brillat-Saverin around the time of the development of the early Burns Suppers, encapsulating a widely held belief that a person and even a nation could be characterised by the food it eats. [498] The use of diet as national cliché is hardly new either as a reinforcement of pride or as a cheap xenophobic insult and often occurring as opposite sides of the same coin. While Nelson's Navy summoned its officers to dine by playing the drum-tune *The Roast Beef of Old England* their choice of cuisine was equally the cue for their French adversaries to disparage them as 'les rosbifs'. [499] Staple diets thus become elevated in the national consciousness, as in de Gaulle's famous summary of the problems of the Fifth Republic of France: '*Comment voulez-vous gouverner un pays qui a deux cent quarante-six variétés de fromage?*'. [500] This French/ cheese identification of course was followed up in a different century and a much different genre by Groundskeeper Willie's 'cheese-eating surrender monkeys' gibe from *The Simpsons*. [501] Naturally such national icons became poetic tropes such as the 'hamely fare' of Burns which Kinsley characterises as connoting 'peasant virtue and strength' (Tyrrell *et al* call it 'alimentary nationalism' in an echo of Roland Barthes's proposition 'chips are the alimentary sign of Frenchness').[502] In this vein, at Paisley's 1808 Burns Supper in the midst of the Napoleonic Wars, one club member or guest raised this 'Scotch Popular Toast':

> Here's plenty o' Bannocks and Barley kail,
> They aye keep a Scotsman hearty an' hale,
> An' tho' when we're scrimpet, we whiles raise a
>   rook'ry   [stunted through poor diet
> Deil feed him on whins wha would greet for French
>   cook'ry![503]   [cry

Scotland's traditional soubriquet 'the Land of Cakes' (ie oatcakes rather than Tunnock's Teacakes) underscored that the country was not seen (rightly or wrongly) as a sophisticated culinary nation. Even F Marian McNeill who is our definitive culinary Scottish nationalist claimed that '[t]he proverbial Scot has been reared on porridge and the Shorter Catechism, a rigorous diet, but highly beneficial to those possessed of sound digestive organs'.[504] The semi-autobiographical board around which the Cotter's family gathers on a Saturday night for a meagre but 'cheerful supper' epitomises that lifestyle or at least the poetic perception of a life built on 'healsome Porritch, chief of SCOTIA's food', the ultimate 'hamely fare'. [505] In this evocation of the Scots table, as Nigel Leask points out, while 'Burns abstains from [overt] patriotic moralising' Burns is at home with 'a familiar trope of culinary chauvinism in the tradition of Scots pastoral'.[506] In its stricter sense, this would have been focussed on the staples of kale and porridge, but in relatively growing prosperity, the 18th century saw the recognition of four dinner dishes based on offal as being considered characteristic of Scotland and the Scots: the sheep's head, black puddings (or white puddings in the North East); tripe; and haggis.[507]

On the more mundane level a haggis was prepared to celebrate a Scots officer's birthday on board Captain Cook's *Endeavour*, lying off New Zealand in 1770, although as a dog was used not a sheep it is hardly a canonical reference let alone a traditional recipe.[508] So while Scots might yearn for the dish on special occasions, visitors to Scotland remained both unprepared and unconvinced. When the English traveller Edward Topham (1751–1820) visited Edinburgh in 1775, he was regaled with a feast of Scots dishes, but neither the form nor the substance of the Scots menu appealed to him.

> This was a Haggis a dish not more remarkable or more disgusting to the palate, than in appearance... I found it really to be the stomach of a sheep, stuffed till it was as full as a foot-ball. An incision being made in the side of it, the entrails burst forth... and presented such a display of oatmeal, and sheep's liver, and lights, with a mofeta [sc: skunk-like smell] that accompanied them, that I could scarcely help thinking myself in [a sulphurous volcanic grotto in Naples].[509]

Even after Burns commemorated the dish, it remained a challenge. Professor Benjamin Stilliman of Yale (1779–1864) visited Edinburgh in 1805 and investigated the cuisine with due scientific inquiry, but ultimate rejection: 'I had never met with the haggess in Scotland, although its praises had been sung by their favourite poet Burns... its taste is fat and heavy, nor did I feel any regret that the haggess was not an American dish'.[510] However, the dish did pop up on North American menus: the Montreal St Andrew's Society was serving haggis as one self-consciously Scottish dish in November 1807 ('A roasted sirloin and plum pudding oppose/A sheep's head, minc'd collops, fat haggis and brose').[511] A few years later, Helen Currie, the Philadelphia poet, commemorated 'On Partaking of a Haggis in the House of a Worthy Scottish Clergyman after Hearing Him

Preach' extolling it as '[t]he very wale o' Scottish food / Unlike the trash of foreign lands'.[512]

At home there continued to be a school of thought in Edinburgh literary circles which saw old Scots traditions as merely boorish. Bishop Gleig in an early critique saw the humour in *To a Haggis*, but dismissed it as a kind only relished by 'Scotchmen... as have not learned, from neighbours on the south side of the Tweed, to banish that national dish from their tables'.[513] While *Blackwoods* took considerable pains in 1823 to attack the principal speaker at the dinner of the Liverpool Scottish Society who, in full highland dress, proclaimed his pride in having dined on haggis. The editor called out the haggis as 'this most hideous and indecent dish', fit only for bare bottomed savages' and 'solemnly protest[ing] against the doctrine that holds haggis to be the national and characteristic diet of Scotland.[514]

This desire of some Scots to assimilate English customs through the creation of 'North Britain' was plain enough until Sir Walter Scott's *Waverley* popularised and preserved the old traditions, albeit in romanticised aspic. A fine, fat haggis had featured prominently at the grandest of the banquets Scott orchestrated for his fine, fat monarch George IV during his 1822 Edinburgh progress. However, the complete displacement of the sheep's head by the haggis took some while (even with the popularity of Burns's poem) and, as with so many Scots 'traditions' finds its proponents in Scott and his coterie. The dish achieved manifesto status from 'Meg Dodds' in her 1826 cookery manual, when she opined that:

> every country is celebrated for some culinary preparation, and that all national dishes are good. The reason of this is sufficiently obvious: had they not been acceptable to the palate, they never could have either gained or maintained their rank. Accordingly, the Spanish olio, the Italian macaroni, the French ragout, the Turkish pillau, and the Scotch haggis, differing essentially as

they do, are, nevertheless, all equally good after
their kind, though here we give precedence to the
'Great Chieftain of the Pudding Race'.[515]

Thereafter, haggis was regularly served at Abbotsford on its
high days from the outings of the Abbotsford Hunt which were
included 'unfailing haggis... and quaichs of Glenlivet', to the
many literary pilgrims.[516] The American portraitist, Charles
Leslie (1794–1859) remembered dining at Abbotsford in 1824
while painting Scott's portrait:

> the next day a haggis appeared on the table. It
> was placed before [Scott], and he greeted it with
> the first lines of Burns's address to the 'Chieftain
> of the Pudding Race'. He repeated them with
> great effect; and at the words 'Weel are ye worthy
> of a grace /As lang's my arm', he extended his arm
> over the haggis.[517]

Beyond the increasing visibility of the dish at Burns Suppers,
it continued to be used in print as the haggis performed a role
as a touchstone of Scottishness ranging from the friendly (eg
Hogg's anecdote concerning the exploding haggis in the *Noctes
Ambrosianæ* in 1828 or in a gastronomic compendium of the
following year)[518] to the dismissive jocularity of Galt at the 1818
Burns Dinner in London:

> The Duke of York, like all the refined of the
> human race, had a very civilized regard for choice
> cookery... the landlord placed before him a haggis.
> It was evidently ill made; the bag was dingy, – alto-
> gether an ugly, flabby, desultory trencher-full of
> 'fat things'. The duke, alarmed at the apparition,
> cried to me, 'Galt, what is that?' Fascinated at
> the sight, I could not resist the temptation, and
> replied gravely, 'a boiled pair of bagpipes'.- Tell it
> not in Gath, – even at the risk of being reviled in

Scotland forever, his Royal Highness immediately
ordered the 'Great chieftain of the pudding race'
ignominiously away.[519]

As part of the Victorian adoption of Balmorality, Queen
Victoria was introduced to haggis at Blair Atholl in 1865 and
promptly gave it her royal approval: 'There were several Scotch
dishes, two soups and the celebrated "Haggis," which I tried last
night, and really liked very much', thus adding another pebble
in the growing cairn of Victorian sentimental Scottishness.[520]
Here the haggis, at once a complex recipe yet equally a simple
dinner, was adopted at the highest and lowest dinner tables in
the land. To paraphrase Budgell's suicide note, the dish which
Walter Scott had served and Queen Victoria enjoyed, cannot
be wrong.

The haggis had now become the formal national dish of
Scotland and the sheep's head became the foundation for sheep's
heid broth ('powsoudie') or Scotch Broth, giving the haggis the
status of being the alimentary sign of Scottishness, as whisky
would be its metonymic libation. As Alex Tyrrell says: 'There can
be few groups that exceed present-day Scots in their assertion
of national identity through the celebration of distinctive food
and drink.'[521]

The heightened symbolism is two-edged, for while the
haggis becomes what it was not – the standard staple of the
common folk in an idyllic pre-industrial Scotland, typifying
Burns as Orpheus in his Ayrshire Arcadia – it allows us to share
a recognisable alimentary icon, which speaks both to Scotland,
and to concepts of Burns as if not 'the peasant poet' at least
a common man. Anthony Cohen coined the phrase: 'Haggis:
the great leveller' describing it, and its place within the Burns
Supper as evoking 'the democratic idea which stands at the very
heart of Scottish political theory and self-identity.'[522]

But as with so many interpretations of Burns, certain
commentators then try to see particular traits in the tropes
that are unwarranted extensions of the symbolism. The

controversial editors of the *Canongate Burns* sought to show
the meal as in some way even 'dissident' which appears to over-
egg this particular pudding: 'The haggis's vast buttock-like
shape culminated in a pronounced phallic-like pin [provoking]
Breugel-like orgiastic appetites'.[523]

The social and culinary reception of the haggis has enough
interpretative problems already without looking to create more.
To a lesser extent than the interpretations of Burns's poems, or
the themes drawn from his life, the haggis is at least a more
appropriate shape to be a polemical football. The choice of
haggis by Hamilton Paul was more a recognition of the highly
performative nature of the poem, alongside its idiosyncratic
status as one, and through the success of the poem soon to be
the pre-eminent, of Scotland's national dishes.

Burns's Inspiration

While poetry about the joy of drinking is commonplace (with
its own Anacreontic genre) there is a poetical joy associated
with the kitchen as well as the cellar. When it came to the
composition of his poem on the haggis, as is often the case,
Burns was influenced by Robert Fergusson whose *Address to
the Principal and Professors of the University of St. Andrew's
on Their Superb Treat to Dr Samuel Johnson* used the haggis as
the opening salvo in flyting or teasing the well-rehearsed anti-
Scottish views of that English writer:

Imprimis, then, a haggis fat,	[*In the first place*
Weel tottled in a seything pat,	[simmered, pot
Wi' spice and ingans weel ca'd thro',	[onions
Had help'd to gust the stirrah's mow [524]	[relish, rude
	fellow's mouth

The haggis alone would be insufficient to reward the doctor, so
Fergusson's poetic menu continues by dishing up, *seriatim,* the

sheep's head, its trotters, white and black puddings and girdle farls. It is this mock-heroic tone that is striking as it distances itself from other food celebrations such as Fergusson's *Caller Oysters*, the opening of Drummond of Hawthornden's *Poemo-Middinia*, or of course, Burns's own Augustan description of the Cotter's family's simple repast.[525]

Taking his cue from 'his elder brother in the muse', Burns alights on the haggis as being peculiarly (in both senses of the word) Scottish and this allows him licence to explore some of his philosophy of nationalism. He takes this unusual culinary preparation and elevates it, transforming it from an occasional meal into a staple dish embodying his view of Scots life and virtues. It is plain that Burns is writing his *Address* with a wider view than satisfying that one audience desire. Just as *To A Mouse* is not merely about a displaced rodent, so *To a Haggis* is not a simple paean to the mundane Scots kitchen. Following a chain of thought started by Nicholas D Smith on Smollett's satirical use of food and menu in a political and nationalist sense, it can be seen that Burns, a fan of Smollett's writing, was significantly influenced by his approach.[526] Lewis Knapp flagged this 'personal motif' for Smollett as 'a strong love of the virtues of country life as opposed to the socially corrupting luxury and affluence of urban existence' and it is interesting to focus on how this becomes equally personal for Burns.[527]

We can see Smollett's imagery from that book as a clear influence in the composition of a key passage in *To a Haggis* when, in the novel, the squire's party with their traditional outlook meet the *nouveau riche* Baynard family and experience an awful, alien dinner –

> At dinner, the lady maintained the same ungra-
> cious indifference, never speaking but in whispers
> to her aunt; and as to the repast, it was made up
> of a parcel of kickshaws, contrived by a French
> cook, without one substantial article adapted
> to the satisfaction of an English appetite. The

> pottage was little better than bread soaked in
> dishwashings, lukewarm. The ragouts looked as
> if they had been once eaten and half digested: the
> fricassees were involved in a nasty yellow poul-
> tice; and the rotis were scorched and stinking, for
> the honour of the fumet.[528]

The influence is far too close to be coincidental. Here we
clearly have all the elements contained in verse five of the
Address: from the 'sneerin' scornful view' of Mrs Baynard to
the 'stinking'/'skinking' soup and 'spew'-ed up 'ragouts' or
'fricassees' beloved of the French cook. Clearly, the menu reflects
badly on the host and is certainly insufficient to sustain the true
virtue of the native son either nutritionally or politically. Burns's
poem acts out Smollett's message out for the listener.

Kinsley describes it, it is an 'almost certainly an occasional
poem' but its origins are disputed.[529] The most detailed story
of its writing, told by Burns's friend John Richmond, (which
Mary Ellen Brown calls 'the proto-celebration') pins it to a
'Haggis Club' meeting near Kilmarnock in 1785, can be set
against the competing claims of Andrew Bruce (in Edinburgh)
or John Morrison (in Mauchline) in 1786. Each effectively tells
the same story of the Ayrshire poet being served haggis and
'extemporaneously' giving thanks in verse, extolling the haggis
as an object of national succour and pride.[530, 531]

Hamilton Paul would likely have been aware of these
conflicting tales and, once again, he adopted the remembrance
of an episode in the 'Life of Burns' into his harmony ritual,
thus maintaining the commemorative theme within the Burns
Supper, but adding the wider homage to Scotland. It is easy to
envisage Burns declaiming the final verse in the same manner
as his other 'worldly' Graces which thanked the landlord Willy
Hyslop for an inexhaustible supply of tup's heads or jugs of
spirit. Just as there are variants of those occasional Graces, here,
it is not inconceivable that all three stories are true – that Burns

was so pleased with the effect of this performative poem that it
became a useful 'party piece' at several different tables.

Its apogee possibly around occurred a few weeks later around
St Andrew's Night in Edinburgh, for as a contemporaneous
English newspaper reported: 'This being St. Andrew's Day, the
same will be observed by all the sons of Caledonia, with the
usual ceremonies of devouring sheep's heads, haggis and barley
broth... and every mark of festivity.[532] This could be how the
impromptu Haggis grace was first published ('applauded into
print' as Kinsley describes it) in a newspaper just after the feast of
St Andrew with a variant closing stanza and which, for the First
Edinburgh Edition, would be refined (albeit in some copies with
the infamous typographical error of 'stinking' for 'skinking') to
the invocation known and used today in the canon of the Burns
Supper ritual. [533]

The Haggis on the Menu

When Hamilton Paul was looking to create a remembrance of
Burns in 1801, his mind turned to capturing as many themes of
the poet as he could. Here, the circular links between Burns, the
haggis and an ideal of Scotland provided a perfect synecdoche
and was immediately adopted as a part of the ritual in subsequent
Alloway dinners. There is no record of the bill of fare at the early
Greenock meetings but Paisley records honouring the haggis at
some of their earliest meetings: 'where the "Great Chieftain of
the Pudding Race" was not forgotten nor unhonoured.'[534]

While haggis is not featured in the 1819 public Burns dinner
in Edinburgh which is described by Lockhart in *Peter's Letters
to His Kinsfolk*, nor does it feature in the 1844 Doon Festival
menu (where SC Jerrold's *Punch* article would without doubt
have added its trademark ridicule of the Haggis to its criticism
of the fare on offer).[535] It looks as if the absence of the dish from
particularly large, public banquets was due not only to its inedible
reputation, but to the prosaic fact that commercial chefs were

unused to cooking it (hence, the unappetising dish served before Galt and the Duke in 1818). Paisley records in 1815 having two large haggises thanks to the 'secretary having furnished the receipt from Ayrshire'.[536] Yet in the Ayrshire homeland, by 1826, Dalry Burns Club's founders had envisioned it as a necessary constituent of the feast: 'Where drink of the best, will be got/ With a haggis and bannocks the table to grace'.[537]

The difficulty in arranging to have even a single haggis on the bill o' fare forced dinner stewards and cooks to extremes. In 1830, the secretary of the Junior Dalry Club was reduced to writing to Jean Armour Burns to seek her assistance, beseeching if 'she would be good enough to prepare, *with her own hands,* a Scotch haggis, and address it to the care of the Postmaster of Dalry, so that the said precious compound might arrive in time to grace the anniversary meeting'.[538] Where haggis was not readily procurable, the dining theme often remained in a simple guise, again reimagining the poet's own Ayrshire fare as in the Johnstone supper of 1813, where after the Memory speech, 'Each of the company was presented with a glass of 'Scotch drink' with oaten cakes and Dunlop cheese, in the good old style of Scottish hospitality'.[539]

Some clubs felt the central importance of the haggis imagery as pivotal and so went further calling themselves after the 'great Chieftain' itself, the notable examples being Dunfermline Haggis Club (at its foundation in 1812 until its merger in 1820 with the Dunfermline Junior Haggis Club) and the Glasgow Haggis Club (from 1885 to date).[540] In Alloa, the first club to hold a Burns Supper was called the Alloa Tripe Club in 1828 with the Alloa Haggis Burns Club following in 1873.[541]

Meg Dodds not only extolled the haggis from both a national and culinary perspective. In her 1826 volume's selection of menus, she recognised the growing trend of Burns dinners (35 are recorded that January) and so she included a complex example of what an ideal a 'Bill of Fare for St Andrew's Day or Burns' Club' might look like.

FIRST COURSE.

COCK-A-LEEKIE.
1st Remove, Bannock Fluke.
2d, Dressed Lamb's Head and Pluck.

A FITLESS COCK. GRATED SMOKED BEEF or SMOKED
SAUSAGE. SCOTCH COLLOPS.
CRAPPIT HEADS.   STEWED TROUT.

SHEEP'S HAGGIS.
Remove
Venison Pastry.
RABBITS SMOTHERED WITH ONIONS.
KIPPER IN SLICES.   LIVER PUDDING.

HARE SOUP.
1st Remove, SALTED RUMP WITH GREENS.
2d, Hind-Quarter of Lamb, with Pouch.

SECOND COURSE.

VEAL FLORENTINE.

SPINAGE DRESSED.   SALAD.   FRITTERS.

ORANGE MARMALADE TART.   **PLATEAU.**
CURED FLORENTINE.
POTTED CALF'S HEAD GARNISHED
PANCAKES WITH CURRANT JELLY   SCOTCH EGGS

MOOR GAME
on buttered toasts.
REMOVE,
SCOTCH RABBIT.[542]

As social conventions changed during the 18th century from
service à *la française* (where all the various dishes on the menu
would be arranged in large groupings laid simultaneously on
the table called 'removes' such that diners would choose from

various plates as they desired) to *service* à *la russe* (the modern habit of each diner receiving a series of identical dishes from soup to nuts), so the haggis, latterly accompanied by mashed potatoes and turnips, became an intermediate course or even sometimes, the main course of the Burns Supper.

The growing presence of haggis on the menu can be seen in Ballantine's *Chronicle* (albeit the number of references is probably understated as the journalists would typically arrive after the meal to report the speeches) where one in eight dinners are reported as having served haggis although there remained many who wondered why, including the Boston Burns Club's chairman, who had to 'confess that my own admiration for the national literature of Scotland does not extend to the national cookery'.[543]

At least he saw a symbolic value in the comestible. On the other hand, the correspondent of the *Lowell Daily Citizen* felt 'agreeably disappointed', in finding that the haggis was a 'palatable sort of suet pudding mixed with oatmeal'. He relished the dish, recommending that it 'need not wait five years to receive its naturalisation papers, [being] evidently well fitted to become a citizen among us without delay'.[544] Regardless of those who found the taste of the dish unappealing, its symbolism was now firmly agreed upon and as haggis became more available commercially its central place on the bill o'fare became ubiquitous.[545]

We can trace the development of these rituals through the records of the Albany Burns Club of the State of New York, who used *To a Haggis* as an effective Grace at the inaugural dinner of the resurrected club in the Union Hotel on 25 January, 1854 when 'the worthy President, occupying the head seat, remained standing while Mr D D Ramsay delivered 'Burns' Address to the Haggis'. The article says haggis is 'an odd dish of hash and one which to a Yankee appetite is grateful'.[546]

A century on, and F Marian McNeill drew up her ideal bill o'fare in 1953, for the nationalist-leaning newspaper, the *Scottish Journal*. It is interesting to compare it to the standards of the previous century. McNeill believed that the food should be chosen to reflect 'the festive fare of hamely folk' and that the bill should be 'written in the Lalland tongue… adorned with brief rhymed tributes to individual dishes'. This is a convention still regularly followed today at Burns Suppers, though it can be difficult to avoid twee neologism.[547] Her ideal was:

HET KAIL
Cock-a-leekie   Bawd Bree

CALLER FISH
Crabbie-claw   Saumont wi' a Gusty Sauce

RARE-BIT
THE HAGGIS
Wi' Champit Tatties, Neeps and Nips

HET JOINTS
Roastit Bubbly-jock wi' Cheston Crappin
Roastit Grumphie wi' Aipple Purry
Sprouts   Curly Kale   Baikit Tatties

ITHER-ORRA EATOCKS
Hattit Kit   Tremblin' Tam
Hotch-potch o' Frit wi' Whuppit Cream

GUSTY KICKSHAWS
Kipper Creams   Finnan-Toasties
Mitey Kebbuck wi' Wee Ait Bannocks
Coffee.[548]

As well as these grand banquets, many Burns Suppers adopted a simpler (and cheaper) menu. In many traditional clubs, the main course of the dinner will be a full portion of haggis, neeps and tatties, preceded by soup and followed by pudding. Today, the menu at a Burns Supper will tend to have fewer courses: a starter, haggis as an intermediate course, a main course and dessert (with tea and coffee). As the arrangers and caterers are minded to capture the traditional Scottish theme in the culinary half of the Burns Supper, the starter will more often than not be a Scottish Soup (Cock-a-leekie, Scotch Broth or perhaps Cullen Skink) or possibly Scotch Smoked Salmon. If the haggis is not to be the principal plate, the main course has more latitude and can either be 'classic' or perhaps a 'signature dish' of the chef's. Finally, Scotch Trifle, Cranachan or the like would be served for dessert.

But in every menu, the pride of place had to fall to the haggis and that pride is literally manifested in the ritual that surrounds it on Burns Night, which is the subject of the next section.

The Haggis in Ritual

Once again, the earliest reference to a formality around the haggis as the centrepiece of a Scottish banquet comes from the reminiscences of Walter Scott,

> I have often heard Scott mention some curious par-
> ticulars of his first visit to the remote fastness of
> one of these Highland friends [in 1786 or 1787]...
> I must not forget his admiration at the principal
> article of the laird's first course; namely a gigantic
> haggis, borne into the hall in a wicker basket by
> two half-naked Celts, while the piper strutted fierce-
> ly behind them, blowing a tempest of dissonance.[549]

Although the scene described is hardly likely to be a strict reportage, and more likely another of his Scottish myths, giving the *chef d'oeuvre* of a feast the honours of a parade is an ancient and not exclusively Caledonian custom. The very old tradition of the Boar's Head Gaudy at Queen's College, Oxford sees the principal platter paraded into the dining room with trumpet fanfare, formality and song. The Society of the Sons of the Clergy in 19th century Glasgow had adopted the St Andrew's Feast etiquette of 'parading' the chief dish of their meal:

> there are always four standard Scotch dishes
> paraded; and which, not strange to say, attract

even more attention than the more fashionable
specimens of French and English cookery. The
four dishes are — a haggis, a sheep's head, tripe,
and black puddings.[550]

By the middle of that century the haggis replaced the sheep's
head at St Andrew's Dinners and became the totemic dish as it
was with the Burns clubs and this change cross-fertilised with
the Burns clubs starting to adopt the St Andrew's processional
ritual as part of their Burns Supper programme. In time, both
St Andrew's and Burns Nights would have essentially the
same haggis ritual by the end of the century. The British army
was a parallel medium both of formalising the procedure and
disseminating it.

Other than Hamilton Paul's initial minute, the earliest
records of a formalised haggis ceremony involving reciting the
Address over the haggis in a directly Burnsian context come
from the USA: in Philadelphia (in 1824) :which the Haggis, held
a conspicuous place, and Burns' celebrated address to the same,
was recited in an appropriate manner.[551] The first newspaper
record of the Haggis being addressed by the Burns Club in New
York was in 1848:

A splendid banquet was provided for the occasion, and a fine haggis, which even the countrymen of Burns acknowledged as well compounded,
showed its 'honest sonsie face' among the principal dishes on the table. Major Sinclair, armed with
the pin belonging to the haggis, recited Burns' ode
to the haggis, as a preliminary to the festivity.[552]

This shows a general acceptance of having both the haggis and
the poem as key parts of the Supper ritual. The addition of the
piper and a procession from the kitchens to the top table can
be seen as early as in New York in 1854. The *New York Times*
reported on the Burns Club's 1890 dinner and the origins of the
now dramatic centrepiece of the evening:

The central feature of the feast was reached when
the piper escorted a procession of six waiters,
each carrying aloft a genuine Scotch haggis. As
'the great chieftains' or haggises were borne up
and down the aisles, the bagpiper discoursed
the old tune 'Bannocks o' Barley' the Scotsmen
cheered until their throats were sore, and the
guests of other nationalities enjoyed the scene...
Piper William Cleland led the procession as he
has done for 36 years.[553]

While there is no 1854 report in the *New York Times*, it records
Cleland as playing in the haggis to be addressed in 1858 which
proves the longevity of the procession ritual.[554] The earliest
processional reference found yet in print was from a Burns
Supper at Tammany Hall, New York in 1856:

At a proper time midway between the sitting-down
and the uprising, that 'chieftain of puddings' the
haggies [sic], was introduced, whereupon the confined corks were released, and the 'wee draps' cir-
culated amongst the hilarious company.[555]

And this was not a unique occurrence, as recorded in Milwaukee in
1859 which again shows the good-natured humour surrounding
the ritual:

One of the characteristic demonstrations of the
evening was the introduction of the 'Haggis' and
the delivered by Mr Robert Menzies, of Burns's
famous Address to that national dish of Scotland.
This was rendered with fine effect, eliciting peals
of laughter from the whole company.[556]

And in Sydney, that year, the company were entertained to see
'foremost amidst the dishes... was a right royal Scotch haggis almost
as big as Geordie's [sc: the landlord's] head' while at an
appropriate pause in the entertainments, 'Professor Anderson also

considerably contributed to the astonishment of the natives by entering, dressed as Rob Roy Macgregor, and plying the blade of his jewelled dirk into the heart of the haggis in lieu of between the ribs of Osbaldiston'.[557]

We have the first evidence that this ritual had crossed back into Scotland in time for the Burns Centenary of 1859 where there are three descriptions of a ceremonial procession of the haggis with a theatrical address: in Ardrossan – interestingly at the public dinner, not at the Ardrossan Burns Club – at Walkerburn, and with the Freemasons of Melrose, where:[558]

> Brother William Scott entered, bearing a real scotch haggis, and recited to the company Burns's graphic poem on the same subject. The 'great chieftain of the pudding race' was then thorough-ly dissected, and its contents partaken of by the brotherhood with great relish.[559]

Statistically, working through the reports in the Ballantine *Chronicle,* Haggis is only mentioned as part of the feast at 100 dinners, while the ceremony and recitation is hardly mentioned at all. This is probably less valid than other statistical analysis of Ballantine as typically the journalist covering the dinner would arrive after the cloth was drawn and so would have no knowledge of what went on before his arrival: Sydney is a case in point, where Ballantine does not mention the haggis being addressed and stabbed, but it is in local newspaper reports.

After 1859, with formality and the increased availability of haggis this ritual became an integral part of the annual memorial allowing the development of the haggis ceremony from Paul's simple recitation of the *Address* to the modern piping in of the haggis.[560] There is clear evidence of a more ritual based ceremony expanding from those Centenary Burns Supper reports, influenced by the St Andrew's rituals combined with the trend of Balmorality, growing over the next decades. Until the end of the 20th century, the UK tradition maintained the more sober approach, but the ritual kept a more florid complexion in the USA and Canada, where haggises are still regularly treated like royalty in the presence of an armed honour guard, massed pipers, legions of chefs and attendant ceremonial whisky bearers (often bearing two bottles held above their head in a saltire shape). Interestingly, some of those practices have come back to Scotland in the last decade without too much unconscious self-parody, in many ways echoing the mock-heroic rituals that Fergusson drew up for the Edinburgh Cape Club. As the contemporary poet and National Makar Jackie Kay captures the spirit in one of her poems, 'The haggis, piped in like a glowing bride. /The bagpipes bellowing till it swells with pride'.[561] So some form of procession around the diners is usual today, normally with a very large haggis (often called a 'chieftain' by haggis-mongers) on a large serving tray nestling on a bed of green salad, or on napkin origami. Occasionally, this can be taken to extremes, such as the Edinburgh hotel which adds stags' antlers at the front of the haggis, and pheasant tail feathers at the back, or the German supper which has brought the haggis in, festooned with large firework sparklers, proving that the bounds of the mock-heroic can be pushed fairly far.

The haggis procession (however formal or informal) is now an indispensable element to the event as there are examples where despite the haggis being absent or even the procession and recitation were both acted out in full without there being any haggis for the company to eat. The Burns Club of London's grand 1918 Supper where polenta was served instead was such a crisis. As William Will announced from the chair:

> Last night, however, we were told that the Scot-
> tish makers of the Haggis were unable to supply
> the 'chieftain' because of the food restrictions...
> (Groans). That is one of the penalties of having
> a Welsh Food Controller. However, the Crite-
> rion people have prepared a dish – let us call it
> Italian Haggis. We were uncertain as to whether

> the Pipers should play the Lament, or pipe in the
> Italian haggis, but we have decided... to play in
> the Italian dish in the usual way. (Applause).[562]

The rituals surrounding the haggis at a Burns Supper may have a deeper significance as part of a wider psychological approach to understanding rituals around consumption. Experiments undertaken by Katherine Vohs and others to make a quantitative assessment of the positive hedonic effect on consumption driven by participation in an attendant ritual are of particular interest here. As Vohs *et al* describe their findings:

> ritualistic behavior potentiates and enhances
> ensuing consumption – an effect found for choc-
> olates, lemonade, and even carrots... Rituals
> enhance the enjoyment of consumption because
> of the greater involvement in the experience that
> they prompt.[563]

The test results show a clear correlation between the consumer who participates in various forms of ritual and their subsequent heightened enjoyment around the eating of both 'treat' foodstuffs (such as chocolate) or basic nutrition (carrots). Participation in ritual, therefore, is shown to enhance the flavour and enjoyment of a dish. Using for example, a child's birthday cake, with candles, accompanied by singing and a wish-making as a paradigm case within a 'rich social context' which opens questions around an equivalently rich, convivial context within the Burns Supper programme. Vohs *et al*, however, have not gone that far and, perhaps crucially in the specific case of haggis state that '[r]esearch on the potential of rituals to alter the taste of truly unenjoyable foods would be welcome'.[564] Does our haggis fall within that next experiment? Perhaps this is a recognition of the words of the great Burns scholar, DeLancey Ferguson that:

> [Haggis] shares with Scotch theology and the
> Scotch climate the responsibility for having made

whisky a necessary of human survival north of the Tweed.[565]

That is as maybe, but it is certain that the Haggis and its ritual are necessary parts of each Burns Supper.

Addressing the Haggis

After the pomp and circumstance of the piper-lead procession, the finale of the Haggis ceremony is the recitation of Robert Burns's *To a Haggis*. Wallace, re-editing Chambers in 1896, said of the poem that 'the "Haggis", to an ordinary mind probably the most unpoetical subject conceivable... Yet, in Burns's hands, it becomes the material for a triumph of Homeric word-pairing and arch humour'.[566] And it is that perception that is the key to understanding its success as a ritual and/or an entertainment. After the haggis (or haggises, or facetiously 'haggi') is piped in one of the guests, usually flanked by the piper and the chef, recites or more accurately performs, the poem. Its very structure calls out for performance. As Kinsley describes it: 'The brisk, cumulative rhythms of this stanza, and its familiar and comic associations, do not allow Burns more here than a hint of the mock-heroic – a hint, however, that is traditionally made explicit in recitation'.[567]

It is, however, a challenge to find early demonstration that reciters (at the very least) stabbed the haggis during the poem. Haggis had featured as the prime dish at a Scottish Hallowe'en party in London in 1807, from when an anonymous rhyming grace is recorded which strongly suggests that people were reciting *To a Haggis* and stabbing the pudding at table in the ritual form we know today:

Till Uncle John, wud be at it,
Lifts up his e'en to consecrate it;
Syne reverently straiks his chin,
An' sticks his faithfu' gully in,   [knife
Ladeing wi' sunkit ilka plate,   [provisions

Bidden the bashfu' no be blate;   [shy
To thee, great keuk o' kintra fare,   [country fare
We owe this wale o' a' wame-ware,   [plentiful belly ballast
'And grant that we ay may have grace
To look a haggis in the face,
Wi' thankfu hearts whene'er we dine,
An' a' the praises shall be thine'.[568]

Absent that possible reference, the performance element
around the recitation of the poem seems to have crept in after
the 1859 centenary, where there is the specific report from
Sydney, plus two ambiguous references, to 'the cutting up' of
haggises and these seem to be the first records of when the
reciter first stabbed the Burns Supper haggis at the appropriate
point in the poem at the lines: 'His knife, see rustic labour dight
/an cut ye up wi' ready slight'.[569] It is now commonplace that
the reciter will at the very least make a theatrical gesture of
wiping the blade of the knife provided on his/her sleeve and
then stabbing the haggis to release a plume of warm reek. This
custom would appear to be firmly rooted by the early 20th
century as F Marian McNeill famously warns how to cut a
haggis to avoid being scalded:

> The uninitiated are advised to note the danger of
> too sudden attack on the 'chieftain'. Some carvers
> begin by carefully cutting a St Andrew's Cross (x)
> on the top, and then turn the flaps over to make
> an aperture.[570]

Following the mock-heroic theme, over the years many reciters
have adopted a more flamboyant presentation, not confined to
'the business' with the knife, but adding gestures and movements
throughout the verses to create a 'semi-staged' version of the
address.[571] This too is often thought of as a modern trend, notably
in the annual performances of Group Captain Reverend Donald
Wallace (1925–2018) at the Chartered Institute of Bankers in

Scotland's London Burns Supper, featuring his trademark *coup de theatre* in chopping off the tops of the lighted candles of a candelabrum at the line 'an heids will sned/ Like taps aff thrissle'. It would be wrong to think of the addition of a dramatic element to be uncanonical or at least untraditional as the concept also seen in costumed and staged poems, in particular *Holy Willie's Prayer* and *Tam o'Shanter*, is over 100 years old. The Scottish Colourist painter, JD Fergusson (1874–1961) described one enthusiast giving the *Address* in 1915:

> I mentioned Burns (of course) and [his friend] told me he was at Golf Club dinner and a butcher who was a great admirer of Burns recited *To a Haggis*. He put so much into it that he nearly collapsed at the end... Being a squeamy veg[etarian], of course you'll think that most ludicrous and disgusting. I think it splendid and inspiring. The man making haggis, selling haggis and reciting the haggis address with real feeling of sympathy with Burns's understanding and sympathy seems to me to be really getting near the real thing.

> Think of this disgusting person a dealer in meat! Worse still, a dealer in tripes – that is entrails, innards, or guts. A maker of haggises, or haggi... Imagine him over a cauldron of boiling haggises, watching them and prodding them with a needle, moving about rhythmically while Burns's words run in his head and at moment of intense emotion, at the *sight* of their fullness of form and the *knowledge* of their fullness of food, of real food that nourishes both through feeling and fact – at these moments, feeling the continuity of idea that comes from having conceived created and completed the work – at these moments this frightful person will get into the fourth dimension, so

> to speak, and recite with the fullness of emotion
> derived from this comprehensive experience,
> marking the rhythm with the needle, and punctu-
> ating the time with prods.[572]

Partly, this semi-staging acts not only as a colourful and humorous ritual but can also assist the auditors' comprehension.

While neophytes might well adopt a Wildean pose in describing the *To a Haggis* as the incomprehensible addressing the inedible, dramatic gesture can be particularly appropriate to audiences with many non-Scots listeners, some of whom, like the protagonist in Helen Simpson's short story *Burns and the Bankers*, could be tempted to find the poem 'as lang as his airm, too. On and on it went, incomprehensible... and smug and ridiculous'.[573] It is certainly a ritual which can often challenge the neophyte as in Madras in 1938, where an Indian guest replied to a St Andrew's toast expressing his confusion over the ceremony and the comestible inverting the standard colonial vision by seeing the inbound Scots and their traditions as the exotic other: 'It is very pleasing to see a strange ceremony of another people... I assure you it is much more curious than a Hindu marriage (laughter)'.[574]

It is this curiosity or incomprehension that drives the debate over the need to gloss the poetry of Burns, a debate exemplified by *To a Haggis*, Alex Watson sees the dramatic ritual as an extended, three-dimensional glossary which 'acts as an interactive glossary on *To a Haggis*, enabling diners to bring their own personalities and cultures to the poem and engage with it in any way they see fit'.[575] Again, looking at the long view, this ritual – the poetic justification of simple, slightly unusual food as the national source of character – is a classic example of Burns's mode of composition of an occasional piece recited *in situ* around the dining table. It is not too difficult to envisage the poet at a friend's kitchen table in the late 1780s, reciting this poem as an apparently impromptu grace as his haggis dinner is served, and stabbing it with some theatre to make his point.

As with the Immortal Memory, this hypothesis rings true because Burns himself seems in some way to have willed it. That was the insight of Hamilton Paul's creation and that explains why this particular dish and its invented ritual are now essential at Burns Night. So, the *To A Haggis* is not just a funny turn at the Supper but a deliberately chosen element characteristically capturing a key part of Burns's message, part of what McGuirk calls 'that inventory of outsized cultural artefacts that Burns takes up to dramatise his counterpoise'.[576] Hamilton Paul would have been aware of the tales about the genesis of the poem and, in stealing the poet's chosen invocation to the national diet, he adopted the remembrance of an episode in the Burns story into his ritual for the Burns Supper. Here the imagery of Burns, Scotland and the haggis become intermingled. It is through Burns's poetic appellation that the haggis becomes the great chieftain not just of the 'puddin' race' but of all Scots comestibles, and perhaps of all Scots. The teasing mock heroics on the page are translated into playful social ritual with a simple form of recitation in Alloway growing, mainly through the American diasporan influence, into a cultural set piece central to the enjoyment of every Burns Supper.

Thus, Hamilton Paul embellished the commemorative theme by using Burns's poem to create an undercurrent which passed around the world and is still consciously, unconsciously or sometimes all-to self-consciously paraded at every Burns Supper in his memory.

CHAPTER TEN

Ale, Sangs an' Clatter

Ae night at e'en a merry core
   O' randie, gangrel bodies,   [rude, riotous; vagrant
In Poosie-Nansie's held the splore,   [carousal
   To drink their orra dudies: [spare ragged clothes
      Wi' quaffing and laughing,
        They ranted an' they sang,
      Wi' jumping, an' thumping,
        The vera girdle rang.[577]   [griddle

CONVIVIALITY IS A KEY theme in Burns's poetry, and it is no coincidence that that should be reflected within the tradition of the Burns Supper. Longfellow once remarked that Scott should be read outdoors, Moore in the drawing-room, Byron in a prison cell but 'Burns, generous, impassioned, manly, social [should be read] in the tavern'.[578] Over and above the solace and companionship of a working man enjoying a relaxing drink with his friends, which Burns often experienced in the Ayrshire and Galloway villages, in more formal and literary settings the precursors of the Burns Supper (whether in Freemasonic lodges, the Tarbolton Bachelors Club, Buchan's Thomson dinners or the Crochallan Fencibles) were occasions for songs and conversation over a social drink, influencing and inspiring not only the poet, but the key players in the development of the Enlightenment.

> If we wish to seek for the beginnings of Scottish literature, we shall find it in the clubs of gentlemen that met in dingy taverns, in dark wynds of

Edinburgh. There they had their gatherings over ale and claret, where they would discuss politics, books, and ballads... It may indeed be said that in taverns Scots modern literature was born, and the first public it addressed was in a public-house.[579]

It was the inspiration of those precursors, not least of all Freemasonry, that allowed Hamilton Paul to craft his first Burns Supper, where (as now) drink, songs and poetry combine as part of the celebration of the Bard.

Drink

Drink was almost always the binding force of all the Enlightenment Clubs and though some societies set sumptuary caps in terms of consumption to maintain the tone, to set the pace or perhaps to keep the peace, by and large the three-decker novel often went hand-in-hand with the three bottle man. Similarly, the tradition of Freemasonic 'harmony' after the lodge meeting involved drinking to such an extent that there was at times a clash between the core Freemasonic principle of self-control on the one hand and being a good host and a better guest on the other. Many lodges, including Burns's own, had had to pass by-laws to fine brethren who were obstreperous through drink or simply careless with the lodge's property, to preserve a level of decorum in a heavy drinking time.[580] In Burns's time, and in the generation after, this remained a tension such that even their clerical brother Hamilton Paul, a truly convivial host himself, described the drinking culture prevailing in Scottish lodges as being 'certainly adapted to withdraw the warm-hearted noviciate from the serious pursuit of business, and indirectly to encourage habits of dissipation, though its rules are directly contrary'.[581]

This thesis is not the place to rehearse the arguments for or against Burns's drinking habits, whether through the prism of Currie's strong temperance views or the wider Victorian perception of Burns's 'frailty', but in the context of social drinking it must be remembered that the conventions of the long 18th century in Scotland linked power, hospitality and alcohol consumption tightly. Burns would have been well aware that the political masters of cities and towns would use drink as a display both of authority and magnificencewith free drink traditionally supplied to the town's inhabitants at New Year and other high days at the Market Cross (typically either hogsheads of wine or special burgh recipes of a lethal cocktail called 'Het Pint')[582] This is why it is perfectly natural to see the first Burns Suppers in the context of emphatic toasting and equivalent imbibing. We do not know what kind of liquor was supplied by Hamilton Paul for the nine gentlemen who met in Burns Cottage on the first Burns Supper, but Paul later contextualised the poet's drinking in the wider social mores of the day where 'many of the most respectable characters in the kingdom for talents, morality, and piety, seldom, when health permits, retire to rest without having a Hawick gill [sc. half an imperial pint of spirits] under their belt'.[583] Again, Hamilton Paul captured these habits in one of his bons mots: when offered a glass of whisky by an elderly paritioner, he accepted because it was 'only flinging water on a droon't moose.'[584]

It would be wrong, though, to assume that alcoholic consumption was (or is today) compulsory at any Burns Supper. John Struthers, in his poem delivered at the Paisley Burns Club in January 1810, was clear that the club sought to set a higher tone in conduct:

Let barking, wild Impiety,
With smirking Smutt, and Ribaldry,
Find out some paltry tribe, who dub
Themselves a FREE-AND-EASY-CLUB;
There, belch out frothy ravings, stale,
And grin upon the thread-bare tale.

> But here, decorum marks the bound,
> We tread on consecrated ground.[585]

Certainly, as the 19th century progressed, the concern over the working class's drinking habits was an increasingly prominent topic. When Wilson was arranging the Doon Festival, one of the reasons for the procession from Ayr to Burns Cottage was to occupy the lower-class men and keep them out of the hostelries of 'The Wicked Toun of Ayr' (although the 2,000 diners were supplied with *Punch's* infamous 'pint of something calling itself Sherry'). By 1859, when we read the reportage in Ballantine's *Chronicle*, we can see an undercurrent of defensiveness about drinking. Many reports are at pains to emphasise that the evening was 'respectable', a journalistic code for it not being a drunken rout. Exceptionally some journalists reported cases of excess, such as the culmination of one large dinner in Glasgow, where a diehard group received some censure in the papers: 'The proceedings, which commenced a few minutes past five o'clock, did not terminate till about half past eleven, by which time many persons had left the hall, and many of those who remained had become rather confused in their jollity'.[586] Several reports go to some length to display this balance between sociability and the avoidance of the temptation to excess: at Perth, in 1859 the drink was 'porter in pint bottles... a small quantity of spirits was distributed, amounting only to three dozen bottles of whisky among not fewer than 900.'[587] The message that is consistent through the reports is one of controlled 'hilarity' without 'licence' and was particularly noted in the towns which made a day of it: with shops closing, bells ringing and a general holiday adding to the general temptation. The report on Ayr's celebrations ends with the uplifting character of the townsfolk: '[d]runkenness, swearing, or brawling were out of the question – there were no such things... the Captain of Police informing us, that he has usually twice the number of cases on an ordinary market day'.[588] This theme is an undercurrent throughout Ballantine, with the adjectives 'respected' and 'respectable' appearing 107 times, with a further 23 Scottish reports instancing the strictures imposed by recent legislation on public houses and hotels which created the first mandatory 'closing time' for inns and public houses. This curfew of 11pm (or as several wits described it in Burnsian quote: 'a good hour avant the twal') restricted the duration of any Burns Supper held in licensed premises.[589]

While there was a clear trend to a soberer approach, there were a few older fashioned events where the older rites of drinking were maintained in the form of the entrance of the punch or toddy bowl after dinner. Punch was a very popular drink across Scotland in the 18th and early 19th century, as merchants and sailors came home from the East and West Indies bearing the traditional ingredients of punch: lemons, strong spirit, sugar and spice. Currie's life described (with his habitual reaction against alcohol) a 'typical' session: 'the marble-bowl was again and again emptied and replenished; the guests of our poet forgot the flights of time and the dictates of prudence'.[590] That 'marble-bowl' was the poet's wedding gift from his father-in-law. It bears a later addition of a silver rim added by Alexander Fergusson of Craigendarroch (to whom the bowl was gifted by Gilbert) inscribed with the last pair of lines from the *Epistle to J Lapraik* capturing the concept of twin sociabilities – not only of sharing a drink with friends but literally sharing it out of the same receptacle, in the camaraderie of being gathered around the punch bowl which was set in the middle of the festal table: 'Come to my bowl, come to my arms, /My friends, my brothers!'[591]

To his friends and admirers, Burns's punch bowl was talismanic and in that current of trying to 'touch' Burns in the Burns Supper, for many years recreating his 'smoking bowl' was seen as an important part of the ritual. That was captured by the anonymous contributor to the *Port Folio* in 1821 who wrote *Verses on Burns's Punch Bowl*, ending thus:

> Sae fill the glass, but e'er we pree,
> Round this dear relic reverently,
> We'll lighten Scotland's downcast e'e.
>   For sair she mourns,
> And toast thy honoured memory
>   Immortal BURNS![592]

The Greenock Ode at the club's 1805 dinner acknowledges the power of the 'social bowl' (or as it is called the following year, the 'inspiring bowl') and through references in the poems from Paisley and Alloway, in the early suppers, the arrival of the punch became a regularly performed closing ritual.[593] In January 1819, Lockhart, in *Peter's Letters*, waspishly wrote about Hogg's use of punch at the third formal Edinburgh Burns Supper when he had 'finished the bottle of port allowed by our traiteur, and was deep in a huge jug of whisky toddy – in the manufacture of which he is supposed to excel almost as much as Burns did – and in its consumption too, although happily in rather a more moderate degree'.[594]

Hogg in his persona as the Ettrick Shepherd and claimed co-celebrant of a 25th January birthday, often is seen as spiriting up (in both senses) the punch bowl after the formal speeches, conjuring the simple inn fireside ritual of the toddy nightcap. He first performed this function in Edinburgh in 1815 (in collaboration with Gilbert Burns, Robert Ainslie, John Wilson and Alexander Boswell), and revelled in the attention and the assumption of Elijah's mantle from Burns's shoulders in a practical sense as toddy-master and in hope as bard. But the reflection of the toddy bowl as Burns's peculiar taste was more widespread than that particular attempt to arrogate the bardic totems. At the foundation of the Dumfries Burns Club, in January 1819, as the Mausoleum Committee morphed into the club which exists today, the members agreed to a subscription to commission a porcelain punch bowl as 'particularly appropriate, as it is well known that Burns preferred the punch bowl at his convivial meetings'.[595] It was duly commissioned from Josiah Spode with a specification of a capacity of three imperial gallons, decorated with Burns's portrait and the subscribers' names, along with a suite of mugs and glasses, allowing the pleasantry 'that the club was baptised in a punchbowl'.[596] This became a famous artefact, with even James Glencairn Burns writing to the club in the 1820s asking for toddy to be mixed in the famous bowl, then bottled and shipped to him in India, which request was complied with cheerfully and commemorated in verse.[597]

The now priceless (and repaired) Dumfries bowl was in pride of place during the centenary, and only nine other dinners were reported to have held to this last vestige of the old ritual.[598] As the Victorian era progressed the use of the punch bowl fell into desuetude in the Burns Supper, leaving, even today, the Dumfriesians as the sole guardians of this species of tribute.

This tale of a balanced approach to alcoholic consumption is probably over-exaggerated in the collated reports of the centenary, as many of the recorded functions were male-only dinners with up to 50 men present and, in the privacy of their hotel dining room, no journalist would record the exact alcoholic intake. It is fair to say that if there had been a national or international bacchanal that would have been captured by the watchful and growing temperance movement, which found itself in a significant dilemma. The report on the centennial in Cupar carries a carefully worded statement on the hard-line anti-drink position:

> Although some leading members of the Commit-
> tee of the Total Abstinence Society were present,
> and took a more or less active part in the proceed-
> ings, the majority of the Committee held aloof, not
> because they do not appreciate the merits and geni-
> us of Burns, or are not fully sensible of the high hon-
> our he has reflected upon the land of his birth; but
> that having lifted up testimony against the drink-
> ing manners and usages of society, they considered

> it quite improper in celebrating this centenary to
> use the agent which, more than anything else, hung
> like a dark cloud around his chequered career, and
> hurried him to a premature grave.[599]

Yet it would be wrong to imagine that the temperance movement
would not, or could not support the remembrance of Burns's
works even if not all of his lifestyle conformed to the ideal they
sought to promote. The largest Edinburgh supper – the 'grand
citizen's banquet in the Corn Exchange'– was held on 'temperance
principles' to the ire of several town councillors, and the ridicule
of some commentators such as Mrs Caroline Norton (1808–
1877) who could not but 'think of three thousand sitting down
to Temperance tea-trays! I'd lief as be a duck and sit in a pond
with my chin upon duckweed'.[600] There were many celebrations
happy to report Burns Suppers or Burns soirées based on
enjoyment without alcoholic stimulation usually consisting of
the consumption of tea often described in journalistic cliché as
'that excellent beverage which cheers but not inebriates'.[601] In
all a total of 44 'dry' events are recorded in Scotland (with three
in England and one each in Ireland, Canada and the USA). This
is a relatively early example of how a particular interest group
could modify the running order of the Burns Supper to match its
own principles and aspirations. The fundamental conviviality
remains, with a sociable group gathered to share a drink and
a bite to eat while remembering the bard, the only substantive
difference being that the drink of choice was non-alcoholic. In
fact, many abstainers were proud that they could accomplish
the balancing act between creating an enjoyable non-alcoholic
celebration of Burns without condoning his perceived alcoholism
so that the 'essential' form of the Burns Supper is recognisable
but its 'accidents' conform to that specific group's social, moral
or political code, but without alcohol.

This compromise worked after the Burns Centenary too
and it was recognised that the celebration could be 'dry' or
'wet' (or even 'extremely wet') depending on the taste of the

organisers and the target audience. Over the 150 years to 2009 and through today, not only ostensible temperance groups, but church fellowships, youth movements, schools and women's groups – even some established clubs, such as Greenock in 1857 – all held Burns Suppers without alcohol in addition to wider community activities such as grand concerts (which although 'dry' during the performance often permitted certain less committed participants to elect to dine and drink before and after).

Again, the concept of celebrating Burns can be adapted and of all the elements one finds, contrary to popular misconception, a Burns Supper need not be an alcohol-fuelled evening. However, just as alcohol is used in the wider social context as a medium of celebration, so in the Burns Supper too it is more common than not. It would be wrong to suggest that there are occasions which make Helen Simpson's short story *Burns And The Bankers* look like social documentary rather than parody (where, for example she describes '[a]n ocean of alcohol was being drained in nips and sips and gulps in a steamingly hot room on a thousand empty stomachs').[602] So while drinking was and is a common but not obligatory part of the proceedings, the linkage between the history of Burns's life and the wider, older tradition of alcohol at club dinners and the happy, celebratory nature of the Burns Supper all add to an important philosophy of conviviality, however any given particular group may seek to define the phrase 'conviviality' as it specifically applies to them.

Entertainment

There is a long-standing joke amongst speakers giving toasts on Burns Nights that the menu card usually describes 'Speeches and Entertainment' implicitly classifying the speeches as not being part of the entertainment. When Burns conjures up scenes of conviviality in his works, 'sangs an' clatter' are a regular accompaniment to the party, whether in the noise and storm of the beggars' riot at Poosie Nansie's howff or the more sedate imbibing by Tam and the Souter by the tavern ingle. The celebration, by definition, of a poetic genius must involve not only reference to his work, but performance of it and that imperative can be seen from the earliest Burns Suppers. Hamilton Paul recognised that Burns as a man enjoyed conviviality, his poems reflect that enjoyment, and his audience welcomes it: those three truths marry up within the context or form of the Burns Supper. So what can we discern from the poems and songs chosen to be featured and performed and enjoyed in successive Burns Suppers? Just as the common assumption that every Burns Supper needed of necessity to be a heavy drinking session has been shown to be incorrect, there are a number of assumptions over the use of song and poetry that do not bear closer scrutiny. These will be discussed in detail below, looking at the songs and the poems separately. In summary, it is important first to recognise that the works chosen for these programmes were not all written by Burns and, second, to recognise that the corpus of Burns's works used in celebration was relatively limited.

In terms of the breadth of cultural reference used across Burns Suppers in the 19th and early 20th centuries, it is important to recognise that the evening's entertainment could include the compositions of major writers (notably Scott, Hogg, Byron, Campbell and Tannahill) being aligned alongside those of genteel amateurs (such as Hamilton Paul, Sir Alexander Boswell, Lady Nairne, Lady Oliphant, and even Robert Burns Junior). These were enjoyed beside the compositions of noted hymnologists and church musicians (of the likes of Neil Dougall in Greenock, James Montgomery in Sheffield or RA Smith of Paisley) who though virtually forgotten have compositions still in featured today's hymnals. All of whom who competed for attention with local poetasters and now-forgotten versifiers of that moment. All of these sources were used in creating the entertainment to complement the poet's own oeuvre. At this point, the Burns

Supper was a forum for simultaneously honouring Burns but also for giving a stage for other poets too: sometimes new writers, other times 'classics', sometimes even writers from other countries or genres. So, up to 1896 at least and really into the 1920s, we must be cautious in accepting Robert Crawford (and MacDiarmid)'s thesis of Burns blotting out competition like the rhododendrons of a great Ayrshire estate forcing out the smaller, weaker native plants. As Crawford sets out this argument:

> The prominence of Burns among icons of Scottishness has ensured that, in vague terms at least, poetry has been viewed as important to Scotland's cultural identity. On the other hand, a smattering of Burns has been used by a lot of folk inside and outside Scotland as an excuse for ignoring all the rest of Scottish poetry. For too many people Scotland is allowed only one poet.[603]

The early Burns Supper celebrants would not have recognised this statement as valid or descriptive of their evening's entertainment as the songs and poems were supposed to take the sentiment of the short toast and amplify it. The entertainments of those early evenings would be a mix of the regional, local, topical and traditional mixed in with favourite works of Burns. Only once the Bureaucratic period gained momentum did the movement start to concentrate on Burns's works alone.

The Songs

Singing was a central part of many dinner entertainments in the late 18th and early 19th centuries (and remains prevalent today). It is not surprising, therefore, to see the use of Burns's songs as a regular part of the early Burns Suppers. Hamilton Paul's Allowa' minutes are vague on detail of the performances, but we can read of communal singing being arranged by Neil Dougall at Greenock in January 1804 where he had 'a most efficient chorus of his friends to render the songs of Burns' as part of a musical entertainment.[604] Similarly under the aegis of Robert Tannahill and RA Smith, Paisley's suppers covered a range of songs and poems. Sometimes these programmes became quite elaborate performances with an ambitious cantata in 1807, where 'McLaren spoke the recitative parts very well; and Messrs. Smith, Stewart, and Blaikie, sung the songs, harmonised in glees by Smith, in their best styles'.[605]

These early suppers used what talent there was to hand: Smith and Dougall being choirmasters they encouraged communal song, Alexander Boswell had a pleasant amateur singing voice and was the *a capella* soloist to his own compositions, while in 1816, RA Smith, serving as Paisley's president apologised for 'never having been accustomed to speak in public, he felt himself quite incapable of such a task; he had however thrown loosely together some few sentences for the occasion, and he craved to be allowed to sing them', which he did, regaling the audience of the evening with a selection of Burns songs while accompanying himself on the piano.[606]

It can be seen then, that in the early period of Burns Suppers there was a vigorous mix of Burns, new Scottish verse, folk song and other English-language poetry. This fine balance, using Burns as the centre, but with subsidiary poetic spokes to build out a wheel, became the norm. Moving forward in time and taking Ballantine's *Chronicle* as the benchmark of the Traditional period, we can make an assessment of how the audiences interacted with the Bard's song works. Within the limitations of the journalistic reportage we can see that a relatively small and defined list of Burns's songs were favoured. There was a growing divergence of style, notably the larger Edinburgh events and in the key Dumfries dinner which only used Burns songs, but in the west of Scotland and abroad a wider range was still sung. Taking one of the most detailed reports, the 'Literary & Artistic Club' held its supper in Glasgow on 25 January 1859. Most of the main toasts (which were quite long in the delivery) were followed by an instrumental air and then also one or more songs, breaking up the pace of the evening. Of the programme only five out of 15 instrumental pieces and 12 out of 21 songs (excluding *Auld Lang Syne*) were by Burns.[607] Across Ballantine, Burns songs did rather better, coming out at 80 per cent (again, excluding *ALS* as a special case of its own).

The other statistic that is evident from the Ballantine *Chronicle* is that the canon of Burns's works featured in 1859 is smaller than thought. One of the 1980s clichés of the state of the Burns Supper and its purported negative effect on the study and appreciation of Burns was a look back to a 'golden period' when Burns Suppers heard a huge range of the poems and songs which were deemed more central and important that the output of amateur orators. Ballantine's data clearly shows no such 'golden period' existed. The 'Top Three' (*Honest Poverty, There Was a Lad, and Scots Wha Hae)* accounted for 32 per cent of all songs sung. The 'Top Ten' was 62 per cent in total, and a further 23 Burns songs added 18 per cent, leaving 20 per cent of other authored/traditional songs.[608] That is a tiny sample of the attributed Burns canon. The choice leaned away from the famous love songs: *Ye Banks and Braes* and *Nanie, O* were in the top ten but the few performances of *My Luve's Like A Red Red Rose* (which not sung in Scotland at all, and only twice in England) or the total absence of *Ae Fond Kiss* are striking. It is possible to surmise that the story behind these two works ('the fause lover' or what is in effect epistolary adultery respectively) was too close to the perception of the 'frailties' of Burns in 1859 to appear comfortable for discussion or even contemplation in a wide Victorian public company. It still seems a very surprising omission.

The creation of the Burns Federation as a central resource for the preservation of the widest forms of the Burns cult could have been expected to accelerate the trend to using only Burns songs at Burns Suppers in support of one of its primary purposes. To an extent, this aim could have the unintended consequence of bringing about Crawford's worry of 'one poet' being sufficient for all Scotland. However, while the desire to 'honour' the works was explicit, it was still rarely exclusive during this period. The trends can be tracked through typical Burns Suppers for the following century in the Bureaucratic period of the Burns Supper.

Internationally, taking as a prime example the 1896 Sydney celebrations in honour of the centenary of Burns's Death, which 'in order to meet all tastes... made arrangements to hold a Burns concert in the Town Hall on Monday 20 July and a Haggis Supper at the Freemasons' Hall, York Street, the following evening'.[609] Here we can see two movements coinciding: the drive to treat Burns (as the Federation sought) as a pre-eminent genius of Scotland (at the concert) and the older desire to maintain a convivial atmosphere around any celebration (at the Haggis Supper). The concert programme had hardly changed in its choices from 1859, with five of the ten programmed songs reflecting 1859's top ten list (those songs being marked below by an asterisk). However, now the audience were expecting a programme entirely of Burns and so it had no traditional or local songs on the docket:

Scots Wha Hae *
A Man's a Man *
Bonnie Doon *
Green Grow The Rashes O *
John Anderson, my Jo *
Duncan Gray
Afton Water
Corn Rigs
Tam Glen
O Whistle and I'll come tae you my Lad
The Lass of Ballochmyle.

The following evening saw the Haggis Supper, and for the moment ignoring the speeches and recitations, we see a different approach to the concert as the supper was light on the poet's works (ignoring the copious quotation from his verse within the speeches). The attendant band equally used *A Man's a Man* and *The Garb of Auld Gaul* as thematic interludes and closed the festivities with Burns's *My Love a Highland Lad was Born* as a prelude to his traditional *Auld Lang Syne*. Similarly, the professional female vocalist gave one lesser Burns song (*Last May a Braw Wooer*) balanced between two sentimental Scottish songs: *The Land o' the Leal* (Lady Nairne – although sometimes erroneously attributed to Burns) and *O Sing to Me The Auld Scotch Sangs* (Bethune) so averaging both out, just half of that evening's entertainment was of Burns's works. Even when a significant part of the programme was devoted to Burns's songs, its delivery could occur in what would seem quite unexpected fashions, unimaginable at several levels today:

> The annual Burns concerts were held in London...
> The Mohawk Minstrels at Islington likewise
> offered a programme, the first part of which was
> chiefly of Burns's songs, delivered by the melo-
> dists of the burnt cork community.[610]

To test this common approach to singing at Burns Suppers over the years, we can look through the Dalry Burns Club's records (*The Cairn*), where records go back to the founding supper of 1826, but details of the evening's entertainments only started to be recorded in detail from 1870. Singing – probably because of its participative nature – has been a key attribute of the club's dinners from the beginning in fact, songs seem much more important to the Dalry Club that the poems. The club records first note the details of the evening's entertainments in 1861 where the members gave two dozen toasts and sang two dozen songs in the evening, of which but four were by Burns (*Corns Rigs, Afton Water, Gloomy Winter's Now Awa'* and *The Bonnie Lass o' Ballochmyle*). We can see that the Dalry Club has remained on the 'eclectic' side of the tradition although Burns works are now in the majority of the performances heard at suppers today. It can be seen that this 'non-exclusive' tradition remained strong until the Second World War, as the majority of songs sung at these suppers until the late 1940s were not written by Burns. From that time, fewer songs (and more recitations) have been included in the programme while the evenings 'ongauins' have shortened to have not the 30-odd toasts and songs, but the 20 plus-or-minus which is that club's norm today, with the emphasis having swung to the poet. The 2018 (number 193) Club dinner saw the company singing seven Burns songs and two others which have important ritual purposes: *The Land O' The Leal* which has been a traditional accompaniment to the toast to 'Departed Members', and *The Star O' Robbie Burns* (by James Thomson) which has only been performed at the club since 2001.

This song merits some critical attention. *The Star o' Robbie [sic] Burns* is felt by some clubs (particularly in the West and Borders of Scotland) to be traditional if not canonical. This paean was composed by James Thompson (1827–1888) to music by James Booth for the 1870 dinner of the Hawick Burns Club. This song creates a sharp debate: some find it almost obligatory while many others regard it as mere maudlin Victorianism with a music-hall pathos and an almost aggressive assertion of the peasant school of Burns interpretation embodied in its chorus:

> Let kings and courtiers rise and fa'
> This world has mony turns,
> But brightly beams abune them a'   [above
> The Star o' Robbie Burns.[611]

It is a great irony that many of the supporters of the song include the most vehement against the practice of calling 'Rabbie', 'Robbie'. Ogden Nash posed the question why 'Bobby Burns' and not 'Wally Scott', or 'Tommy Hardy and Bernie Shaw'? Sometimes in Burns studies, the smaller the issue, the greater the noise.[612] The song in question is not, therefore, a compulsory part of the structure of a Burns Supper, and it would be a shame to reduce the time available to share in the poet's songs to include this one.

In summary, looking at the performance of songs at Burns Suppers, from the earliest through the development of the formal supper through to today, Burns's songs were central to almost every event but with a relatively small selection of them being regularly used and a very common theme of using other Scottish or traditional songs and ballads as an integral part of the evening, showing the genius Burns surrounded by a wider, Scots tradition.

The Poems

Turning to the poems, early Burns Suppers were not defined as showcase vehicles which were focussed entirely upon the Bard's oeuvre. As the Greenock Burns Club records, its 1810 dinner saw that '[m]any appropriate toasts were drunk and seldom have we heard such good singing. Poetical effusions were also composed, recited and met with applause'.[613]

As above with the songs, by reviewing Ballantine's *Chronicle* for the entertainment of 1859, data can also be captured on the recitations of his major poems in the subsequent Traditional period (in this case excluding *To a Haggis* which is analysed elsewhere). An immediate point noted is that the total number of recitations was less than one third of the total number of songs sung, probably reflecting organisers' wishes to balance a programme between the spoken word (which was already heavily underpinned by the speeches) and music. The reportage is very light in detail for most of the overseas events (including Ireland) and many general references to 'poems and songs' are scattered about, so the analysis around the poems is less robust but still gives a good indication of which were most popular and noteworthy. As with the songs, this appears to be a narrower selection of his poems than one might expect.

Unsurprisingly, then as now, *Tam o'Shanter* is by far the most popular recitation, at 39 per cent of the recorded Burns recitations, including the *tour de force* rendition by the centenarian Walter Glover who claimed Burns's acquaintance.[614] The other great set-piece, *The Cotter's Saturday Night* garnered 21 per cent of the recitations. Of course, both are long works, so by choosing them, the organisers limited the number of other poems or songs that could be performed, therefore, no other poem achieved double figures of recitations. The next three most popular *(Man Was Made To Mourn, The Twa Dogs, and To Mary in Heaven)* contributed broadly equally to 22 per cent, leaving 16 other poems performed once or twice (but, surprisingly, neither *To A Mouse, or To a Louse)*. It might be safe to assume that Holy Willie's 'wanton leg' probably ruled him out of mixed performance in those days of Victorian sensibilities.[615]

In 1859, there was a greater preponderance of Burns poems on running orders when compared to the eclecticism in song choice. Still in many venues new 'gifts' of song or verse would be performed. Several of the dinners using Isa Craig's prize-winning Crystal Palace poem, for example. However, in addition to the extensive quotation of Burns's words (both poetic and epistolary) incorporated in the speeches, it was (and is) rare to find poems by other respected writers on the programme with the exception of tributary poems such as the homage of two American writers: Fitz-Green Halleck's *To a Rose*, Brought From Near *Alloway Kirk, in Ayrshire, in the Autumn of 1822* and John Greenleaf Whittier's 1840 poem *Burns. On Receiving a Sprig of Heather in Blossom,* being used to contextualise the 1859 enthusiasm to repair the 'neglect' of the living poet, compensated by heightened adulation in the Burns Centenary year.[616]

In the Ballantine reports, there are glimpses of that performative urge that Crawford flags in his bardic theory of Burns. Adding 'show' was not confined to the ritual around the haggis: in Beattock two gentlemen co-recited the *Twa Dogs* (a fair assumption being that one spoke Caesar's lines and the other acting as The Poet and his Luath), while the narrative force within *Tam o'Shanter* calls out for a three-dimensional representation with five staged or semi-staged events of that master work being recorded.[617] In particular, three towns built the day's festival around a re-enactment of the poem before an evening's dinner: West Wemyss, Auchterarder and, atmospherically by torch light, Auchtermuchty.[618] Many modern reciters of *Tam* think that they are being innovative in switching out the lights at the poem's line: 'In an instant a' was dark', but a Mr Johnstone of Castle-Douglas had come up with this *coup-de-theâtre* in 1859 when he 'caused a good deal of amusement' by 'the total eclipse of the lights at the moment Tam, unable to contain his admiration of the "supple jade and strang," shouts out "Weel done, Cutty Sark"'. [619]

Interestingly, while there appears a level of self-censorship or at least careful selection of what could be performed, three events created a staged version of *The Jolly Beggars* following Burns's concept of *Love and Liberty: A Cantata* off the page and onto the stage. This gritty tale of low life in Ayrshire remained controversial and equally attracted praise for its insight and much condemnation for its perceived coarseness, so it was rare to hear of its performance (although Lockhart records an earlier incidence, at the Edinburgh 1819 dinner in *Peter's Letters* and it was performed by the Dunbar Burns club at its Dinner in 1820).[620] In Stonehaven 40 years later, it was 'the great treat of the evening viz: "The Jolly Beggars" acted in real character' and a similar approach was seen at events in Thornhill and Strathaven.[621] The most elaborate was in Liverpool where the late refusal of Thackeray to be the key speaker left the organisers with a programming gap for their planned Burns Supper which was plugged late in the day by adding *The Jolly Beggars* as the finale of extended concert preceding a curtailed dinner: '[t]he cantata, as a whole, was the most interesting musical performance of the evening'.[622]

Looking at how the poetry programme developed at a club closely associated with the foundation of the Federation, the records of Alexandria Burns Club (number 2 on the Federation roll) give a more interesting picture of the use of the poems from 1981 to 2018. Poetry is a key interest of this club, with each Burns Supper typically having around four poems performed from a good broad repertoire: 14 different recitations are recorded (with 16 unspecified poems) with all of them being by Burns. *Tam o'Shanter* is virtually ubiquitous, featuring every year except 2005 (when it was deliberately dropped to prove a point that the club members' 'wide knowledge of the bard's works' meant 'that it is not always necessary to include *Tam O'Shanter* or *Holy Willie's Prayer* in the programme' – both poems returned in 2006 by popular demand!). *Holy Willie's Prayer* is the next most popular, with 16 outings, with another Willie – *Willie Wastle* – close behind with 15.

Advice to a Young Friend (with 9), *The Unco Guid* (8), The *Mouse* (7), the *Louse* (6), *Twa Dogs* (5) are the other repetitions over the period. Semi-staging has become a common feature at Alexandria where one can see Tam in his traditional bonnet and blue breeks or Willie Fisher in his nightshirt and candlestick, and hear the *Address to The Unco Guid* recited while standing on a Cutty Stool. The *Twa Dogs* has been performed a two or three-handed recitation (and also with puppets), while a live mouse timorously made an appearance. [623]

What we see over the years at Alexandria Burns Club is typical of the entertainment produced by members of a committed Burns Club for their fellow aficionados. The running order is quite extended covering four main speeches, around five recitations, about the same number of songs or musical interludes and the 'ritual' use of Burns's verses in asking for Grace and, of course, in the ceremony of the haggis during dinner. To be successful, this calls for a strong pool of talented performing members and an audience happy to spend five or more hours at the table.

By the time of the end of the Great War, recitations of poems not by Burns were hardly heard at Burns Suppers (although there were some who gave poetic speeches composed for the evening – a tradition still to be found in the Lassies/Reply where these toasts are often given in rhyme – poetry would be too strong a word) but appears to be after the Second World War that the same trend caught up with the songs. (Similarly, whereas 19th century Burns Suppers piped in the haggis to any rousing tune –*The Campbells Are Coming* being often cited – from the mid-20th century a Burns tune – often *There Was a Lad* or *A Man's a Man* – would be first choice).

This is very much what could be expected at a modern Burns Supper (at the traditional/formal end of the scale) which will still typically alternate the now shorter speeches with poems and songs. The typical approach is to follow a postprandial programme of this shape:

> The Loyal (or Patriotic) Toast(s)
> The Immortal Memory
> > Interlude/Performance of poem, song or music
> The Toast to the Lass(i)es
> > Interlude/Performance of poem, song or music
> The Reply to the Toast to the Lass(i)es
> > Interlude/Performance of poem, song or music
> Vote of Thanks or Concluding Remarks
> The Company: *Auld Lang Syne*

The three interludes would reflect the talent available for the evening and the audience's interests with a mix of music, song and recitation. It is important to remember that both professional and amateur singers will have a fairly short repertoire, while reciters typically have one longer poem and a few 'party pieces' so because of that there is a dynamic towards concentrating on relatively small, defined canon of Burns's works for the purpose of live entertainment.

In summary, every programme reflects a particular organiser's taste, tradition (or desire to escape from it) and the pressures of time on the running order. There is often criticism that the focus is on a diminished subset of Burns's works which creates a repetitive strain to the annual event. From the records we have between 1810 and today, that concern is misplaced. At a purely anecdotal level, the songs that appear to have been sung most often in 2009's anniversary year were:

My Luv is Like a Red, Red Rose
Ae Fond Kiss
A Man's A Man
Comin' Through The Rye
Ye Banks and Braes o' Bonnie Doon
Green Grow The Rashes O
Flow Gently Sweet Afton
There Was A Lad
Scots Wha Hae

And a relatively few others – but not a significantly smaller range than can be seen from the statistics of Ballantine's *Chronicle*, and now (absent *the Star O' Robbie Burns* and maybe a rare *National Anthem*) it would be unusual even in the least formal Burns Supper to include a non-Burns song. When it comes to celebrate Burns in a convivial setting, it appears that a much smaller canon of his songs has been used consistently over the decades than had previously been thought.

Similarly, in reviewing the use of his poems, nowadays the two *tours-de-force* are *Tam o'Shanter* with *Holy Willie* in second place and with *The Cotter's Saturday Night* and *Halloween* out of current critical favour. These two set piece poems have moved from simple recitations into semi-staged performances in the latter case typically finding the performer in nightcap and nightgown bearing a candle, and in the former typically boisterously galloping around the stage or dining room, flashing lights on and off for lightening and *pace* the dominie of Castle Douglas, plunging the company into darkness to await the sally of the 'hellish legion'. The modern programme typically would not run to two long poems, so shorter familiar pieces such as *To A Mouse* and *To A Louse* are popular exemplars of his works although the choice is often driven by the particular repertoire of the performer rather than an aesthetic choice to complement the evening's theme. It is interesting to note that, while the poems and songs of Burns are widely regarded as being of sufficient worth to warrant an annual commemoration of their writer's genius, the canon of his works performed at Burns Suppers – even from the earliest occasions – has been relatively limited to perhaps a dozen key works of Burns in total and these poems were regularly admixed with not only hagiographic verses, but other popular traditional, emblematic or merely comic Scots work.

By looking at contemporary supper programmes over the last two centuries, it is possible to challenge two often rehearsed arguments. The first is that the Burns Supper, by deifying Burns, stultified wider Scottish poetry. This was certainly not true during the 19th century as, until the inter-war years of the 20th century, Burns Suppers regularly used works from other poets and songwriters. It is certainly true that the Bureaucratic period saw a codification (and shortening) of the running order which squeezed out the works of other poets and songwriters in the main. It is not obligatory to have Burns works alone, and perhaps that trend can at last be corrected.

The second canard, that there was a 'golden age' of Burns Suppers where knowledgeable 'Burnsians' shared a wider range of the poet's songs and poems than happens today, is definitively untrue. The early celebrations saw a range of performance talent included with songs given by (more or less) gifted amateurs, by professionally engaged performers or in the round by the assembled company. Then and now, the singers' repertoire and the audience's desire centred on a core of around ten songs, and fewer poems. Burns's oeuvre is much larger and more varied and so while it would be impressive and interesting to widen our engagement with his lesser known works, the love of his core songs and poems has always been clear and they sit at the heart of the Burns Supper entertainments.

CHAPTER ELEVEN

Beginning and Ending the Evening

The auld kirk-hammer strak the bell
Some wee, short hour ayont the *twal*,
Which rais'd us baith:[624]

HAVING ISOLATED AND DISCUSSED the three core elements of the Burns Supper ritual there are a number of other traditional parts which are common. The format has developed over the last 150 years to create a programme almost entirely using Burns's own words in the key rituals of the evening. While we have no comment from Paul on how he opened and closed his prototype suppers, it is safe to assume that even a churchman from the faction Burns called 'the candid liberal band' would give thanks by saying Grace before (and probably after) the service of dinner but the closing moments of his dinners are less obvious.[625] Modern tradition sees most suppers opened with the pronouncement of Grace by either the event's chairman or a visiting clergyman (more often than not using the words of *The Selkirk Grace*) and they close with the communal singing of *Auld Lang Syne*, where the participants stand to sing Burns's verses while performing the well-known traditional hand-holding ceremony. How and when did these two rituals become part of the tradition?

Opening the Proceedings: Saying Grace

The dinner at a modern Burns Supper will very often commence in Burns's words with the *Selkirk Grace* most likely in the

'Scottish' version. Although given current contemporary attitudes to organised religion this practice, which would have been virtually universal a generation ago, it is now often omitted or retained more as a charming tradition as opposed to a formal religious invocation.

Any dinner in the early 1800s would have been opened by a minister offering thanks to God (and there would have also been a prayer at the end of the meal, but that custom is dead). Burns early admirers faced the twin problems of Burns's own religious beliefs, and more urgently, the condemnation of his personal religious practice and individual morality by the majority of the Church of Scotland. These issues would make it difficult for all but the most liberal (or unorthodox, in at least one sense of the word) to imagine using the poet's own poetic Graces as an acceptable wording to give thanks to God.

After Burns's death there was no shortage of clerical criticism of the poet who had christened himself 'Poet Burns, wi' your priest-skelping turns'.[626] Many (in likelihood, most) ministers were openly hostile to the poet's memory but in the main, the score-settling saw the living dog-collared asses happily kicking the dead poetical lion. As part of that post mortem battle, the invention of a feast in Burns's memory drew the ire of the Reverend Dr William Peebles of Newton-upon-Ayr (1753–1826) who devoted a generous helping of bile in his own poetic magnum opus. He coined the abusive term 'Burnomania' (why not 'Burnsomania' one wonders?) in a vain poetic attempt to discredit the rapidly growing phenomenon. Peebles had been lampooned by Burns on several occasions and took his late revenge by describing the poet as a 'bard of immorality and infamy' mocking the Greenock Burns Club's particular ambitions in verse.[627] Interestingly, Peebles looks to have avoided starting a literally parochial dispute within Ayr by critiquing the Greenock society and not Provost Ballantine's Allowa' Club which was composed of significantly influential men within the Royal Burgh and the County of Ayr. Peebles's stance was roundly decried by Hamilton Paul as 'narrow minded'.

On the one hand, Paul openly recognised that 'it has not been satisfactorily demonstrated that Burns ever was what we call an orthodox believer' (*Air Edition*, p.xxvii) but he sought to refute Peebles and his like, not only on the consequential phenomenon of celebrating the Bard's anniversary, but more importantly to actively endorse Burns's clerical satires on the basis that '[t]he shafts of ridicule are the best weapons for exposing absurdity' in a search for 'rational piety'. These encomia align with modern thinking, but nearly found Paul on trial at the General Assembly. JG Lockhart sensed the potential for a fight, and characterised it in a typical 'Maga' article: 'nobody but a fool, will ever attempt, either to exaggerate or extenuate errors... as to the blasphemy of many of Burns' allusions, it is really quite an insult to common sense to attempt their defence'.[628] Paul was not without influential literary supporters. Hogg, in the Hogg/ Motherwell Edition of the Works, later said of the reverend gentleman: 'Rev Hamilton Paul. There is a hero for you. Any man will stand up for a friend, who while he is manifestly in the right, is suffering injury or malice of others; but how few like Mr Paul have the courage to step forward and defend a friend whether he is right or wrong'.[629] As discussed, he championed the anniversary celebration of Burns for another 14 years until his death as a popular, bibulous bachelor in 1854.[630]

There was, however, some level of clerical support for Burns, too, beyond Paul. In 1844 at the Doon Festival, for example, the dinner was opened by: 'The Rev Mr Cuthill, of Ayr's Auld Kirk, [who] asked the blessing, in language brief, impressive and appropriate'.[631] The steady growth of this affectionate and widespread celebration of Burns had some softening effect of the views of the strictly Calvinist camp, and that thaw in attitude hit a high point at the Birthday Centenary of 1859 where we see a broader acceptance of Burns by the clergy – tellingly summarised by the minister of Geelong in Australia who told his Burns Supper audience: 'that some years ago a person of his profession would have felt it an insult to be asked to be present on such an occasion; but that time had passed'.[632]

The wider arc of acceptance by the kirk is embodied in the career of one of the most influential Scots churchmen of Victorian times, the Reverend Dr Norman Macleod (1812–1872). As a young parish minister in Ayrshire in 1838 he point-blank refused to attend a Burns Supper, declining the invitation in highly critical terms:

> Only consider the matter seriously as a Christian man, and say how we can, with the shadow of consistency, commemorate Burns after sitting down at the Lord's Supper to commemorate the Saviour? I have every admiration for Burns as a poet; but is it possible to separate the remembrance of his genius from the purposes for which it was so frequently used..., however much I may admire the beautiful poetry of Burns... I cannot, I dare not, as a Christian minister do this; neither can I but in the strongest manner disapprove of any dinner to his memory.[633]

By 1859 however, Dr Macleod, then minister of the Barony Kirk in Glasgow, felt able to sit on the platform of the City Hall centenary dinner and to speak about the poet while others were stridently denouncing the event. Despite his asseveration that he had not been called to the platform 'to pass any judgement on [Burns] as a man, but only as a writer', his focus on the poet's 'failings' (articulated at some length in front of an unimpressed James Glencairn Burns) brought a mix of cheers and hisses from the audience, leading to an early close to the worthy preacher's homily.[634] Another decade on, Macleod had reached a point where he was unsupportive of the controversy created by the conservative Calvinist Reverend Fergus Ferguson who preached and published a highly critical sermon entitled *Should Christians Celebrate the Birthday Of Robert Burns?*[635] This posited the ultra-Presbyterian thesis that the poet, as irrefutably evidenced by his critical depictions of the church, let alone in the conduct of his daily life, was proven to be an incorrigible atheist, and therefore was a condign influence against Victorian Christian values. As Ferguson put the attack – in words not far from Macleod's 1838 opinion – 'you cannot divide his influence – extracting the sweet and wholesome from the poisonous –He has one influence and that influence is an evil one.'[636]

This stirred up a controversy in the press, mostly defending Burns in the round and the positive elements captured at his popular birthday celebrations.[637] Thomas Watson denounced Fergusson poetically as being '[l]ike a vile highland adder he wriggles and turns/ And he bites at the dust of our own Robert Burns', which earned the thanks of Colonel Burns for 'the admirable castigation'.[638] The debate was effectively closed when Queen Victoria dismissed the poor minister's crusade by writing of her fondness for Burns to Thomas Carlyle: 'Her Majesty also alluded with some force of words to the bad taste and folly of the attack made on the memory of the poet by the Reverend Fergus Ferguson'.[639]

That ultimate level of Establishment support allowed Macleod to write that, while deprecating drunkenness as a generic Scotch characteristic, 'the songs of Burns have done more to bind the sentiment of an old nationality, than any other power – except the Presbyterian Kirk!'[640] Late in life, Dr Macleod, at the summit of the Kirk's patronage as Dean of the Thistle, continued to refine his views on the poet and spent his closing years in the Queen Empress's service, reciting *Tam o'Shanter* and *A Man's A Man* to her and her daughters as they worked their spinning wheels at Balmoral.[641]

In the Church of England, too, there were distinguished churchmen who saw merit in Burns, notwithstanding his moral and social irregularities. The Right Reverend Arthur Stanley (1815–1881) served as Dean of Westminster and the respect he commanded as a liberal theologian made him another confidante of the Queen. He famously characterised Burns as the 'prodigal son of the Church of Scotland'.[642] Theologically, too, he recognised a moral quality in Burns and, in his Installation Address as Lord Rector at St Andrew's University in 1875 he abjured the undergraduates 'to go to Burns for your Theology'.[643] A theme echoed across the Atlantic by Reverend Henry Ward Beecher who said: 'I think that Robert Burns has taught men the thoughts of God in Nature more than a great many pulpits have'.[644]

The religious acceptance of Burns reached its apogee on 7 March 1885 on the day the ubiquitous Burns orator, Lord Rosebery, unveiled the bust of Burns in the Poets' Corner of Westminster Abbey announcing to the dean and chapter that 'in handing over to the Abbey the bust they were bringing the very choicest offering they could bring to the shrine of the Empire'.[645] That rehabilitation allowed the gathering presence of ministers around the Burns Supper board and, since then, the Kirk has provided many notable Burns orators, including the Reverend James ('Jimmy') Currie who claimed to perform at over 40 Burns Suppers a year in the 1970s and '80s.[646]

While clerics could now be actors in the celebrations, the second religious issue remained moot and the use of Burns's own Grace Compositions was still highly problematic.[647] While possible to love the sinner but hate the sin, what about the sinner's direct use of devotional verse? Could it, in conscience, be used as an acceptable religious invocation at the poet's own anniversary celebrations, or was that a further mock to religion? Even today where religious practice is so highly flexible to be near-syncretic, some of Burns's Graces are patently too flippant to be used except ironically.[648] The compositions linked to the Globe Tavern, Dumfries known as *Grace Before Meat* and *Grace Before And After Meat* are good examples of that problem as they end with injunctions to 'bring in the spirit'.[649] Of the remaining Grace verses, one, while having no scoffing quality, is potentially theologically inappropriate as it focuses on human rather than divine love and is therefore, less amenable to clerical use:

O Thou, in whom we live and move,
　Who mad'st the sea and shore,
Thy goodness constantly we prove,
　And grateful would adore.

And if it please thee, Pow'r above,
　Still grant us with such store;
The *Friend* we *trust;* the *Fair* we *love*;
　And we desire no more.[650]

Which leaves two possibilities that appear capable of being used as public prayers without causing clerical or doctrinal offence. One is this:

O, Thou, who kindly dost provide
　For every creature's want!
We bless thee, God of nature wide,
　For all thy goodness lent:
And, if it please thee, heavenly guide,
　May never worse be sent;
But whether granted, or denied,
　Lord bless us with content.
　　　　　　　　Amen!!![651]

Or (of course) the other is *Selkirk Grace* itself, either in a Scots or an English version.[652]

In 1859, the use of the poet's own words as the prayer was still unusual enough for it to be mentioned as exceptional in some of the Ballantine reports.[653] As the *Selkirk Grace* was relatively unknown, it receives but one mention (Aston Hall, Birmingham) with half a dozen uses of *Grace Before Dinner* being recorded.[654] The debate was summed up from the Chair at Bridge of Weir:'he was not ashamed to make the following suggestion, namely, that as we were met, like many others, 'to spend a night with Burns', the 'Grace' should be in the words of the poet himself.[655] Or in an even more festal fashion in Liverpool, where 'the whole audience joined in singing, to the tune of 'Martyrdom', Burns's grace before meat: 'O thou who kindly dost provide...'. [656]

Just as the Birth Centenary year broke the mould of the silent Immortal Memory, so it marks an early turning point in the ability to use the religious words penned by Burns in a religious context. The Scottifying process of the Victorians appears to have moved away from the English words of the 'Content Grace' to embrace the Scots form of the *Selkirk Grace*, with its redolence of Old Mortality and an inherent appeal to the spirit of the Covenanters. This trend gained momentum in 1896, coinciding with the Death Centenary and over the following century, it became a concrete fixture in the typical Burns Supper and remains so today, ensuring that for every dollop of 'dirt' in Byron's memorable phrase, there is a corresponding splash of 'deity' in the tradition of the Supper table.

Closing the Proceedings: Singing *Auld Lang Syne*

The communal singing of *Auld Lang Syne* to mark the end of a Burns Supper is virtually mandatory now, though Hamilton Paul makes no record of it being sung at his early Burns Suppers, nor is it mentioned in the newspaper reports of the first club diners. It first appears in this context in the report of the Burns Supper from Philadelphia in 1818 after a particularly diasporic toast to Scotland ('The Scotsman's creed: honor to the parent, respect to the aged, love to the fair, and laurel to the brave') and it occupied a role as the closing song of the formal toast list at several other US Burns Suppers in that period, signalling the 'open floor' for volunteer toasts to follow it.[657] It is only at Manchester in 1829 that it is recorded as being used 'before the meeting broke up' for the first time.[658] Yet at some point between then and 1859, the song became ubiquitous as the final act of every Burns Supper, 'Scotland's National Finale' as one reporter described it, and it remains so to this day.[659]

Its national impact as a song, or perhaps *the* song, of the nostalgic diaspora is driven by, but extends beyond, its place in the Burns Supper ritual. Kinsley glosses 'syne' in his notes by quoting Jamieson's *Etymological Dictionary*: 'To a native of this country, [syne] is very expressive, and conveys a soothing idea to the mind, as recalling the memory of joys that are past'.[660] In the verses of *Auld Lang Syne* we see that exact recollection: childish and rural pursuits are interrupted by the roar of 'braid seas' (whether they be physical and diasporic or a metaphorical description of the realities of adult life at home) but are never forgotten. So on the one hand we have an archetype of nostalgia (both in the sense that it would have had in Burns's time as a form of melancholia linked to an absence from one's home country and in the transferred sense, current from the 1920s, as sorrowful regret for past times) yet, on the other hand, the antidote to the condition in another example of the healing power of conviviality, where the bonds with the past can instantly can be recreated through the grip of hand and sharing of a cup, or kiss.

Burns's capture of the phrase and the early success of the lyric and music meant that the song and sentiment were quickly taken up as one of the core values of Scottishness. A mimetic marriage of Burns and Scott occurred at the same time as the Burns Supper was establishing itself. The highly popular stage play *Rob Roy Macgregor, or Auld Lang Syne* was a hit from 1819 across the UK and North America with a gala performance played before George IV in Edinburgh in 1822.[661] In fact, versions of the play remained in the repertory for over a century linking kilts and *Auld Lang Syne* indissolubly in the public mind. That linkage grew stronger with every singing of the song by Scots who sojourned abroad, who emigrated to new lands, who returned to their natal place in retirement, or even those who stayed at home.

This is not the place to explore the trans-national impact of this song in its guise as the anthem of the New Year which makes it, according to the *Guinness World Records*, one of the three most sung songs on our planet. That phenomenon came after the growth of the Burns Supper, and the modern form of words and music was widely used throughout the century after Burns's death and was cemented as the New Year institution when Guy Lombardi, the Canadian band leader, used it from 1929 in his New Year's radio broadcasts. Its ubiquity as the harbinger of the New Year, means in Murray Pittock's phrase that 'the settled global reach of "Auld Lang Syne" in particular has lifted it clear of Burns's cultural frontiers'.[662] This was demonstrated when staff and students at Glasgow University went to some practical lengths to prove this in November 2009, by creating a new world record for the most different languages singing the same song simultaneously, with 41 translations of *Auld Lang Syne*, including Arabic, Bangla, Catalan, Chichewa, Czech, English, Esperanto, Estonian, Frisian, Gaelic (both Irish and Scots), Georgian, Hindi, Igbo, Latin, Malay, Maori, Persian, Romanian, Scots, Swahili, Thai, Ukrainian, Urdu, Vietnamese, Welsh and Yoruba.[663]

So while this song is a feature of the modern Burns Supper, that arises in no small part because of its wider role in all Scottish meetings with a particular enthusiasm amongst the North American diaspora of Scots. This theme of nostalgia is the closing of any gathering of Scots and their fellows and friends from Hogmanay to Burns Night to St Andrew's Celebrations where it appears as a simple song of remembering 'the good old days' in the golden haze of youth or the blue remembered hills of the home country. As a title, commentators find *Auld Lang Syne* is as hard to translate as À *la Recherche de Temps Perdu*, but the idiom is best caught by something like 'The Days of Long Ago' – although it is dangerous to gloss such complexity expressing that wistfulness so prevalent in Scottish thought and writing. A theme that was immediately perceived by Burns: 'is not the

Scotch phrase 'Auld lang syne' exceedingly expressive – ...There is more of the fire of native genius in it than in half a dozen of modern English Bacchanalians'.[664]

The concept of a farewell song to conclude an evening's conviviality in Scotland pre-existed *Auld Lang Syne* in the form of the traditional air and lyric *Good Night and Joy Be Wi' You A'*, which was a popular tradition, particularly at the ending of Scottish balls, until late Victorian times.[665]

Burns was well-acquainted with this air, and used it for *The Farewell To The Brethren of The Tarbolton Lodge* to set his memorial request enjoining his brethren to perform an annual, tearful toast. Just as he reworked this particular song himself, it would be the subject of repeated re-covers in the early 19th century with each of Alexander Boswell, Lady Nairne and Scott writing new versions of increasing complexity.[666] Burns counselled Johnston to place this song appropriately at the end of Volume Six of the *Scots Musical Museum*, marking its traditional function as the closer of a festivity in general.[667] While that traditional use of the song had fallen into desuetude today, it lives a life as a folk song known as *The Parting Glass* in the repertoire of the Irish diaspora.

Burns's *Auld Lang Syne* displays the opposite trajectory, and became almost public property in a way previously unheard of. As the Burns Supper started to squeeze out all non-Burns references and contributions, the opening of the event by using one of his Graces and its closing in communal singing *Auld Lang Syne* rounded out the Pauline rite.[668]

The first recorded reference to singing the song while exchanging 'a haun' in acting out the injunction in verse five, is not in a Burns Supper report, but in a travelogue from 1825. An American writer, Nathaniel Carter, visited Irvine and met Dr John Mackenzie and David Sillar a few months before they held the first Irvine Burns Club dinner. Carter and his companion spent a pleasant time with these living relics of Burns until was time to take leave, which 'was performed by rising round the table, locking hands, and chanting Auld Lang Syne in full chorus.'[669]

The song became a firm favourite on supper programmes before the 1859 Burns Centenary with reports from over the world such as Baltimore (1834), New Haven (1837), and Melbourne (1848) recording the song being sung at the end of dinner, the company standing and holding hands.[670] While few years later, in 1850, it even featured as a classic Dickensian set-piece in *David Copperfield* between David and Mr Micawber:

> As the punch disappeared, Mr. Micawber became still more friendly and convivial. Mrs. Micawber's spirits becoming elevated, too, we sang 'Auld Lang Syne'. When we came to 'Here's a hand, my trusty frere', we all joined hands round the table; and when we declared we would 'take a right gude Willie Waught', and hadn't the least idea what it meant, we were really affected.[671]

Certainly when Thackeray was touring the USA in 1853 it was a common enough concept to relate to his audience:

> At a Burns Festival, I have seen Scotchmen singing Burns, while the drops twinkled ontheir furrowed cheeks; while each rough hand was flung out to grasp its neighbour's; while early scenes and sacred recollections, and dear and delighful memories of the past come back at the sounds of the familiar words and tune.[672]

So while there are occasional references to this practice, the first body of depth that can be analysed is Ballantine's *Chronicle*. Given the journalistic format, the data outwith Scotland and England is hard to make robust assessment, but the broad numbers make it plain that while not yet mandatory, the performance of the song was seen by many as integral, to the extent that it was the most performed of all Burns's songs during

the celebrations, with 15 per cent of the recorded events closing
with a communal singing of *Auld Lang Syne*, with about one
in ten involving the entire company holding hands as at Irvine:
'"Auld Langsyne' [sic] having been, according to the invariable
custom of the Club, sung by the company standing and hands
joined, the happy gathering broke up'.[673] Or as reported in
Milwaukee, Wisconsin:

> In accordance with the simple, but touching cus-
> tom of all Scotch social gatherings, the whole
> company now stood and, joining hands around
> the tables, united in that song which Burns wrote,
> not for Scotland alone, but for the whole world –
> 'Auld Lang Syne'.[674]

By the end of that century, the convention of closing the Burns
Supper by the guests standing and holding hands in a circle
was commonplace. It has not been possible from reports or
reminiscences to establish when the more complex ritual we
know and use today – hands side by side until crossing the arms
over the chest to hold hands and tighten the chain at the cue
'an here's a haun...' developed – but, over the 20th century, the
intricacies of the performative element became in some ways a
tribal ritual. Failure to adhere to the strict protocol often still
calls near-Calvinist wrath down on the heads of the offending
parties who stray from the traditional words or movements. The
1952 *Burns Chronicle* thundered over the issue, reprinting an
article of 18 years previously, which itself referred to ineffective
pleas made in 1926 and forgot to mention the strictures of a
similar peeve in 1937: 'No song continues to be misquoted more
than 'Auld Lang Syne', and both at Burns and other gatherings
there is still a deplorable diversity of style and words... The
song that everybody sings is the song that no one knows'.[675]
The frequency of repetition of these strictures points to the
Federation's absence of success.

This use of *Auld Lang Syne* as a shibboleth (quite literally in terms of the often heard pronuncuation of 'syne' as 'zyne'), but contary to the purists, many Burns Suppers now use a curtailed version of the song, two verses and choruses to lessen the strain of the performance on long-sufferring guests. Robert Crawford calls *Auld Lang Syne* 'deft, warm and resolute' with a 'brilliant use of a refrain' which characteristics explain its near universal popularity and its presence as the closing moments of virtually all Burns Suppers.[676] That co-existance or perhaps even ambiguity being the key feature which allows each participant in the closing rite of any Burns Supper to supply his/her own interpretation of the purpose of this particular Burns Night in the wider context of gatherings 'at home and abroad'.

CHAPTER TWELVE

Female Participation in Burns Suppers

Auld Nature swears, the lovely Dears
  Her noblest work she classes, O:
Her prentice han' she try'd on man,
  An' then she made the lasses, O.

Green Grow, &c.[677]

Women Attending the Burns Supper

THERE IS A POPULAR characterisation of the Burns Supper as being an all-male function (or potentially even describing it as an event with misogynistic overtones). This is a concept probably driven in part by the early Freemasonic influences and their reinforcement by many of the Burns Clubs during first century of the Federation movement. However, this chapter looks at the contemporary evidence to show that this is an unfair generalisation, for while the early Burns Clubs and public dinners had been all male it was through dinners commemorating the poet that women first started to be invited to join in public dinners early in the 19th century.

The masculinists within the Burns Movement have often appealed to the tradition of the exclusively male membership of Burns's Tarbolton Bachelors' Club. In a secular echo of the debate on the priesthood, the argument runs that if Burns himself had created a closed male society in Tarbolton, how could his cultists break their hero's mandate? As with so much Burns 'lore', this argument is founded on a fallacy.

The Tarbolton Bachelors Club's membership was constitutionally defined as single-sex (in the memorable phrase: 'Every man proper for a member of this Society, must have a frank, honest, open heart') but all their activities were not exclusively male.[678] In keeping with another regulation that every member has to be 'a professed lover of one or more of the female sex', the club met once a year to hold a ball. It is mentioned in passing in Currie's biography, quoting a memorandum written by Burns himself: 'We resolved to meet at Tarbolton on the race-night, the July following [sc: 1782], and have a dance in honour of our society. Accordingly, we did meet, each one with a partner'.[679] The poet's sister remembered benefiting from the need to balance the boys and the girls at the dance:

> Isabel... had the pleasure of dancing at the same Ball. She was attending the sewing school in Tarbolton, and on her way home to Lochlea, she met her sister Annie, who took her back with her because a member of the Club, Matthew Patterson, had lost his sweetheart and was in despair for a partner; so a girl of eleven years old supplied her place for one night![680]

So, as with the Freemasonic calendar's highlight of 'Ladies Night', here is a further example of a balance between competing convivialities. While convention would have frowned on a woman participating in a debate, one thinks of Dr Johnson's strictures on a woman preaching, the club – whose members were all supposed to have participative relationships with the females of the village – wanted a one mixed event. They were bachelors, not hermits.

For the first 15 years of Burns Suppers there is no record of any female guests in attendance (although some have been confused by Primrose Kennedy's Christian name into an erroneous belief that a woman dined in July 1801).[681] Not even Agnes McLehose, Burns's 'Clarinda', could join her friend Robert Ainslie at the Edinburgh 1815 celebration. She recorded in her journal: '25ᵗʰ Jan[uary], 1815 – Burns's birthday. – A great dinner at Oman's. Should like to be there, an invisible spectator of all said of that great genius'.[682] The following year, the first step in moving from a male-only event was to invite ladies to witness the 1816 London dinner from the balconies of the banqueting rooms (a rule followed in London in both in 1819 and 1832). Hogg gallantly challenged this first (quite innovative then, but timid-looking perhaps today) step, writing to his wife saying, 'I thought this a curious thing that ladies be admitted in their hundreds to smell a good dinner, without being permitted to eat or drink'.[683]

It is true that the more common mode of involvement of women in Burns Suppers in the first 40 years was, more often than not, confined to the serving of food and drink at the venue. Sometime the records reveal some recognition of these auxiliaries, with the early Greenock Club meetings being punningly known as 'Mrs Cottar's Saturday Nights' after Mrs Cottar who ran the Henry Bell Tavern in Greenock. Similarly, the poem praising Mrs Jean Neil Montgomerie of Montgomerie's Inn which was the first home of the Dalry Burns Club:

There are wives that can bear and can nurse up braw
    bairnies   [children
Bake scones, sew, make kebbocks, and spin,   [cheeses
But there's few that can mix up a haggis, sae nicely
As the wife of Montgomerie's Inn.[684]

There are several examples of female participation through the writing of verse by female poets to be recited at the dinner, to be read by a male guest. The much-anthologised poems of Anne, Mrs Grant of Laggan, are recorded as having been read aloud, while poems specifically for recitation were written by Mrs GG Richardson (for Dumfries); Helen Currie (Philadelphia); Mrs C

Tinsley and Elisabeth Sheridan Carey (Sheffield) and Eliza Cook (Cardiff). Isa Craig's Crystal Palace prize poem is shown to have been recited at several events in Ballantine. As the general social rule was that men met in clubs or public occasions to dine *en garcon*, therefore, the Burns Supper was no more masculinist in the first half of the 19th century than other forms of social dining but did allow some female voices, albeit indirectly.

The possibility of attendance as equal guests first appears in Albany, NY in 1829 where 'nearly 400' men and women joined in a 'splendid gala at the Knickerbocker Hall' to celebrate Burns together but this mixing of the sexes still appears exceptional at that date.[685] The first public dinner where women sat down at table with men in Britain was the Caledonian Society's dinner held in London in January 1842. Here the Caledonians were accompanied throughout the evening by their female guests celebrated Robert Burns in a proudly maintained tradition of the Society: 'in 1844, no fewer than 140 gentlemen and 72 ladies were present... It is an old boast that to the Caledonian Society of London belongs the honour of having first initiated the good custom of inviting ladies to sit at table at public banquets'.[686]

The broader canvas of the 1844 Burns Festival saw a celebration which included both men and women. All along the processional route 'various platforms were constructed for the accommodation of the ladies' and there was wholesale female inclusion at dinner too.[687] The festival dinner was a grand affair with 2000 seated in a specially built pavilion at Alloway. Men and women sat in equality and were intermingled throughout the hall. This included four female guests of honour at the top table: the poet's sister Isabel with her two daughters and Jessie Lewars. As Blackwood's described it: 'the distinguishing feature of the pavilion was the number of ladies who were present. A great room exclusively filled with men, is at best a dull and sombre spectacle; '[688]

At the conclusion of the Lord Eglinton's toast to 'The Memory of Burns' the females in the company joined in the accolade by standing and waving handkerchiefs while the men drank off their toast. The innovation of joint dining – perhaps driven by the chivalric themes which had long inspired Eglinton and his coterie combined with the national, all-encompassing ambition of the organisers of creating an *omnium gatherum* in honour of the Bard – failed to catch the wider imagination and, in the subsequent 15 years, Burns Suppers were apparently all male again in line with prevailing convention, outside the Caledonian Society of London which was steadfastly mixed sex in its annual January jamboree.

The depth and breadth of the global celebration in 1859 broke that *status quo* again primarily due to the inclusive vision of Colin Rae Brown who explicitly sought the participation of 'Scotsmen and Scotswomen everywhere'.[689] In looking at the gender tone of the 1859 centenary, Robert Crawford flags a concern over the 'masculine or masculinist' nature or attitude of the Burns clubs. In particular, he looks at the Paisley 1859 dinner and goes on to underscore the charge:

> [O]ften the tone of the clubs may have been masculine or masculinist in a way that lacks the sophistication of Burns's best poetry, not least of 'Tam o'Shanter'. A rare instance of women being admitted to a nineteenth century Scottish Burns Supper came in 1859 when at the Exchange Rooms in Paisley 270 gentlemen (many in full Masonic costume) celebrated the centenary of the Bard's birth. All the toasts were addressed to 'gentlemen', but towards the end of the proceedings 'a goodly selection' of about 100 ladies were admitted to the gallery. They sat there confronted by a large transparency of 'Tam o'Shanter crossing the Brig of Doon, and his mare's tail in the clutch of the vindictive witch'. They had been put in their place. [690]

So, far from this Supper being, as Crawford describes it, 'a rare instance of women being admitted', a more detailed look at Ballantine's reports shows that there were many women involved in the Burns Centenary and they were often welcomed, not just in the roles of relicts (or relics) up on the top table or as waiting staff in the hall or even in the guise of professional or semi-professional singers performing Burns's songs on the stage. Analysing Ballantine's *Chronicle,* a significant 24 per cent of all the events reported had female guest participation, showing that, while still having a majority of masculinist approaches, the Burns Centenary had a significantly greater outreach to female participation than is usually imagined. In fact, women played a recognisable, if not fully equal, part in Burns Suppers. Their 'place', by the Burns Centenary, was a growing one.[691]

The reportage is quite clearly ungrudging over the direct participation of both genders. Of course, the success of 1859 was due to it not being solely a combination of all-male Burns Clubs but through the Burns Centenary being based on a wider international reach and appeal to both men and to women. Whole communities foregathered, social élites met to dance, even factories and businesses regaled their male and female workers.[692] Many societies, notably temperance groups, who already held regular mixed meetings in their ordinary course of business and so their dinners and soirées were equally open to both sexes. There was even a striking innovation with one Ladies Only Dinner in Aylth where, after dinner, the gentlemen were allowed to join for the toasts, but otherwise had the tables turned on them.[693]

There were Mixed Dinners – almost half of the mixed events were where ladies joined in the formal Burns Supper (ca 12 per cent of all events). As in 1844 dinner, this was often seen as a very unusual, but enjoyable, departure from the norm, which 'added much to the éclat, and made the evening not only the most brilliant but altogether the greatest novelty of the kind ever witnessed'.[694] A few of the other dinners (ca 4 per cent) invited the ladies to join them at the conclusion of the dinner (sometimes sharing in the final course of fruit or dessert) and hear the speeches and entertainments. In Cupar, for example, '[a] fter dinner, about 40 ladies were admitted and served with cake and coffee, whose presence tended to enliven the proceedings of the evening'.[695] Though one lady, writing to the local papers in Connecticut, felt 'slighted that we were not invited to partake of the "Haggis"', though there may have been some men who would have gladly swapped that with her.[696] A similar percentage had a female audience in the gallery, or in boxes around the room. In Glasgow, at the City Halls, 'the ladies' stewards accordingly retired, and in a minute or two ushered in a most brilliant assemblage of the fair sex who, on taking their places in the galleries, were cheered with loud and long-continued cheers'.[697] Although this elevated status did not always meet the full approbation of the female guests, as 'Agnes' wrote after her experience attending Melbourne's dinner:

> No doubt it may be considered by you gentlemen as a great privilege for us female creatures to be allowed to look on you eating and drinking and making yourselves happy. Indeed for my part I do like to see men enjoying themselves, but still I like better when we have some share in that enjoyment. It won't do, Sir, for us to sit in a gallery alone, with nobody but ourselves to talk to and nobody to help us to anything... Now, Sir, I think that if there is to be any festival again it would be far better to leave the ladies at home altogether than treat us so shabbily.[698]

While 56 per cent of the instances of female involvement centred on the traditional formal dinner in the three formats above, the remaining 44 per cent opted for a more fluid format, although universally with a toast list headed by the 'Immortal Memory'. In the main these were found in Scotland. There were a number of balls – bringing female participation in through dancing rather than dining, either after an all-male dinner or as the principal celebration of the evening (28 per cent of all mixed events or 7 per cent of the grand total).

> No assemblage to do honour to the memory of Burns could be complete which did not include our lovely Marys and our bonny Jeans wisely resolved that the dinner – exclusively devoted to the inferior sex – should be followed by a ball, in order that the fairer and more divine portion of creation might have an opportunity of participating in the pleasures of the glorious festival.[699]

Some evenings were arranged as 'soirées' (12 per cent of mixed events, or 3 per cent of all events) – in a catch-all description, broad groups congregated to commemorate and celebrate in a more open format but typically having toasts, readings of his poetry and songs.

It was a widespread, but still not universal, desire to include men and women in the Burns Centenary celebrations. It is important to notice that the percentage of female involvement across the range of events was higher in 1859 that either the full formal haggis ceremony or the exact use of the phrase 'Immortal Memory' for the principal toast.

During the next 60 years in the history of the Burns Supper, the male dining tradition reasserted itself. There were, however, several notable mixed Burns Clubs and Burns Suppers, mainly found in the metropolitan *monde* of London or New York, or in a community spirit in 'the colonies'. In 1868, the New York Burns Club had a spirited debate over inviting female guests to sit at the dinner table in January 1869. The controversy continued after the event, with the president outlined the great difference that their inclusive dinner provided:

> About one hundred ladies, of rare beauty and exalted social position, graced the occasion and

placed the propriety of the presence of the gentler
sex at the banquet board upon a basis of respect-
ability against which vulgarians beyond the reach
of woman's restraining influence, and bacchanalians who are always unhappy when they are
decently sober, may rail until doomsday, but will
never settle.[700]

That event appears to have been enjoyable and successful,
and was repeated the following year, however this 'novel feature'
was not universally approved as 'The Original Burns Club' held
a rival stag dinner elsewhere. That male-only club exists to this
day as The Burns Society of the City of New York, dating its
foundation from 1871, the other club failed. This is a depressing
counter-indicator of the pro-mixing argument.[701]

Colin Rae Brown started holding a private anniversary
dinner at his Knightsbridge home in 1863, which developed
in 1868 into the London Burns Club. Under his guidance,
the club included female guests at its Burns Suppers from the
beginning. By 1885 he was proposing the Immortal Memory
'in which the ladies lovingly joined in' which remains the
tradition of the club up to the present day.[702] It was widely
perceived that Scottish clubs retained a fondness for the old,
single sex dinner, one commentator remarked on Rae Brown's
anniversaries that they 'differ[ed] a little from the sober
Scottish clubs... it needs not be remarked that female suffrage
obtains in southern Burns clubs'.[703]

Internationally, the Burns Supper had often a community
aspect which would be naturally more gender inclusive. Although
often maintaining a strict male membership criterion, female
assistance and attendance was encouraged by institutions like
the Brisbane Caledonian Society and Burns Club where women,
though not allowed membership, formed a 'crucial component
of the social side' of the Burns Suppers but typically from the
mid-Victorian period until after the Great War, the numerical
majority of Burns Suppers were centred on traditional clubs and

were, therefore, highly formal and demonstrably male but this was neither universal, nor, importantly, mandatory.[704]

As briefly mentioned above, the first recorded all-female Burns Supper was on 25 January 1859 in Aylth, Scotland where, in role reversal, gentlemen guests were allowed to join for the speeches and subsequent dancing.[705] After that there were few attempts to replicate a women-only guest list, notably in Ellon in 1893 where the local editor opined:

> It [is] a pity that ladies should be debarred from taking part in the celebrations of the Burns anniversary... These are the days of women's rights. And what right can the women of Scotland more fitly demand that of paying tribute to the man who has sung more sweetly of Scotland's lassies than any man who ever lived.[706]

This led to the formation of the Peterhead Ladies Burns Club, as the editor said after their first female only supper in 1896: 'the ladies are the boys!'[707]

After the First World War, women's groups started to hold their own 'Burns Nights' of tea and musical entertainments with a guest speaker providing a toast or speech to commemorate the Immortal Memory.[708] This led relatively quickly to a number of female societies, notably the Co-operative Women's Guild, starting to hold their own Burns celebrations along fairly traditional lines, but with no male guests (except perhaps some performers). The first of these appears to have been in Earlson in Berwickshire in 1920 (two years after female suffrage was first won in the UK) which was to be an annual fixture until at least the mid-1930s.[709] Throughout the 'thirties, there were many such Burns Suppers held across Scotland and the North of England'. There were 'fraternal' associations who had parallel female lodges or branches who decided to followed this lead. Accordingly, there is a significant history of Female Loyal Orange Lodges holding women-only Burns Suppers in

Scotland and in Canada throughout the 1930s.[710] Although there is less evidence the female adjunct of Freemasonry, the Order of the Eastern Star records many similar events mainly in the USA.[711]

There was certainly an apparent desire not only to hold both more Burns Suppers with positive female engagement, but also to have women fulfil an equal role in the growing Burns organisation. This desire clashed with the formal male hierarchy seen in the Federation in the time after the death of Colin Rae Brown. As this period had the closest link between the Burns Club and Burns Supper in many eyes, a natural way to break this bottleneck was for the foundation of women's only Burns Clubs, effectively fighting fire with fire.[712] The first to hold its own meeting was Kyle Ladies Burns Club, founded in Shotts, Lanarkshire which met initially in January 1920, drafting a formal constitution in 1925 although not federating until 1927 (as number 388). By the outbreak of World War Two, there were nearly 30 such societies. The historian of the Federation, James Mackay, called this: 'a reflection of the sexism which pervaded all aspects of society at that time and which is still [1985] regrettably a tendency in the Burns movement'.[713] The minutes of the last ladies' Burns club founded, Irvine Lasses, bear that out even 50 years after the first ladies' Burns club, for in 1976 they looked back on their first year: '[w]hen our club was first founded there were people who refused to take us seriously, but as the year progressed, it was heartening to realise that we were earning respect from other Clubs... and were not just frivolous members'.[714]

This was primarily a Scottish phenomenon, as only four out of 37 federated ladies' Burns clubs were founded outside Scotland, with a handful on non-federated clubs.[715] The fact that there was a single English LBC is testament to the more inclusive approach favoured by 'southern' Burns clubs. All of those international clubs, and most of the others, have faded away, however there are five ladies' Burns clubs still in existence today as federated Burns Clubs and without grammatical irony they continue to send 'Fraternal Greetings' to fellow Burns Clubs to be read at their suppers. [716]

Similar ideas were prevalent in the 1990s when some women sought to break the remaining all-male drinking image of the anniversary events by seeing the Burns Supper through a different prism: that of Jean Armour. There was an all-female charity Burns Supper held in 1992 in the Kelvingrove Museum and Art Gallery in Glasgow which was erroneously flagged as the first of its kind in Scotland and one press commentator suggested that it should have in honour of Jean Armour: 'journalist Ruth Wishart had a Jean Armour supper from which BBC Radio Scotland benefited with a lively programme broadcast last night'.[717] Here, the format would be taken wholesale and feminised. All the perceived mistakes of the stag supper would be replicated but in female terms, with Bonnie Jean in the role of *Bona Dea*. Jean Armour Suppers can still be found from time to time. The real demographic change to wide female inclusion took off through the large public Burns Suppers outwith the Federation: West Sound Burns, the Scottish Bankers (which 'mixed' in the 1970s) and the Society of Scots Lawyers in London. As the Caledonian Society of London had found nearly 150 years before, mixed events were not only fun, but brought in twice as many paying participants.

While being careful not to overstate the evidence above, it can be seen that there was a significant number of Burns Suppers which adopted a mixed male and female approach to convivial celebrations from very early in the phenomenon. Even today there remain many male-only Burns Suppers both in Burns Clubs and in other societies (whether of Scots roots or in golf and rugby clubs for example) however, the trend is for a wider range of social participation by age, by race and by gender, reflecting current social models of diversity but also of the perception of Burns's inclusiveness in his poetry, writings and life.

The Toast to the Lass(i)es

The other core Burns Supper tradition involving the relationship between males and females is the 'Toast to The Lasses' and its 'Reply' which now feature on virtually all Burns Supper toast lists.

The links between toasting and women are quite fundamental in the origin of toasting in its general concept and so drinking either to a specific woman or to generic womankind/ womanhood was a common feature of dinners and parties.[718] It was important enough for Burns to include explicitly in Rule 5th of the Tarbolton Bachelors Club which mandated a 'general toast to the mistresses of the club' to be performed before each meeting concluded.[719] In the period up to 1844, the toast features regularly in the early toast lists, and was of course a toast given by a man to the other men, and the occasional replies were also performed by a male speaker. 'Burns lore' often characterises this toast as a way that the men diners thanked the female cooks or serving staff, but there is no evidence that this is indeed the case (except in a few specific examples) so each toast looks simply to be a stock tribute or sentiment to 'the female' in general, whether described as 'The Ladies' or very often in the early American suppers, as 'The Fair'.

It was not a universal or necessary custom, however, to toast the ladies within the Burns Supper. Looking at the toast lists recorded by Dalry Burns Club (from 1861) other than drinking the health of Mrs Mongomerie in the last year of her life (1863), there was and is no general toast to the ladies/lasses/lassies even today. From 1875 Jean Armour was toasted (initially joined with the 'family' or 'descendants' 'of the poet') but from 1878, the toast became specifically 'The Memory of Jean Armour' which still features at their anniversary dinners today.[720]

During the first century of the Burns Supper, it would have been very unusual to hear a woman make a speech. So even when present and toasted, ladies – even Queen Victoria – remained silent.[721] At other dinners and different clubs, initially, 'The Ladies' was the typical form of words given as part of a list that would often feature over a dozen toasts. It was in 1859 that the toast started to adapt into a more Burns-flavoured part of the proceedings, by the humorous and affectionate use of the Scots word 'lasses' to replace the standard 'ladies'. One of the first uses of this locution was at Glasgow University in 1859: where Mr NS Kerr replied and gave 'the ladies' or, as he preferred calling it 'the lasses' with which he coupled the name of 'Jean Armour Burns' – 'Bonnie Jean'.[722] As part of the development of Scottish customs around Hamilton Paul's Burns Supper format, this innovation was well received, particularly in the United States where the words 'lasses' and 'lassies' were used interchangeably.[723]

While the New York 'mixers' in 1869 were keen to encourage equality, it did not yet extend to speaking right although Revd Dr Chapin, in replying to the toast to 'Woman' said, 'I hardly know why you should call upon me to speak for Woman – who is certainly so well able to speak for herself'. [724] It took more than a few years for that encomium to bear fruit and the earliest record of direct female participation, in what we now would call 'The Reply to the Toast to the Lasses', was at the Caledonian Club of New York's Burns Supper in 1876 where the toast "The Lasses" found respondents in School Commissioner Mathewson and Mrs CH Kerr, the gentleman delivering an appropriate speech and the lady singing.[725]

This concept of direct female participation seems to have spread relatively slowly, it was in between the wars that women first claimed the right to stand and reply to the toast with their own spoken response at a time when formal female participation was widening within the Federation and elsewhere.[726] The earliest menu card showing a female replying to the toast found to date is from 1920 in London where Mrs John B Rintoul gave the speech.[727] By 1939, even the *Burns Chronicle* reported that '[e]ach succeeding anniversary of the poet's birth finds women in greater numbers expending their gift of rhetoric in paying tribute to his memory'.[728]

This trend appears to be increasingly prevalent after the sesquicentennial of 1946, again, this mirroring wider developments in female social roles at formal events. During the war, women had performed roles traditionally perceived as male in what was felt to be an equality of gender in fighting for survival. Several male bastions fell early on, with the Dundee Courier headline in 1940 announcing that a 'Lady Pipes in Haggis at Carnoustie', when a Miss McBeth joined Rosie the Riveter in the wartime pantheon of feminism.[729] After the coming of the peace, there had been a spontaneous female version of the Ba' Game in Orkney that year, so why should women not take roles within the Burns Supper starting with replying on their own behalf? In Motherwell in 1948, being a leap year, one Burns Supper reversed the male/female polarity and had a 'Toast to the Laddies', and a 'Reply'. Another spur of that tradition, which commenced around that time, is that the senior pupils of Ayr Academy Literary & Debating Society started to hold Burns Suppers – the second time that a party of school pupils had done so – and here the toast alternates in successive years between a 'Toast to the Lassies' and a 'Toast to the Laddies' with the opposite sex presenting the 'Reply' to ensure a balance.[730]

The content of the Toast and the Reply from the earliest days had a light-hearted element and a reference to Burns's loves and love lyrics. The period immediately following this saw a significant change in the demeanour of the Toast to the Lasses. Driven by a combination of the increasing acceptability of satire and humour in public entertainment, the toast started to drop its connectivity with Burns and became increasingly a vehicle for a funny speech (typically reflecting 'the war of the sexes') and often in the 1970s involving 'blue' humour particularly (though not exclusively) at male-only functions. The Federation, in classic Bureaucratic approach deprecated the trend, but failed to realise that allowing more positive humour in mixed company would overcome some of the crass failures. The *Burns Chronicle* in 1975 grudgingly acknowledged that 'there is a measure of humour and light heartedness about the toast to *The Lassies* and its reply' but warned of the dangerous consequences of permitting too much licence, or as the writer called it 'questionable aberrations (fortunately rare) such as the Lanarkshire miners' group who attempted a year or two ago, to "modernise" the image of their supper by employing two strippers and a blue comedian'.[731]

In parallel, the growing women's movement and equality debate allowed the Reply speech to be more assertive and to develop into an equal-but-opposite speech, often taking the form of a 'roast' of the male guests and mankind in general. In a throwback to the first Burns Suppers and the Odes of Hamilton Paul it is not uncommon to hear these speeches in some form of verse. At times, the male humour was crude and offensive, and the female counterattack could seem strident and polemical. The last decade has seen the worst excesses of both diminish and today, most (but not all) Burns Suppers include this pair of witty speeches where each sex casts a light-hearted critical eye over the other with a reference to Robert (and maybe Jean) and his/her own emotions. It would be fair to say, however, that not all performers (male or female) get this difficult balance right, not unlike that other potential train wreck of a speech: the best man's at a British wedding. As the philosophy of gender changes in our society, we will see further developments here. In 2016 for example the playwright Jo Clifford became the first trans woman to give 'The Reply to the Toast to the Lassies'.[732]

As the male and female roles have become equalised, the title 'Reply to the Toast to the Lassies' has, from about 2002, started to be replaced by a parallel 'Toast to the Laddies' which has a pleasing euphony but more importantly, allows the female guests to stand and toast the men bringing a complete equality to the proceedings.[733] These speeches albeit common, however, are not fundamental as the Immortal Memory or *To the Haggis* and so the Lasses and the Reply should be seen as common, but not absolutely essential (or indeed canonical) when arranging a Burns Supper.

Of course, women speakers are not now confined to this single role within the proceedings, and women will rightly take the chair, give the Immortal Memory, address the haggis and perform poems and songs: so female participation in Burns Suppers has been broadly reflective of wider prevailing social custom, but it is important to understand that the Burns Supper was not necessarily an exclusive male preserve for over 150 years and it is certainly not so now.

Conclusion

Colonel James Glencairn Burns, who was received with enthusiastic applause, said – ... My mother told the late Mr. McDiarmid of Dumfries that my father once said to her – 'Jean, one hundred years hence they'll think mair o' me than they do now'. How truly his prophecy has been fulfilled the proceedings here and elsewhere amply testify.[734]

OUTSIDE THE PERFERVID world of the study of Burns, could it be thought that the success and longevity of the Burns Supper is far less to do with memorialising an obscure ploughman poet, or rather more likely to be an excuse to break the post Hogmanay monotony of *Janvier Blanche* with a convivial party? Mary Ellen Brown suggested that 'the complete history of the Burns Suppers... can certainly never be written', but however daunting the data pool (and with this Author occasionally feeling like McSisyphus pushing his enormous haggis up an endless hill), this book has captured over 3,200 Burns Suppers to review its importance and development. [735] The Burns Supper is recognisably, at times almost parodically, Scottish yet it is not exclusively owned by the Scots. In January 2009, it was an experience shared by an estimated nine million people, in over 3,500 events taking place on each continent of the globe. It is instantly recognisable, and is an enjoyment for millions and a shibboleth for a declining core of mainly Scots detractors. In some ways it is easier to define it by what it is not and, in so doing, this thesis seeks to make other researchers think more closely about the paradigms against which they judge this phenomenon (for good or ill). The Burns Supper shares characteristics with many other forms of celebration, but the combination of its characteristics is unique, enduring and of broad appeal.

Just as in the children's traditional tale of the five blind men and the elephant, where each pundit touched a single part of the animal and thus misled themselves into thinking that the pachyderm was like a snake (by touching only the trunk), or a sail (the ear), or a rope (the tail), or a tree (the leg), so recent research has measured the Burns Supper against imperfect analogies. The Burns Supper is not a pilgrimage to a geographical literary site (although 1844 showed that characteristic as a one-off in monster meeting terms and the Burns Birth Place Museum remains a popular tourist attraction in its own right) its use spread in the first years quickly from Ayrshire becoming established around the world as a polycentric and de-centralised celebration. Nor is it built into the foundations of the many statues erected to the poet that might be smaller shrines for international homage. Burns has many statues, but many, many more annual Burns Suppers. Equally, it is not a centenary or secular celebration. While 1859's events have been a recent inspiration to researchers (largely thanks to the entertaining and illustrative nuggets that can be dug out of Ballantine's stupendous treasure-trove of a *Chronicle*), the resounding success of that centenary was driven by the ordinary round of smaller annual suppers which had been enjoyed over the previous 50-odd years (the fact that most other centenary years – 1896 and 2009 excepted – failed to achieve escape velocity emphasises this).

Neither is it a solely Scottish phenomenon. For while it was created out of and driven by Scots at home and abroad it was quickly adopted in the United States (at least by 1817) and Australia/New Zealand (1826/1840) and elsewhere (not quite 50 years after the poet's death) as a celebration of pioneering humanity regardless of birthright and is found now in numerous, predominantly but not exclusively Anglophone, countries and communities. It is not a story of the formal Burns Clubs or the successes and failures of the Burns Federation, which has been a source of antagonism between a generation of angry young litterateurs versus grumpy old die-hards, bringing little credit to either, but not at all impeding the growth of the hated/loved object of dispute. It is patently not a saint's day (though it shares many characteristics with the global phenomenon of St Patrick's Day and its Guinness-sponsored slogan 'be a little Irish for the day'). Nor is it a national, bank or government holiday.

Hamilton Paul created an enjoyable, memorable and replicable format for the Burns Supper in 1801. Its three key elements (addressing the haggis, toasting Burns, and performing Burns songs and poems) remain the core features of the celebration today. However, it has not come down the generations without developing, and it may be surprising to some that, for example, it was not always exclusively all male: with albeit modest, but growing, levels of female participation from 1829. Also unexpected has been the analysis that the formalities around the Haggis Ceremony were heavily influenced by the St Andrew's Day rituals, particularly in the United States of America, and only became canonical in the form we now know, after the 1859 Burns Centenary. Lastly, it was even later than that that the key toast of the evening resolved its formal toast in the words the 'Immortal Memory' as a ubiquitous formula.

Given the sheer weight of primary source material (which, iceberg-like can only be a fraction of the number of celebrations held over the last two centuries of Burns Suppers – the discovery of the Sunderland Burns Club's 1804 foundation being a classic example) these findings will be open to refinement in future, particularly around early dates. In time, it is hoped to turn the research into the Burns Suppers recorded here (which have just over 10,000 pieces of primary evidence) into a 'big-data' project that would allow academics and Burnsians to add instances from their own, diverse records.

The Burns Supper is a series of constitutionally unconnected meals of varying size and formality, most of them with men and women joining in, some steadfastly male only; some with vast quantities of alcohol and many relying on tea and restraint, held in an array of locations from five star banqueting halls to farm kitchen tables, from school dinner halls to pubs; each its own party, but each aware that many, many others are following a similar path in a defined and instantly recognisable tradition around that night in a form that, as Robert Crawford concedes, 'though modern intellectuals and poets have often decried Burns Suppers, they are in some ways true to the nature of their subversively clubbable subject', which is exactly what Hamilton Paul set out to achieve in 1801.[736]

Burns's poetry has been a pleasure to many millions of readers over the years, and better than that is to hear it read out loud, to match the word and the cadence or to hear the lyric and the music. The Burns Supper captures particular performative themes that tie closely to the poet's life. Much of Burns's work is 'three dimensional' and calls out for our participation in the performance. Few poets have that quiddity, and it is that essence which was captured by Reverend Hamilton Paul. Just as Burns's love of social engagement (across class, politics and certainly gender) is evident from reading or listening to his works, the performance of those poems and songs in the clubbable *environ*, brings them to their performative home. As Ian Duncan described him 'Burns is the great poet – unrivalled in modern British literature – of enjoyment as the deep-structural principle of psychic and social life'.[737]

The driver in the Burns Supper is that we are not a passive audience but are active members of the company, even if 'only' through the acts of eating and drinking while enjoying the events of the evening. And that is a convivial evening which is a living engagement with Burns, poetry, song and the Scots tongue. That cornerstone affects the holistic reception of Burns, for as Murray Pittock addresses the paradox, we see that the academic and the convivial reception of Burns must be symbiotic: for to understand the works one must understand the man and his global popular appeal: 'If Burns scholarship must spread, so must Burns Suppers... Burns as scholarship and Burns as performance must both be spread globally'.[738] That is only appropriate, for Burns worked actively to create a personal, bardic persona within his enjoyment of the convivial world. Typically, Hamilton Paul confirmed that view in his first minute when he described that July night at Burns Cottage for its appeal in being a 'party was such as Burns himself would have joined with heartfelt satisfaction' so let us embrace that broader than imagined concept, in a milieu that Burns himself would recognise and enjoy.

Participate in your next (or even your first) Burns Supper in that spirit and you will have a deeper understanding of the poetry and humanity of Robert Burns while having a great party.

Abbreviations

a) **Burns's works:**

Poems Chiefly in the Scottish Dialect, (Kilmarnock, 1786), is cited as **Kilmarnock Edition.**

Poems Chiefly in the Scottish Dialect, (Edinburgh, 1787), using the 'skinking' version, **First Edinburgh Edition.**

The Works of Robert Burns. [etc.]; James Currie (ed.), (London/Edinburgh 1800), **Currie Edition.**

The Poems & Songs of Robert Burns, [etc.], Hamilton Paul, (ed.), (Ayr, 1819), **Air Edition.**

The Works of Robert Burns, The Ettrick Shepherd & William Motherwell, (eds.), (Glasgow, 1836), **Motherwell/Hogg Edition.**

The Life and Works of Robert Burns, Robert Chambers (ed.), revised by William Wallace, (Edinburgh, 1896), **Chambers/ Wallace Edition.**

The Letters of Robert Burns, J. DeLancey Ferguson (ed.), G Ross Roy (Second Edition ed.), (Oxford, 1985), as **Letters.**

The Poems and Songs of Robert Burns, James Kinsley (ed.), (Oxford, 1968): *Poems* **K. [number]** for poems and *Poems,* **vol, page,** for other references.

The Oxford Edition of the Works of Robert Burns is abbreviated,

- Nigel Leask (ed.), *Volume I: Commonplace Books, Tour Journals, and Miscellaneous Prose* as **Oxford** WRB **(I)**;

- Murray Pittock (ed.):
  - o *Volume II: The Scots Musical Museum, Part One* as Oxford WRB (II) with individual songs shown as [SMM **Volume number, Roman numeral],** and
  - o *Volume III: The Scots Musical Museum, Part Two* as Oxford WRB (III).

b) **Hamilton Paul: Manuscripts**

McKie Collection: cited as **McKie** MS, **[curatorial letter]**
Zachs Collection: cited as **Zachs** MS, **[date]**

c) **Other Sources:**

James Ballantine, *Chronicle of the Hundredth Birthday of Robert Burns,* (Edinburgh & London, 1859) is cited as **Ballantine** with individual references to **page [number], ([event name]).**
Burns Chronicle is cited as BC, **([year]), [page number].**
Please note that, in this edition, some silent editing within quotations has been made to conform to modern standards and spellings.

Endnotes

1 A companion volume to this, *The Burns Supper: A Comprehensive History* (Edinburgh: Luath, 2019) is also available which provides both further analysis and a full set of critical apparatus.

2 *Air Edition*, 295.

3 Ballantine, *Chronicle*; Anon., *The Burns Centenary:* (Edinburgh, 1859); James Gould (ed.), *Poems, Letters, and Speeches in Connection with the Centenary Birthday of Robert Burns, etc.*, Mitchell Library (Glasgow), Burns Room 4:82.

4 Robert Crawford, *The Bard,* (London, 2009), *passim.*

5 TM Devine, *The Global Scot: Emigration, Empire and Impact*, Public Debate to Mark the Opening of the Scottish Centre for Diaspora Studies, University of Edinburgh, 30/10/2008.

6 Raymond Bentman, 'Robert Burns's Declining Fame', *Proceedings of the British Academy*, 121 (2003), 191-211; Murray Pittock, '"A Long Farewell to All My Greatness": The History of the Reputation of Robert Burns'. Murray Pittock, (ed.), *Robert Burns in Global Culture*, (Lewisburg, 2014), 26-46.

7 *Poems*, K.618

8 *Poems*, K.58: Second Epistle to J. Lapraik.

9 Davis D. McElroy, *Scotland's Age of Improvement: A Survey of Eighteenth Century Clubs and Societies*, (Washington, 1969); Peter Clark, *British Clubs and Societies, 1580 – 1800* (Oxford, 2000); Corey E. Andrews, *Literary Nationalism in Eighteenth-Century Scottish Club Poetry* (Lewiston, 2004) and 'Drinking and Thinking: Club Life and Convivial Sociability in Mid Eighteenth Century Edinburgh' *SHAD*, Autumn (2007), 65-82; Rhona Brown and Gerard Carruthers, 'Commemorating James Thomson, "The Seasons" in Scotland, and Scots Poetry', *Studies in the Literary Imagination*, 2013, vol.46(1), 71-89.

10 Mark Wallace, *Scottish Freemasonry 1725 – 1810: Progress, Power and Politics*, (St Andrews: Unpublished Ph.D. Thesis, 2007), 294-315.

11 David Stevenson, *The Beggar's Benison. Sex Clubs of Enlightenment Scotland and Their Rituals*, (East Linton, 2001) and Julie Peakman, *Lascivious Bodies: A Sexual History of the Eighteenth Century*, (London, 2004).

12 Clark, *British Clubs*, 60.

13 Ron Ballantyne, 'The Mystery of 3000 "Disappeared" Burns Busts', *BC* (Winter, 2010), 33-35.

14 Adam Smith, *The Wealth of Nations*, Campbell, Skinner, Todd (eds), (Glasgow Edition, 1981), I, 145.

15 Bob Harris, 'The Enlightenment, Town and Urban Society in Scotland, c.1760 – 1820', *Scottish Historical Review*, vol CXXVI, no. 522 (October 2011), 1097 – 1136, 'Cultural Change in Provincial Scottish Towns c.1700 – 1820', *The Historical Journal*, vol. 54, March 2011, 105-141, and John Strawhorn, 'Ayrshire in the Enlightenment', in G. Cruickshank (ed.) *A Sense of Place: Studies in Scottish Local History* (Edinburgh, 1988), 188-199.

16 Andrews, 'Drinking and Thinking', 81.

17 James Grant, *Old and New Edinburgh*, (London, 1880), ii, 230-237. Cockburn called the Antemanum 'a jovial institution which contained, and helped to kill, all the topers of Edinburgh'. Henry, Lord Cockburn, *Memorials of His Times*, (Edinburgh, 1856), 224.

18 Robert Collis, 'Jolly Jades, Lewd Ladies and Moral Muses: Women and Clubs in Early Eighteenth-Century Britain', *Journal for Research into Freemasonry and Fraternalism*, 2:2 (2011), 202-235; James Buchan, *Crowded with Genius: The Scottish Enlightenment*, (New York, 2003), 214-271.

19 Grant, *Old and New Edinburgh*, ii, 122.
20 *Ibid*, 126.
21 Hans Hecht, *Robert Burns: the Man and his Work*, Jane Lymburn (trs.), (Alloway, 1986), 107.
22 Clark, *British Clubs*, 219.
23 Wallace, *Scottish Freemasonry*, 316-325.
24 McElroy, 146.
25. Billy Kay, Cailean Maclean, Knee Deep in Claret, (Skye, 1983), 90; Hecht, Robert Burns, 110, and 199; Wallace, Scottish Freemasonry 319. There is some question of him also being a member of Canongate Kilwinning Lodge.
26 Some hold that 'The Court of Equity' was a club, (see Purdie, McCue and Carruthers (eds), *Maurice Lindsay's The Burns Encyclopaedia)*, 95: but that appears to give an occasional poem (the poem called *Libel Summons* by Kinsley, K.109) an exaggerated importance. McElroy, 152; Andrews, *Literary Nationalism*, 256-262. This appears much more like a group of drinking friends than a description of the form and ritual of a club.
27 Dudley Wright, *Robert Burns and Freemasonry*, (Paisley, 1921) and *Robert Burns and his Masonic Circle*, (London, 1929).
28 *Letters*, L.77: to John Ballantine, 14/1/1787.There is no substantial evidence that Robert Burns was formally elected as poet laureate of Lodge Canongate Kilwinning. It is likely he performed for them but in no formally mandated capacity. Naturally, after his posthumous fame, elderly gentlemen of less than robust memory constructed a more definitive story.
29 *Letters*, L.77: to John Ballantine, 14/1/1787; *Letters*, L.500: to John Leven (March? 1792). *Poems*, K.189, 'A Birth-day Ode'. The details are first published in Donald A Low, 'A Last Supper with Scotland's Bard', *BC* (1996), 188-191.
30 Wallace, *Scottish Freemasonry*, 2. (The same might be said of the Burns Supper). David Stevenson, 'Survey: Four Hundred Years of Freemasonry in Scotland', *The Scottish Historical Review*, (October 2011), 280-295 and *The First Freemasons: Scotland's Early Lodges and their Members*, (Aberdeen, 1998).
31 Ibid., 108.
32 Ibid., 70.
33 *Air Edition*, 295.
34 *Ibid*.
35 Peter Westwood, 'Burns Cottage', *BC* (Homecoming 2009), i – xlvii, at xxii. The innkeeper from 1803 'Miller' Goudie is best remembered by Keats's dismissive recollection of some years later. 'Then we proceeded to the Cottage he was born in – there was a board to that effect by the doorside – ... We drank some toddy to Burns's memory with an old man who knew Burns – damn him and damn his Anecdotes – he was a great bore'. Letter, John Keats to Thomas Keats, 17/7/1818, Hyder Edward Rollins (ed.), *Letters of John Keats 1814 – 1821*, (Cambridge, MA 1958), I, 331-332.
36 *Air Edition*, 295.
37 *Ayr Advertiser*, 9/3/1854.
38 James Paterson, *The Contemporaries of Burns and the More Recent Poets of Ayrshire*, (Edinburgh, 1840), 387. Hew Scott, *Fasti Ecclesiæ Scotiæ, Part I: Synod of Lothian and Tweeddale*, (Edinburgh/London, 1866), 213.
39 East Ayrshire Museums, Accession No: McKie, IX, 35.
40 Zachs Ms.
41 *Air Advertiser*, 27/6/1810. Paterson, *Contemporaries*, 383-384. Chambers used Paul's recollections extensively, see: W&R Chambers Archive, National Library of Scotland, Acc. 13178 Dep 341, no 517, 'Manuscripts of the Rev Hamilton Paul'.
42 The early *Currie Edition*, erroneously gave 29th as the poet's birthday.McKie Ms a: *BC* (1892), 'Some Hamilton Paul Manuscripts', 91-94.
43 *Auld Ayr*, 'Laying the Foundation Stone of Burns' Monument', 180-184.
44 In analysing the Burns Supper *per se*, it is not necessary to focus on the constitutional status of any given club or event. The long-running argument over precedence between Greenock and Paisley Burns Clubs is legendary and, to an extent comical. Neither held the first Burns Supper and really neither can be called the first Burns Club.
45 *Poems*, K.115.
46 Crawford, *The Bard*, 198.
47 *Kilmarnock Edition*, iv,v; *First Edinburgh Edition*, v; *Air Edition*, xlv -vi and xlvii..

48 This refers to the Burns portrait 'done at the expence, and at the direction of, several gentlemen of the neighbourhood' to be hung outside the cottage to advertise its new function as an aleshop. Not all critics thought that this either an appropriate manner in which to commemorate the birth-place of the Bard. 'R.M. of Glasgow' visited the Cottage weeks before the first Supper and was scathing about it: 'in the whole design there was exhibited such a poverty of intellect, such a deplorable beggary of taste, and such a woeful display of ignorance and folly, that for a moment, I was unable to decide whether it was most deserving of laughter, ridicule, indignation, or contempt'. *The Monthly Magazine,* No. 73, 1/6/1801, 408-409. By 1817, it had been brought indoors, Andrew Bigelow, *Leaves from a Journal,* (Boston, 1821), 33. 'Another proof of "to what base uses we may turn, Horatio, is the exhibition of the head of Robert Burns on the signs of our grog shops. He, who was endowed with the divine spirit of poetry, is hung up as the representative of the spirit of rum'. *Haverhill Gazette* (Mass), 11/12/1830.

49 *Air Edition,* 296-297.

50 Zacks MS, 1801.

51 'Manuscripts of the Rev Hamilton Paul'.

52 Currie's mistake over the date of Burns's birth caused the 1802 and 1803 suppers in Alloway and Greenock to be held on 29 January. After the Alloway Supper on the 29 January 1803, the diners checked Ayr's parish records finding that the 25th was the true date. This was reported in the newspapers, (eg *The Star,* 8 February 1803), yet Paisley kept to the 29ᵗʰ until 1818 when a leading member, RA Smith, obtained an affidavit from the Session Clerk of Ayr attesting to the 25th. The adherence to the 29th appears to show that there was little correspondence between the 'ancient Scots clubs' at that time.

53 *Air Advertiser,* 28/1/1813.

54 Roland Quinault, 'The Cult of the Centenary, c.1784 – 1914', *Historical Research,* 71:176 (October 1998), 302-323.

55 Holger Hook, *Empires of the Imagination,* (London, 2010), 120-128.

56 Quinault, *op cit,*; Joep Leersen, Ann Rigney, (eds)., *Commemorating Writers in Nineteenth-Century Europe. Nation Building and Centenary Fever,* (London, 2014).

57 Murray Pittock and Christopher A. Whatley, 'Poems and Festivals: Text and Beyond Text in the Popular Memory of Robert Burns', *Scottish Historical Review,* April, 2014, 56-79, at 64.

58 The *Air Advertiser* was founded in 1803 by John Wilson (of *Kilmarnock Edition* fame) and his brother Peter. The latter sold his share to Paul for £600 in 1810 who edited the paper until 1813. He sold his shares in 1816 for £2,500 upon being presented to the parish of Broughton. Carreen S, Gardner, *Printing in Ayr and Kilmarnock: Newspapers, Periodicals, Books and Pamphlets Printed from about 1780 until 1920,* (Ayr, 1976), 45.

59 James Storer and John Greig, *Views in North Britain, Illustrative of the Works of Robert Burns,* (London, 1805), 27. Rather oddly, their acknowledgments for help and advice include Dr William Peebles.

60 M. 'Sketch of a Short Excursion Lately Taken in The West of Scotland', *The Belfast Monthly Magazine,* 2.10 (1809), 341-345, at 343.

61 Pittock and Whatley, 56.

62 Clark McGinn, *The Ultimate Burns Supper Book,* (Edinburgh, 2005).

63 Angus Macdonald, *Greenock Burns Club (The Mother Club) 1801–2001,* (Greenock, 2002), 10. Although it is a tradition of the club, there is no record of Burns's personal friends in Greenock attending any of the early Suppers.

64 Neil Dougall, *Poems and Songs,* (Greenock, 1854), 37-38.

65 Archibald Brown, *The Early Annals of Greenock,* (Greenock, 1905), 19, gives the shorter version recited, while Dougall, 37-38, shows a longer version.

66 Macdonald, *Mother Club,* 20-21.

67 Macdonald, *Mother Club,* 24.

68 *Tyne Mercury,* 21/2/1809.

69 *Ibid.,* 8/2/1803.

70 *Durham County Advertiser,* 3/2/1816. There are annual reports from 1811 (*Tyne Mercury,* 12/2/1811) including 1816, 1818, and from 1818 to 1828.

71 *Durham County Advertiser,* 28/2/1824. It had ceased to exist by 1859, see Ballantine, 485 (Sunderland). A new Sunderland Burns Club was formed in 1897 and closed in 2011 after garlanding Burns's bust in the Winter

Gardens for the last time. *Sunderland Echo*, 27/2/2011.

72 Fergusson composed a similar summons for the Cape Club: University of Edinburgh, Laing Ms, La II, 334/1.

73 Brown, *Paisley Burns Clubs,* 44.

74 David Semple, (ed.), *The Poems and Songs and Correspondence of Robert Tannahill*, (Paisley, 1876), 483.

75 Semple, *Tannahill,* 'Summons to attend a Meeting of the Burns Anniversary Society', 44-45; 'Burns Anniversary Meeting [1805]', 45-49, 'Once on a time, almighty Jove'; 'Burns Anniversary Meeting [1807]', 50-54, 'While Gallia's chief, with cruel conquests vain'.; and 'Burns' Anniversary Meeting [1810]'. 'Again the happy day returns, See also: 'Dirge. Written on Reading an Account of Robert Burns' Funeral', 41-34.

76 Robert Tannahill, *Letter to John Struthers,* 26/9/1807, Coulter Burns Collection, National Library of Scotland, MS 23150.

77 Semple, *Tannahill,* 'Burns Anniversary Meeting [1810]', 54-61; *Letter to James Clark,* 17/12/1809, 434-435.

78 *Greenock Advertiser,* 2/2/1810.

79 Nancy Marshall, *Burns Supper Companion,* (Edinburgh, 2007), p.43.

80 Brown, *Paisley Burns Clubs,* 111-114.

81 Semple, *Tannahill,* 'Epistle to J Buchanan', 103-107 mentions Buchanan's painting of Burns for Kilbarchan Club. There may have been a dinner in 1804 or 1805 (see the bald statement in Semple, *Tannahill,* 'Buchanan was chosen the first Chairman of the Kilbarchan Burns Anniversary Club in 1804', 114) but there is some doubt, see Brown, *Paisley Burns Clubs,* 95-97. Kilmarnock, *Air Advertiser,* 4/2/1808. Similarly, Kilmarnock claims 'a well-authenticated tradition[…] that the anniversary of the birth of Burns was annually celebrated at a very early date by a few choice spirits who met together-in a haphazard way without thought of handing down to posterity any memento of their proceedings'. Duncan McNaught, 'Kilmarnock Burns Club', in *BC* (1895), 90-99, at 90.

82 Robert Tannahill, Letter to James King, 3/8/1806, National Library of Scotland, MS 582 fol. 681.

83 John Kennedy, *The Poetical Works of John Kennedy, Kilmarnock,* (Ayr, 1818), 'An Address to the Burnsonian Society, Royal Ayrshire Militia', 107-112. Tom Barclay, (ed.), *Records of the Ayrshire Militia From 1802 to 1883,* (Ayr, 2011), 58-69.

84 William Innes Addison, *The Snell Exhibitions from the University of Glasgow to Balliol College, Oxford,* (Glasgow, 1901), 82.

85 *Glasgow Herald,* 10/2/1806.

86 *Morning Advertiser,* 30/1/1809.

87 There is no discovered contemporary source, but the meeting is referred to in a report in the *Caledonian Mercury,* 10/6/1819. For 1822, James Douglas, *Glimpses of Old Bombay and Western India With Other Tapers,* (London, 1900), 82.

88 Brown, *Paisley Burns Clubs,* 172.

89 Peter Forbes, *Poems, Chiefly in the Scottish Dialect,* (Edinburgh, 1812), 'Circular Letter Sent to the Friends of Robert Burns, Inviting Them to Meet at the Author's House, on the 25th January, 1811, the Anniversary of his Birth'. 58-59.

90 'To the friends of Burns, on reading the contents of his Poems', Forbes, *Poems etc.,* 3-9.

91 Ebenezer Henderson, *Annals of Dunfermline A.D. 1801—1901* (Glasgow, 1879). In 1760, several Dunfermline farmers formed 'The Chicken Pye Club', which was still active in 1812 inspiring the naming of the Haggis Club: see John M Leighton, *History of the County of Fife,* (Glasgow, 1840), III, 219. The extant Glasgow Haggis Club was founded in 1886.

92 See also James Aikman, *Poems, Chiefly Lyrical, Partly in the Scottish Dialect,* (Edinburgh, 1816), 90-96, 'Verses to the Memory of Robert Burns, Recited at the Meeting which is annually held at D_____ on the 25th of January [1813] in commemoration of his Birth-day'. And his 'Ode to the Memory of Robert Burns' (nd)., 97-104. See Corey Andrews, *The Genius of Scotland,* 223-225, who reviews Aikman's poem, but fails to link its purpose to the Burns Supper.

93 Robert Burns World Federation Website: www.cobbler.plus.com/wbc/newsletter/john_murison_collection/the_dunfermline_united_burns_club.

htm (last accessed 1/5/2018); the club federated in 1896 as number 85. As no Burns SupperBurns Suppers were held in 1940-1943, 2016 was the 200th dinner organised by the club.

94   *Glasgow Herald*, 31/1/1812; *Air Advertiser*, 6/2/1812; Strang, 328.

95   *Air Advertiser*, 28/1/1813 and 4/2/1813.

96   William Glen, Charles Rodgers, (ed.), *The Poetical Remains of William Glen*, (Edinburgh, 1874), 105-109.

97   McKie MS M.

98   ANON., *A Walk from the Town of Lanark to the Falls of the Clyde on a Summer Afternoon*, (Glasgow, 1816).

99   *Air Advertiser*, 10/2/1814.

100 Letter, James Hogg to George Thomson, 28/11/1814, in James Hogg, Gillian Hughes, Douglas S Mack, (eds), *The Collected Letters of James Hogg*, (Edinburgh, 2004-2008), I, 219.

101 Letter, James Hogg to John Aiken, 14/1/1815; *Hogg's Letters*, I, 229-230. *Caledonian Mercury*, 2/2/1815.

102 William Roscoe, 'Elegy, on the Death of the Scottish Poet Burns', *Morning Chronicle*, 28 July 1800.

103 William Maginn, Shelton Mackenzie (ed.), *Miscellaneous Writings of the Late Dr Maginn*, (New York, 1855), I, 118.

104 Willison Glass, *The Caledonian Parnassus: A Museum of Original Scottish Songs*, (Edinburgh, 1812), 'Anniversary of the Birth of Robert Burns', 54-55.

105 *Scots Magazine*, vol. 78 (1816), 154-155.

106 ANON [Assumed to be William Grierson], *An Account of the Masonic Procession, Which Took Place at Dumfries, on the 5th June 1815, At the Laying of the Foundation Stone of the Mausoleum to be Erected Over the Remains of Robert Burns*, (Dumfries, 1815). ANON, *The Nithsdale Minstrel*, (Dumfries, 1815), 'VERSES Delivered at the Public Dinner on Occasion of Laying the Foundation Stone of BURNS'S MAUSOLEUM, 5th June, 1815', 166-170.

107 William Grierson, John Davies (ed.), *Apostle to Burns*, (Edinburgh, 1981), 292.

108 Robert Burns House Museum, Dumfries; *Handbill, Anniversary of Burns, 18 January 1820*, MS Accession number: DUMFM:1965.623.

109 Robert Burns House Museum, *Minute Book of the Burns Club, No. 1*, MS accession number DUMFM:0198.422. Also, ANON [Philip Sully], *The Centenary Book of the Burns Club of Dumfries*, (Dumfries, 1920).

110 Not all of the 'ancient' Scottish Burns clubs have an uninterrupted history prior to the World Wars. Dumfries did not hold dinners in 1828, 1831-1833, 1835, 183; or 1849 (due to a cholera epidemic); 1879 ('in respect of the general distress and depression prevalent in the County'), or 1901 (Queen Victoria's death). Paisley failed to meet in 1820 due to the radical riots and held no meetings for 38 years between 1837 and 1874. Irvine cancelled 1832/3 and 1849/50 (cholera epidemics); and 1853 and 1906 (death of the Hon Secretary), and 1901 (Queen Victoria). Kilmarnock held no meetings between 1814 and 1841 nor from 1850 to 1854; Greenock Burns Club failed to meet in 1807 and 1808.

111 *Edinburgh Evening Courant*, 27/1/1816.

112 'Peter Morris' [John Gibson Lockhart], *Peter's Letters to his Kinsfolk*, (Edinburgh/London, 1819), i,106-143.

113 *Caledonian Mercury*, 20/1/1816; *Scots Magazine*, Vol.78 (1816), 154-155.

114 *The Edinburgh Annual Register*, 1816,.8.

115 *Letter, Gilbert Burns to Jean Armour Burns*, 27/6/1816, Robert Burns Birthplace Museum, object 3.6430.

116 *The Sun*, 5/6/1816.

117 Philip Sully, *Robert Burns and Dumfries, 1796 – 1896*, (Dumfries, 1896). Irvine Burns Club debated a triennial and a biennial proposition in 1830, both were 'rejected by a considerable majority'. http://www.irvineburnsclub.org/ourhistory.htm <last accessed 1/5/2018>

118 *The Edinburgh Magazine*, 1819, 28-29.

119 '3rd [June, 1819]. Attended a meeting of the stewards of Burns's dinner... In settling the airs to be played after the toasts, I proposed after the city of Edinburgh to have 'I'll gang nae mair to yon town', which allusion to the unwillingness of the Scotch to return northward did not seem to be much relished'. Thomas Moore, Lord John Russell (ed.), *Memoirs, Journal and Correspondence of Thomas Moore*, (London, 1853), 321-322.

120 Sully, *Centenary Book,* 130-131.

121 History of Irvine Burns Club: http://
www.irvineburnsclub.org/ourhistory.
htm <last accessed 1/5/2018>.

122 *Currie Edition,* i, 330.

123 Tanja Bueltmann, Andrew Hinson,
Graeme Morton, (eds.), *Ties of
Bluid, Kin and Countrie: Scottish
Associational Culture in the Diaspora,*
(Guelph, 2009).

124 *Calcutta Journal,* Vol.II, 156.

125 *New York Daily Advertiser,* 7/2/1820.

126 Bueltmann, *et al, Ties of Bluid,* 41-42.

127 An abbreviated version of this section
appeared in the *Burns Chronicle*
(2015), 'Early Burns Celebrations in
America', 47-59.

128 Ambrose Bierce, *The Devil's
Dictionary,* (New York, 1911), 96.

129 Low, *Critical Heritage,* 44-46.

130 Rhona Brown, '"Guid black prent":
Robert Burns and the Contemporary
Scottish and American Periodical Press'
in Sharon Alker, Leith Davis and Holly
Faith Nelson (eds.), *Robert Burns and
Transatlantic Culture,* (Farnham, 2012),
71-86, at 79.

131 Carol Thompson Gallagher, *The Scots
Who Built New York,* (New York NY,
2006), 19.

132 *Pennsylvania Packet,* 25/12/1790.

133 *State Gazette of South-Carolina,*
26/2/1789; *Hampshire Chronicle,*
11/3/1789;

134 *Pennsylvania Packet,* 25/12/1790;
Albany Spectator, 12/12/1804;
Commercial Advertiser, 8 /12/1804;
Albany Gazette, 6/12/1804.

135 John M. Duncan, *Travels Through
Part of The United States and Canada
In 1818 And 1819,* (Glasgow, 1820),
ii,235.

136 *The Balance and Columbian
Repository,* 7/2/1804.

137 *Caledonian Mercury,* 1/6/1818; Richard
Rush, *Memoranda of a Residence at the
Court of London,* (Philadelphia,1833),
253-255.

138 *Morning Chronicle,* 28/5/1818.

139 Franklin Didier, *Franklin's Letters to
his Kinsfolk,* (Philadelphia, PA, 1822),
II, 38-39.

140 James Thom (born 1802, emigrated
1836, died 1850), the self-taught
sculptor of the life-sized Tam o'Shanter
and Souter Johnnie figures was present
at Burns Supper in New York City
(Blue Bonnet Tavern, 1831) and in
Newark, NJ (1837).

141 *The Star,* 8/2/1803.

142 *The Poetical Works of Robert Burns,*
(Salem, NY, 1815).

143 *Poulson's American Daily Advertiser,*
3/2/1817; Helen Currie, *Poems,*
(Philadelphia, 1818), 'Intended for the
Burns Club, *but not presented to it',*
109- 115.

144 *Ibid.,* 5/2/1819.

145 Frederick Pattison, *Granville Sharpe
Pattison: Anatomist and Antagonist:
1791–1851,* (Alabama,1987), 106.

146 *New York Daily Advertiser,* 2/2/1820.

147 *New-York American for the Country,*
2/2/1822, James B. Sheys, 'Ode to the
Memory of Burns, Written for his
Anniversary, Jan. 25th, 1822', *Ladies'
Literary Cabinet,* 9/3/1822, 143.

148 *New-York Evening Post,* 27/1/1825;
Statesman, 4/2/1825; *Georgian,*
5/2/1825; *Charleston Courier,*
9/2/1825.

149 Robert Ernst, *Immigrant Life in New
York City, 1825 – 1863,* (Syracuse, NY,
1994), 236.

150 *National Advocate,* 29/1/1828.

151 *Sun,* 4/2/1840.

152 *Athenaeum,* 25/1/1832, 133.

153 *Boston Traveler,* 17/2/1832.

154 *Georgian,* 18/2/1824; *Baltimore
Gazette,* /2/1830.

155 *New York Mirror,* 30/6/1838; *Newark
Daily Advertiser,* 6/2/1843.

156 Jeffrey J. Mclean, 'The Macarthurs
and the Mitchells: Wisconsin's First
Military Families', *The Wisconsin
Magazine Of History,* (Winter 2010),
14-27, at 17. Robert Shields, 'An 1851
Celebration in Wisconsin', *BC* (1901),
47-64.

157 *Glasgow Herald,* 11/3/1857.

158 *Sacramento Daily Union,* 28/1/1856.

159 Anon, *Celebration of The Hundredth
Anniversary of The Birth of Burns:
Boston Burns Club, January 25th,
1859,* (Boston MA, 1859),4.

160 *Signs of the Times,* 2/2/1828.

161 *Rhode-Island Republican,* 5/2/1829.

162 David M. Kinnear, *The Albany Burns
Club,* (Albany, 1919), 5.

163 Frederick Douglass, 'On Robert Burns
and Scotland', John W Blassingame
(ed.), *The Frederick Douglass Papers.
Series One: Speeches, Debates and
Interviews,* (New Haven & London,
1982), II, 147-148.

164 Ballantine, 605, (Washington, DC).

165 Ballantine, 604, (St Louis, MO).

166   Ballantine, 550 (Boston, Parker House); 584 (New York, Astor House). Henry Wadsworth Longfellow declined the Boston invitation 'due to lumbago', asking his friend John Fields 'to make a little speech for me … and also eat my part of the haggis which I hear is to grace the feast. This shall be your duty and reward'. Letter No. 1716, Andrew Hilen (ed.), *The Letters of Henry Wadworth Longfellow,* (Cambridge, 1972), iv, 117.

167   'The Centennial Anniversary of the Birth of Robert Burns', *Journal of the Illinois State Historical Society*, (Apr – Jul, 1924), 205-210; Ballantine, 604 (Springfield, IL).

168   *Newark Daily Advertiser*, 31/1/1837.

169   *Weekly Miners' Journal* (Pottsville), 1/2/1862.

170   Terry A Johnston, Jr, *Him on the One Side and Me on the Other,* (Columbia SC, 1999), 124-125. The Campbell brothers emigrated from Scotland and later enlisted in the opposing armies. Both their regiments wore uniforms with Scottish attributes – although it is unlikely that the New Yorkers wore kilt dress in the field.

171   *Cincinnati Commercial Tribune*, 27/1/1862; Ballantine, 564 (Chicago):and 560 (Charleston).

172   Ron Chernow, *Grant*, (London, 2017), 510.

173   San Francisco Scottish Thistle Club (number 31), Newark Burns Club (number 32) (both in 1886) and then Chicago Caledonian Society (number 51 in 1892); Mackay, *Federation*, 225-226; *BC*, 1893.

174   Bueltmann, *Clubbing Together*, 94-97.

175   Murray Pittock, 'Introduction', in Murray Pittock (ed.), *The Reception of Robert Burns in Europe*, (London, 2014). 1-7, at 1.

176   Oliver Wendell Holmes to JS Tyler, Boston, 7/12/1858, in [Anon] *First Editions of Ten American Authors Collected by J Chester Chamberlain of New York,* (New York, 1909), 114.

177   Ballantine,122 (Dumfries, Assembly Rooms).

178   Susan Manning, *Poetics of Character: Transatlantic Encounters 1700 – 1900,* (Cambridge, 2013), 243-244.

179   Fiona A Black, 'Tracing the Transatlantic Bard's Availability', in Alker, *et al, Robert Burns and Transatlantic Culture,* 57-69.

180   Bueltmann *et al, The Scottish Diaspora,* 192.

181   Gillian I. Leitch, 'Robert Burns as a Symbol of Montreal Scottish Identity, 1801 – 1875', *Burns in the Scottish Diaspora Conference*, Napier University, Edinburgh, July 2009.

182   Michael Vance, 'A Brief History of Organised Scottishness in Canada', in Celeste Ray (ed.), *Transatlantic Scots* (Tuscaloosa AL, 2005), 96-119, at 101.

183   Elizabeth Waterstone, *Rapt in Plaid: Canadian Literature and Scottish Tradition*, (Toronto, 2001), 41.

184   'Happy 250th Birthday Robbie Burns!', *Heritage Toronto News*, 22/1/2009.

185   *Kingston Chronicle and Gazette*, 6/2/1836.

186   William Wye Smith, Scott McLean & Michael Vance (eds), *Recollections of a Nineteenth Century Scottish Canadian,* (Toronto, 2008), 18. William Wye Smith, *The Poems of William Wye Smith,* (Toronto, 1885), 'Burns – For a Scottish Gathering', 118-120.

187   Bueltmann *et al, Ties of Bluid*, 26.

188   Mackay, *Federation*, 225.

189   *Calcutta Journal*, 12/1/1796 and 19/1/1796.

190   *Caledonian Mercury*, 10/6/1819, *Asiatic Journal*, (1819),100.

191   *Madras Chronicle*, 29/3/1814; Douglas, *Glimpses*, 82.

192   Steve Newman, 'Localizing and Globalizing Burns's Songs From Ayrshire to Calcutta: The Limits of Romanticism and Analogies of Improvement', in Evan Gottlieb (ed.), *Global Romanticism: Origins, Orientations, and Engagements, 1760 – 1820*, (Lanham, MD, 2015), 57-80.

193   Douglas, *Glimpses*,62.

194   *Calcutta Journal*, 8/12/1819.

195   Douglas, *Glimpses*, 22.

196   Sulley, *Dumfries*, 41-42. James Kennedy, 'LINES, Occasioned by James Glencairn Burns Requesting a Quart Bottle of the Punch Drunk at His Father's Anniversary Birth-day Club, and to Forward the Same to Calcutta by the Earliest Opportunity', *Poems & Songs* (Dumfries, 1824), 115-117.

197   *Asiatic Journal*, vol. 14 (1834), 22.

198   John William Kaye, *The Life and Correspondence of Major-General Sir John Malcolm GCB*, (London/Bombay, 1856), ii, 29.

199 *Calcutta Journal,* (November/December 1819), 59; *Blackwood's Magazine,* March 1820, 675.

200 Mary Ellis Gibson, *Indian Angles: English Verse in Colonial India From Jones to Tagore,* (Athens, OH, 2011), 21.

201 The inauguration dinner for Lodge 'Star of Hope', (Agra) in September 1844 with its toast to 'The memory of Robby [sic] Burns'. *Freemasons' Quarterly Magazine,* Vol.2 (1844), 495-496.

202 'Oscar', 'Lines: Written for the Anniversary of Burns's Birth-day', *Calcutta Journal,* 7/2/1823.

203 Ballantine, 44, (Glasgow, City Hall). [George Anderson Vetch], *Pilgrimage to the Shrine of Burns During the Festival with The Gathering of the Doon and Other Poetical Pieces', by An Indian Officer,* (Edinburgh, 1846), 14-15. See also his 'An Exile's Tribute', in George Anderson, and John Finlay (eds.), *The Burns Centenary Poems; A Collection of Fifty of the Best [etc. etc.],* (Glasgow, 1859), 186-188.

204 Ballantine, 512, (Bombay).

205 David Hepburn & John Douglas, *Chronicles of the Caledonian Society of London: 1837 to 1905,* (London, 1923), 114.

206 Ballantine, 4, (Glasgow City Hall); and Hepburn & Douglas, 114.

207 Ballantine, 55 (Glasgow, City Hall); 34 (Edinburgh, Dunedin Hall).

208 Mackay, *Federation,* 226.

209 Menu Card: *The Calcutta Burns Club, 1938.* National Library of Scotland: NLS PB4.209.112/6; Mackay, *Federation,* 227.

210 Elizabeth Buettner, 'Haggis in the Raj: Private and Public Celebrations of Scottishness in Late Imperial India', *Scottish Historical Review,* vol. LXXXI (2002), 212-239, at 220.

211 Bueltmann *et al, Scottish Diaspora,* 239-241; Benjamin Wilkie, *The Scots in Australia, 1788 – 1938,* (Suffolk, 2017).

212 *Tasmanian and Port Dalrymple Advertiser,* 26/1/1825. The newspaper carried an Erratum; to point out that the Immortal Memory was drunk, not 'with three times three' but 'IN TOTAL SILENCE'.

213 *Launceston Examiner,* 20 and 24/1/1849; *Cornwall Chronicle,* 24/1/1849.

214 *Colonial Times and Tasmanian Advertiser,* 1/12/1826, *The Sydney Gazette,* 2/12/1826.

215 *The Australian,* 30/12/1826

216 *The Sydney Gazette,* 3/12/1835.

217 *The Sydney Monitor,* 17/1/1840; *The Sydney Herald,* 24, 25/1/1840; *The Australian,* 23, 25/1/1840.

218 Robert Burns Club of Melbourne: http://www.scotsofaus.org.au/robert-burns/ <last accessed 1/5/2018> Ballantine, 537, (Sydney).

219 Gordon Ashley, *The 250th – Is It All Down Hill From Here?,* Unpublished paper at GU Robert Burns Conference, 14/1/2012, 2. (Thanks to the author for sharing a draft).

220 *London Daily News,* 23/6/1846.

221 Alex Tyrell, 'No Common Corrobery': The Robert Burns Festivals and Identity Politics in Melbourne, 1845-59', *Journal of the Royal Australian Historical Society,* (December 2011), 161-176.

222 *The Maitland Mercury & Hunter River General Advertiser,* 7/2/1846

223 *Port Philip Gazette & Settlers' Journal,* 27 /1/1847.

224 *Geelong Advertiser,* 24/12/1847; *Melbourne Argus,* 27/1/1847.

225 *Geelong Advertiser,* 26/1/1848.

226 *The Maitland Mercury,* and *Hunter River General Advertiser,* 15/2/1845.

227 *Melbourne Argus,* 21/1/1848, see also 19/1/ 1849, and 28/1/ 1850.

228 *ibid.*

229 Tyrell, 'Corrobery', 164.

230 Patrick Buckridge, 'Robert Burns in Colonial Queensland: Sentiment, Scottishness and Universal Appeal', *Queensland Review,* 16:1 (2009), 69-78, at 73.

231 *Melbourne Argus,* 10/1/1859.

232 *New Zealander,* 5/2/1859.

233 *Sydney Morning Herald,* 25 /1/1859.

234 Ballantine, 534 (Sydney); 514 (Geelong); 525 (Melbourne); 540 (Tarrangower); 548 (Yaas); see also *Gippstead Guardian,* 4/2/1859. The additional events were held in Adelaide, Ballarat (John o'Groats), Ballarat (Bath's), Beechworth, Bendigo, Brisbane (North), Brisbane (South), Deniliquin, Melbourne (Mechanics Inst), Sydney (School of Arts), Troy, Tasmania, Wagga Wagga and Yachandandah.

235 Bueltmann, *Clubbing Together,* 119.

236   Mackay, *Federation*, 225. Both societies had disappeared by the 1920s.

237   Bueltmann *et al, Scottish Diaspora*, 245.

238   Liam McIlvanney 'Editorial: Burns and the World', *International Journal of Scottish Literature*, (Spring/Summer 2010), 1-12, at p.4.

239   Letter, James McIndoe to JR Thornton, BC (1897), pp.127-128.

240   *New Zealand Gazette*, 5/12/1840.

241   *New Zealander*, 26/06/1850; *Daily Southern Cross*, 3/12/1850.

242   *Otago Witness*, 10/2/1855, 19/01/1856; John Barr, *Poems Descriptive and Satirical*, (Edinburgh, 1860), 181-183.

243   Lyttleton Colonists' Society and Literary Institution, *Lyttleton Times*, 2/2/1856; or Auckland Mechanics Institute, *New Zealander*, 14/1/1857.

244   *Otago Daily Times*, 19/1/2010 and 'John Barr' in *Dictionary of New Zealand Biography*, (Wellington, 1990). Barr attended Paisley BC's 1875 dinner as a guest.

245   Brad Patterson, Tom Brooking, and Jim McAloon, *Unpacking the Kists: The Scots in New Zealand*, (Quebec, 2013).

246   Tanja Bueltmann, 'No Colonists Are More Imbued with Their Natural Sympathies than Scotchmen', *New Zealand Journal of History*, 43,2 (2009), 167-181, at 168.

247   Tanja Bueltmann, *Scottish Ethnicity and the Making of New Zealand Society: 1850 – 1930*, (Edinburgh, 2011), 122.

248   Letter, James McIndoe to JR Thornton, BC (1897), pp.127-128.

249   *Lyttelton Times*, 21/1/1867.

250   *Wellington Independent*, 26/1/1859; *Hawke's Bay Herald*, 22/1/1859.

251   *Hawke's Bay Herald*, 22/1/1859.

252   David Kennedy, *Kennedy's Colonial Travel, &c.*, (London, 1876), 167.

253   Bueltmann, *Clubbing Together*, 106.

254   Mackay, *Federation*, 225-226; *Burns Chronicle* (2018).

255   *Calcutta Journal*, Vol.II, part 64, p.156.

256   *Singapore Free Press*, 7/1/1936; Bueltmann, *Clubbing Together*, 169.

257   Hong Kong St Andrew's Society: http://www.standrewshk.org/mavista/cms/en/dinners <last accessed 1/5/2018>. Shiona Airlie, *Thistle and Bamboo: The Life of Sir James Stewart Lockhart*, (Hong Kong, 2010), 32.

258   Charles Burton Buckley, *An Anecdotal History of Old Times in Singapore,*

(Singapore, 1902), I, 278 (1835); 306 (1836); 320 (1837); 398-399 (1843); 239 (1843). *Singapore Free Press*, 1/12/1836.

259   *The Straits Times*, 28/06/1848, 31/12/1850.

260   Graeme Morton, *Ourselves and Others*, 259.

261   'By CAM', *Singapore Free Press and Mercantile Advertiser,* 25/2/1913.

262   Bueltmann, *Clubbing Together*, 190.

263   John M MacKenzie, Nigel R Dalziel, *The Scots in South Africa: Ethnicity, Gender and Race, 1772 – 1914*, (Manchester, 2007), 18-19.

264   Ibid.

265   Nigel Worden, Elizabeth Van Heyningen, Vivian Bickford-Smith, *Cape Town: The Making of a City*, (Kenilworth SA, 2004), 121; *The Colonist*, 28/02/1828.

266   Thomas Pringle, *Ephemeridies or Occasional Poems Written in Scotland and South Africa*, (London, 1828); Nigel Leask, '"Their Groves o' Sweet Myrtles": Robert Burns and the Scottish Colonial Experience, in Pittock (ed.), *Robert Burns in Global Culture*, 172-188, at 184-185.

267   MacKenzie & Dalziel, 243; Margaret Harradine, *Port Elizabeth*, (Port Elizabeth, 1994), 37.

268   *Natal Witness* (nd), quoted in Gould, iv, 251. Ballantine, 289 (Jedburgh). See also 34 (Edinburgh, Dunedin Hall); 492 (Wrexham); and 543 (Toronto).

269   JJ Hulme, 'Gallant Gentlemen 1855 – 1865. The Cape Colony Volunteers of a Century Ago', *The South African Military History Society: Military History Journal*, (June 1971). The Scots Company became an independent unit in 1861 and was disbanded in 1866 following an inspection which determined 'The Scotch Volunteer Rifle Corps was only mustered for inspection with great difficulty. Its drill was indifferent and, apart from a few good shots, musketry was poor and received no attention as part of unit training. Clothing was of an expensive national character and resulted in a great variety of dress on parade'.

270   Bueltmann, *Clubbing Together*, 137.

271   Harradine, 77; Bueltmann, *Clubbing Together*, 143; Mackenzie & Dalzeil, 243-245.

272   Bueltmann, *Clubbing Together*, 143

273   Mackenzie & Dalziel, 263.

274 *Ibid.*, for 1880s: 139, for up to 1905, 141-142; beyond South Africa, 142.

275 Andy Hall (ed.) *Touched by Robert Burns,* (Edinburgh, 2008), 137.

276 Leith Davis, 'The Robert Burns 1859 Centenary: Mapping Transatlantic (Dis)location', Alker *et al* (eds), *Robert Burns and Transatlantic Culture,* 187-205, at 189.

277 ANON, *Poetic Tributes to the Memory of Burns,* (Newcastle, 1817).

278 *Ibid,* 4.

279 Richard Welford, *Men of Mark 'Twixt Tyne and Tweed,* (London/Newcastle-upon-Tyne, 1895), iii, 191-198.

280 Letter, Cadell & Davies to Gilbert Burns, London, 22/3/1819, quoted in D. McNaught, 'The Earnock Manuscripts', BC (1898), 7-40, at 34.

281 John Holland, James Everett (eds.), *Memoirs of the Life and Writings of James Montgomery,* (London, 1854 -1856), iii, 196-199.

282 BC (2009), 570.

283 James Montgomery, *The Pelican Island,* (London, 1827), 127-128.

284 Holland & Everett, iii, 255-256.

285 *Blackwood's Magazine,* August 1819, 521-529.

286 *Morning Post,* 5/2/1822.

287 John S Howie, 'Dalry Burns Club', BC (1953), 68-69.

288 *Belfast News-letter,* 16/1/1829; *Freeman's Journal,* 28/1/1840.

289 'A Few Hints for Dalry Burns Club', *The Cairn,* at www.dalry burnsclub.org <last accessed 1/5/2018>

290 Christopher A Whatley, *Immortal Memory: Burns and the Scottish People,* (Edinburgh, 2016).

291 William [Ramsey] Maule MP: History of Parliament Online: *http:// www.historyofparliamentonline. org/volume/1790-1820/member/ maule-hon-william-1771-1852;* [Sir] Alexander Boswell [Bart] *http:// www.historyofparliamentonline.org/ volume/1790-1820/member/boswell-alexander-1775-1822* (last accessed 1/5/2018); Robert Howie Smith (ed.), *The Poetical Works of Sir Alexander Boswell of Auchinleck,* (Glasgow, 1871), xlvi.

292 *Caledonian Mercury,* 30/5/1816.

293 *Morning Chronicle,* 28/5/1818.

294 *Ibid.,* 29/5/1819; 7 /6/1819.

295 Cockburn, *Memorials,* I,356. Richard Cronin, *Paper Pellets. British Literary*

Culture After Waterloo, (Oxford, 2012), 18-32.

296 [Lockhart], *Peter's Letters.*

297 Brown, *Paisley Burns Clubs,* 96-97.

298 John Strawhorn, *The History of Ayr: Royal Burgh and County Town,* (Edinburgh, 1989), p.138.

299 [ANON] A Burgess, *Brief Historical Reminiscences of the County and Town of Ayr,* (Ayr, 1830), 132-133. One of the Presidents of this Club was Dr John Taylor of Ayr, the radical Chartist politician. His Anniversary Ode can be found in *Ayr Advertiser,* 4 February 1836: W Hamish Fraser, *Dr John Taylor, Chartist, Ayrshire Revolutionary,* (Ayr, 2006).

300 James Glencairn Burns was on home leave, having been found wanting in his Commissariat duties by a formal Board of Enquiry, and was in England to rebuild his career. Robert Burns Junior also benefitted from the political attention, being permitted to retire from the Stamp Office in August that year, on a pension of £120 pa, to recognise 'the great literary talent of his father'.

301 Letter, James Hogg to Margaret Hogg, 16/1/1832; *Hogg's Letters,* III, 14-15, at p.14.

302 *The Mirror of Literature, Amusement and Instruction,* 4/2/1832.

303 *Motherwell/Hogg Edition,* 'Song for The Anniversary of Burns', v, 275-276; 'Robin's Awa', v, 278-288. David Vedder, *Poems, Legendary, Lyrical & Descriptive* (Edinburgh, 1842) 237-239.

304 *Caledonian Mercury* 2/2/1832.

305 *Caledonian Mercury,* 2/2/1832.

306 Gordon, *Memoir,* ii, p.291.

307 *Literary Gazette Journal of the Year,* (1832), 60.

308 Pittock and Whatley, 3.

309 Tyrrell, 'Paternalism', 54-55.

310 *Blackwoods Magazine,* September 1844, 56.

311 Tyrell, 'Paternalism', 47-49.

312 Care should also be taken over how to characterise the parade as the Incorporation of Shoemakers of Ayr (who owned Burns Cottage at that time) had the privilege of parading through the Royal Burgh in fancy dress and held irreverent and possibly slightly subversive shows in the form of Mock Coronations and Royal Weddings for 'King Crispin'. *Auld Ayr,* 174-176.

313   *Punch*, August 1844; *Banner of Ulster*, 9 August 1844.
314   S.C. Hall, *A Book of Memories of Great Men and Women of the Age*, (London, 1871), 325.
315   James Paterson, *Autobiographical Reminiscences*, (Glasgow, 1871), 188. (Emphasis added).
316   Ballantine, 44, (Glasgow, City Hall). *Pilgrimage to the Shrine of Burns*, 9-10.
317   Colin Rae Brown, *Noble Love and Other Poems*, (London, 1871), 57-68.
318   *Tait's Edinburgh Magazine*, September 1844, 545-553, at 545.
319   Whatley, *It Is Said*, 640.
320   *Aberdeen Journal*, 25/6/1844.
321   MacKay, *Federation*, 43 (emphasis added).
322   Ibid., 44-45.
323   Ballantine, 81, (Glasgow, Kings Arms Hall).
324   Leith Davis, 'The Robert Burns 1859 Centenary', at 204; Ann Rigney, 'Embodied Communities: Commemorating Robert Burns, 1859' *Representations*, (Summer 2011), 71-101, at 75. The first use of telegraphic greeting was in 1854, when Irvine Burns Club sent greetings to the Glasgow Ayrshire Society, see *Morning Post*, 3 February 1854.
325   Ballantine, 'Preface'.
326   Ibid.
327   *Glasgow Herald*, 10/1/1859; P. Hately Waddell, *Robert Burns: A Lecture*, (Ayr, 1859).
328   Ballantine, 92-116, (Ayr); Nimmo, 87-93, (Ayr).
329   Ballantine, 70, (Glasgow, Royal Hotel).
330   Carol McGuirk, 'Burns and Nostalgia', in Kenneth Simpson (ed.), *Burns Now*, (Edinburgh, 1994), 31-69, at.32.
331   WE Henley, quoted in *BC*, (1907), 118.
332   Ballantine, 57 (Glasgow, City Hall).
333   James J Coleman, *Remembering the Past in Nineteenth-Century Scotland: Commemoration, Nationality and Memory*, (Edinburgh, 2014), 16. Whatley, *Immortal Memory: Burns and the Scottish People*, (Edinburgh, 2016) and 'Robert Burns, Memorialisation, and the "Heart-beatings" of Victorian Scotland.' in Pittock (ed.), *Robert Burns in Global Culture*, 204-228; Johnny Roger, *The Hero Building: An Architecture of Scottish National Identity*, (Farnham: Ashtead, 2015), 49-70 and 127-140; Kirsten Carter

McKee, 'Burns and the British Empire: Viewing a Scottish Monument from an Imperial Perspective', *Architectural Heritage*, April 2014, 21-39.
334   Rae Brown was a Master Mason of Lodge number 175; Sneddon, a Past Master of Lodge number 109 and Mackay, a Master Mason in Lodges number 109 and number 405. See Archibald Chalmers, *The Burns Federation: 'The Actions Of Men Are The Best Interpreters Of Their Thoughts'* on http://www.grandlodgescotland. com/index.php?option=com_ content&id=376&Itemid=29 <last accessed 1/5/2018>
335   *Inverness Courier*, 20/3/1851.
336   McBain, *Burns' Cottage*, 118.
337   Tanja Bueltmann, 'Manly Games, Athletic Sports and the Commodification of Scottish Identity: Caledonian Gatherings in New Zealand to 1915', *The Scottish Historical Review*, (October 2010), 224-247 at 226.
338   *Northern Argus*, 11/4/1882.
339   Peter Ross, *Scotland and the Scots*, (New York, 1889), 131,132.
340   Vance, 'Organised Scottishness in Canada', 96-119, at 104.
341   Graeme Morton, *Ourselves and Others: Scotland 1832 – 1914*, (Edinburgh, 2012), 259.
342   Earl of Rosebery, *Burns Centenary, 21st July 1896*, (Dumfries, 1896).
343   Mackay, *Federation*, 141-142.
344   Anon, *Ritual of the Robert Burns Society of America*, (Canton, [1910]).
345   Lauren Jenifer Weiss calculates that 54 Burns Clubs were founded in Glasgow in the second half of the 'long nineteenth-century' which represents 32% of all the literary clubs in the City over that period. Lauren Jenifer Weiss, *The Literary Clubs and Societies of Glasgow During the Long Nineteenth Century*, (University of Stirling: unpublished PhD Thesis, 2017), 80.
346   *Scotsman*, 26/1/1884.
347   William Stewart, *J. Kier Hardie, A Biography*, (London, 1921), 19.
348   Mackay, *Federation*, 142-144.
349   *Glasgow Herald*, 2/12/1947; *BC* (1948), 37.
350   JFT Thomson, 'Suggested Lines for Organising a Burns Supper', *BC* (1979), 31-32.

351 J. Mackay, 'A Vade Mecum for Burns Night', *BC* (1982), 15.

352 Macdiarmid, *Drunk Man*, 57.

353 Annie Boutelle, *Thistle and Rose: A Study of Hugh MacDiarmid's Poetry*, (Loanhead, 1980), 100.

354 *Ibid.*, 169.

355 MacDiarmid, *Burns Today and Tomorrow*, 123.

356 *Ibid.*, 76.

357 MacDiarmid, *Drunk Man*, 55 at ll.37-40.

358 Hugh MacDiarmid, 'Your Immortal Memory, Burns!' *Universities & Left Review*, (Autumn 1959), 74-75.

359 Boutelle, 74.

360 *Montreal Pilot*, quoted in Gillian Leitch, 'Robert Burns as a Symbol of Montreal Scottish Identity, 1801 – 1875', *Burns in the Scottish Diaspora Conference Papers*, (Edinburgh, Napier University, 2009).

361 MacDiarmid, 'The Future of the Immortal Memory', 3.

362 *Independent*, 28/1/1996.

363 Edwin Muir, 'The Burns Myth', *New Judgements: Robert Burns Essays by Six Contemporary Writers*, William Montgomerie (ed.), (Glasgow, 1947), 7.

364 Ian Nimmo, *Robert Burns: His Life and Tradition in Words and Sound*, (London, 1965), 97.

365 John Buchan, *Immortal Memory, 25th January, 1918*, The Burns Club of London Archives.

366 Brown, *Paisley Burns Clubs*, 61-65; Semple, *Tannahill*, p.382.

367 Brown, *Paisley Burns Clubs*, 61-65.

368 Semple, *Tannahill*, Letter to James King, 4/6/1809, 429.

369 *Air Advertiser*, 1/2/1810; *Glasgow Courier*, 3/2/1810.

370 Mackenzie MacBride (ed.), *With Napoleon at Waterloo, [etc.]*, (London, 1911), 143-144; Charles Dalton, *The Waterloo Roll Call*, (London, 1904), 250.

371 *Findlay's Edition of Burns' Poems, Printed for The Army*, (Dublin, 1816). Also a two volume 24mo 1819 edition likely addressing the military market. *The Poetical Works of Robert Burns*, 2 vols. (Edinburgh, 1819). This was reissued in 1835. An unspecified edition of Burns was included in the 'Soldier's Libraries' created by the HEIC in Bengal in 1822; *The Soldier's Companion, or Military Recorder*, vol.1 (1824), 399.

372 George Vetch, *Poems*, (Calcutta, 1821), 'A Wild Wreath', 105-107.

373 *Glasgow Herald*, 26/1/1901, *BC* (1937).

374 David Goldie, 'Robert Burns and the First World War', *International Journal of Scottish Literature*, Issue Six, (Spring/Summer 2010). http://www.ijsl.stir.ac.uk/issue6/goldie.pdf <last accessed 1/5/2018>

375 'Caledonians Not To Hold Burns Supper' *Colorado Springs Gazette*, 13/12/1914 their position was modified the following year: 'Caledonian Society is to Give Burns Dinner Affair won't be so elaborate Because of War Relief Work Being Done'. *Ibid.*, 21/1/1917.

376 *Scotsman*, 26/1/1915.

377 *Ibid.*

378 Dalry Burns Club, *The Cairn*.

379 Kinnear, *Albany Burns Club*.

380 John Foord, 'The Immortal Memory'. *Speech Delivered at the Annual Dinner of the Burns Society of the City Of New York at Delmonico's, January 25, 1916*, (New York NY, [1916]), 10.

381 *Trenton Evening News*, 25/1/1916.

382 Robert Crawford, 'MacDiarmid, Burnsians, and Burns's Legacy' in David Sergeant, Fiona Stafford (eds), *Burns and Other Poets*, (Edinburgh, 2012),182-194 at 182.

383 *Yorkshire Evening Post*, 6/2/1915.

384 *The Times*, 26/1/1915.

385 Robert W. Service, *Collected Poems*, (New York, 1940), 306-309.

386 Edwina Burness, 'The Influence of Burns and Fergusson on the War Poetry of Robert Service', *Studies in Scottish Literature*, vol.21, issue 1, 135 -146; *Highland Light Infantry Chronicle*, (April 1917), 54.

387 *Scotsman*, 11/2/1918.

388 Revd Lauchlan MacLean Watt, 'A Plea For The True Text'. *BC* (1937), 48-53, at 50-51.

389 Nicol, *Till The Trumpet*, I, 263. A week later the New Year was celebrated with both armies joining in *Auld Lang Syne*, *ibid.*, I, 268.

390 Graham Seal, *The Soldiers' Press: Trench Journals in the First World War*, (London, 2013), 73.

391 *Scotsman*, 12/5/1915. Quoting *Poems*, K.391.

392 Israel Cohen, *The Ruhleben Prison Camp*, (London, 1917), 86.

393 *Southern Reporter*, 30/1/1919.

394 *BC* (1919), 4.

395   Clive Dunn, Gillian Dunn, *Sunderland in the Great War*, (Barnsley, 2014), 19.

396   *Aberdeen Press & Journal*, 27/1/1940 or *Dundee Courier*, 25/1/1940.

397   Annan Burns Club, *Fraternal Greeting: 1940*. Burns Club of London Archives.

398   *Glasgow Herald*, 24/1/1942.

399   Francis Douglas MP (Socialist, Battersea North), *Hansard*: HC Deb 18/12/1941; vol.376, cc2083-4. This was no more successful than the intervention in favour of haggises by Robert Houston MP (Conservative, Liverpool West Toxteth) in 1916 (HC Deb: 15/11/1916, vol.87, cc792-3).

400   *Daily Mail*, 26/1/1940.

401   Imperial War Museum, Major AAH Fraser RAMC, *Private Papers, Documents 24015*.

402   *Aberdeen Press & Journal*, 29/1/1943.

403   *Derby Daily Telegraph*, 29/1/1944.

404   http://www.bbc.co.uk/ww2peopleswar/stories/32/a8947632.shtml <last accessed 1/5/2018>. See also Steve Murdoch and Andrew MacKellop', Introduction', p. xxvii, and Dauvit Horsbroch, '"Tae See Oursels As Ithers See Us;" Scottish Military Identity from the Covenant to Victoria, 1637 – 1837', 105-129, in Andrew MacKellop, Steve Murdoch (eds), *Fighting For Identity: Scottish Military Experience c. 1550 – 1900*, (Leiden, 2002).

405   Carlton Younger, RAAF in Stalag 357, Fallingbostel discussing the 'effects of distilled PoW alcohol' on Burns Night, 1944. Imperial War Museum, Sound Department, catalogue number 23329. See also Changi Caledonian Society in TPM Lewis, *Changi – The Lost Years: A Malaysian Diary 1941-1943*, (Kuala Lumpur, 1984), 159.

406   Andrew Winton and Allan Carswell, *Open Road to Faraway*, (Dunfermline, 2001).

407   *Evening Telegraph*, 26/1/1946; *Dundee Courier*, 24/1/1946.

408   *Scotsman*, 26/1/1946.

409   Tom Sutherland, 'Burns in Beirut', *Studies in Scottish Literature*, vol. 30 (1), 1-8, at p.6.

410   Tom Sutherland, Jean Sutherland, *At Your Own Risk: An American Chronicle of Crisis and Captivity in the Middle East*, (Golden, 1996).

411   *Chambers/Wallace Edition*, iv,.502.

412   James K Hopkins, *Into the Heart of the Fire. The British in the Spanish Civil War*, (Stanford, 1998), 182-184. Also, *Daily Worker*, 8/2/1937. Some 375 of the 600 men in the battalion were casualties (including Caldwell).

413   http://www.international-brigades.org.uk/content/poem-burns-night (last accessed 1/5/2018).

414   Kevin Thompson, 'Bowhill People Celebrate 70th Anniversary', BC (Spring, 2011), 24-29.

415   *Observer*, 20/5/1951.

416   Glasgow University Library, Special Collections, Ms Morgan: Morgan/H/1/1 and Scraplook No. 13, Ms Morgan/C/13/p2663.

417   MacKay, *Federation*, 147-148; BC (1960), 45-48, at 45.

418   Natalia Kaloh Vid, 'Censorship and Ideology in Literary Translations: The Case of Robert Burns' Poetry in the Soviet Union', Floriana Popescu (ed.), *Perspectives in Translation*, (Newcastle upon Tyne, 2009), 77-94. *Burns Chronicle* (1965), 'Samuel Marshak: Obituary',80 and John Gray, 'A Tribute to Robert Burns in Moscow, USSR', 82-85.

419   *Daily Worker*, 25/1/1956.

420   Alex Anderson and Ronald Searle, *By Rocking Chair Across Russia*, (Cleveland & New York, 1960), 15-24.

421   *Glasgow Herald*, 1/1/1963; *Burns Chronicle* (1965), 82.

422   *Glasgow Herald*, 25/1/1984. Leningrad had celebrated a 'Burns Jubilee' in 1982, CD Macaulay, 'Political Culture and Foreign Policy Making', in Mario D Zamora (ed.) *Anthropological Diplomacy: Issues and Principles, Studies in Third World Societies* (June 1982), 115-138, at 125. Gordon Hepburn, 'The Logistics of Arranging a Burns Supper in Moscow USSR', BC (Autumn, 2003), 41-44; 'To Russia Again', BC (1977), 70-72; BC (1978), 109, and BC (1979) 68.

423   http://www.scottishmoscow.org/Supper.php <last accessed 1/5/2018.> The Scottish Government's claim that 'on Burns Night on January 25 each year, more glasses are raised to a haggis in Russia than anywhere else in the world' is patently wrong considering the number of events in the USA and in Canada. *Scotland's Links With Russia*, http://www.gov.scot/Resource/Doc/923/0013226.pdf <last accessed 1/5/2018>.

424 See /www.facebook.com/kyivlions/ <last accessed 1/5/2018>.

425 Donald A. Mackenzie, quoted in MacDiarmid, *Drunk Man*, 54. Sir Chi Chen was for many years the Minister of Legation from China to the Court of St James.

426 *The Children's Newspaper*, 29/1/1944.

427 *Glasgow Herald*, 27/1/1944. BBC *Year Book*, 1945, (London, 1945), 80. BC (1945), 6-7.

428 *The North-China Herald and Supreme Court & Consular Gazette*, Volume 82 (1907) 296; *China Reconstructs*, Volume 30 (1981), 40. 'Burns Dinner in Yokohama 1913; *Japan Chronicle Weekly* Edition 810/820, 231. Pat Wilson, 'Burns in China', BC (1983), 58-61.

429 http://www.gunghaggis.com,<last accessed 1/5/2018.> Since 2007, Seattle, WA has also held a GungHaggis event annually.

430 http://www.vancouverhistory.ca/ chronology1928.htm. <last accessed 1/5/2018.>

431 Brian Hennessy, John Hennessy (eds) *The Emergence of Broadcasting in Britain*, (Lympstone, 2005), 219.

432 *Aberdeen Press and Journal*, 26/1/1923.

433 HR Rivers Moore, 'The Wireless Transmission of Music', *Music & Letters*, (April, 1923), 158-161, at.158.

434 http://www.mauchlineburnsclub.com/ history.htm <last accessed 1/5/2018>

435 Hajkowski, 135-167. There were four programmes which were linked to the Burns Supper: on 19/1/1938 'Scottish Cookery: A Burns Supper' by Elizabeth Hughes Hallett, focussed on recipes; 'Children's Hour', 25/1/1945 has a small Burns Supper for children; 'The Immortal Memory: an extract from the toast at the bicentenary supper of the Ayr Burns Club', 25/1/1959; and 'Robert Burns Night in the South East: 'preparations' 23/1/1961.

436 *London Calling*, Volume 2, (London, 1959), 23.

437 *Jedburgh Gazette*, 20/1/1956, *London Calling*, Vols 844-852, 23.

438 Thomas Keith, 'A Discography of Robert Burns 1948 to 2002', *Studies in Scottish Literature*, vol.33, issue 1,387-412. See also R. Peel, 'Burns on Record', *Burns Chronicle* (1966), 45-54.

439 Mackay, *Federation*, 144; Nimmo, *Words and Sound*.

440 Donny O'Rourke, 'Supperman: Televising Burns' in Simpson (ed.), *Burns Now*, 208-217.

441 *Falkirk Herald*, 15/1/1955.

442 *Aberdeen Evening Express*, 4/1/1958, 28/1/1961.

443 BC (1963), 115.

444 http://ssa.nls.uk/film.cfm?fid=5034 <last accessed 1/5/2018>. Title: [IRVINE BURNS CLUB]; Date: [ca. 1971] [Templar Film Studios, Glasgow]. .

445 TV *Times*, 23/1/1973, BC (1973), 102; *Aberdeen Press & Journal*, 31/1/1975; BC (1977), 28.

446 O'Rourke, 214-215.

447 MacDonald, *Mother Club*, 111.

448 Nimmo, *Words and Sounds*, 87-88.

449 BC (1980).

450 *Glasgow Herald*, 25/1/1984.

451 The first Burns Supper which is recorded to have claimed to be 'the largest in the world' was held in the City Hall, Glasgow in 1935 for 900 unemployed men, *Glasgow Herald*, 29/1/1935 and appears to have been an annual event from 1934 until the war, see *Glasgow Herald*, 27/1/1934 and 25/1/1938. Communal Singing from the 1935 event was broadcast on BBC Radio.

452 Helen Simpson, 'Burns and The Bankers', *Getting A Life*, (New York: Vintage, 2002), 83.

453 http://www.burnssupper2009.com <last accessed on 20 March 2009>

454 Walt Whitman, 'November Boughs: 7: Robert Burns as a Poet and Person', *North American Review*, 143 (1886), 427-429, at 428.

455 Without diminishing the significance of this happy event, the statement that 'this represents the first such event in the cottage in 207 years', is not correct. Certainly, the Allowa' Club last met in the Cottage in 1809, meeting latterly at the King's Arms in Ayr. But the 'Original' Burns Club held their dinners there from 1821 until the building of the hall abutting the Cottage in 1847. They dined in that new hall annually until 1881. See McBain, *Burns Cottage*, 83-84.

456 Frank Shaw: Speech to 'Burns and Beyond' Conference, University of Glasgow, 15 January 2011.

457 Nigel Leask (ed), *Oxford WRB I*, 'First Common Place Book,' 65.

458 *Poems*, K.115, *The Farewell. To the Brethren of St. James's Lodge, Tarbolton,* ll.29-32.

459 Brown, *Paisley Burns Clubs*, 37-55.

460 Letter, Robert Tannahill to James Clarke, 2/2/1807, quoted in Brown, *Paisley Burns Clubs*, 65.

461 Leith Davis, 'Negotiating Cultural Memory; James Currie's "Works of Robert Burns,"' *International Journal of Scottish Literature*, issue 6 (Spring/ Summer 2010); Andrews, 'Vendors'.

462 Lord Byron, *Journal*, 13/12/1813: 'What an antithetical mind! – tenderness, roughness – delicacy, coarseness – sentiment, sensuality – soaring and grovelling, dirt and deity – all mixed up in that one compound of inspired clay'. Quoted in Low, *Critical Heritage*, 258.

463 Davis, 'Negotiating Cultural Memory'.

464 Richard J Finlay, 'Heroes, Myths and Anniversaries in Modern Scotland', *Scottish Affairs*, (Winter 1997), 108-125, at 114-115

465 Finlay, 'The Burns Cult and Scottish Identity in the Nineteenth and Twentieth Century', Kenneth Simpson, (ed.), *Love and Liberty. Robert Burns: A Bicentenary Celebration*, (East Linton, 1997) 69-78, at 76. Colin Kidd, 'Burns and Politics', Gerard Carruthers (ed.), *The Edinburgh Companion to Robert Burns*, (Edinburgh, 2009), 61-73, at.61.

466 Leerson and Rigney, *Commemorating Writers*, 59.

467 Wilkie Collins, 'Burns as a Hat-peg', *Household Words*, 12/2/1859, 241-243 at.241.

468 Nimmo, *Words and Sounds*, 96.

469 Robert Burns, *Poems Selected by Don Paterson*, (London, 2001), vii.

470 Neil Ascherson 'Now Does It Add Up?' *London Review of Books*, 12/3/2009, 3-5, at 3.

471 DeLancey Ferguson 'The Immortal Memory', *The American Scholar*, (Autumn 1936), 441-450, at 445.

472 JFT Thomson, 'Suggested Lines for Organising a Burns Supper', BC (1979), 31-32, at 32.

473 BC (Spring 2009), 43-44 at 43. From the author's experience, 14-18 minutes is the most effective timing for an Immortal Memory speech.

474 DeLancy Ferguson, 'Immortal Memory', 441; Edwin Muir, *Scottish*

475 *Journey*, (London, 1935), 90; Lewis Grassic Gibbon and Hugh MacDiarmid, *Scottish Scene or the Intelligent Man's Guide to Albyn*, (Bath, 1934), 51.

475 DeLancey Ferguson, 'Immortal Memory', 444-445.

476 Jeffrey Mark, 'Mr Churchill Runs the War', in *Life*, 9 December 1940, 16.

477 *New-York Daily Advertiser*, 3/2/1818.

478 Philadelphia (annually from 1818); Paisley (1822); Sheffield (1822); Edinburgh, the Edinburgh & Ayrshire Gentlemen (1825, 1830), Newcastle-upon-Tyne (1825), Leeds (1826) and Baltimore (1835).

479 Ebenezer Picken, 'Verses on the Death of Robert Burns', *Miscellaneous Poems*, (Edinburgh, 1813), I, 70-73, at 73.

480 Macdonald, *Mother Club*, 35.

481 *The Calcutta Review*, (April 1906), 307- 308, at 308.

482 Brown, *Paisley Burns Clubs*, 260 -262.

483 Ballantine, 203, (Cawdor).

484 With even greater ritual, the Robert Burns Society of Australia, in 1933, reported that '[t]he toast of the 'Immortal Memory' was drunk with 'lights out', the company facing an alcove, where stood an illuminated model of the thatched cottage in which Burns was born'. *Sydney Morning Herald*, 25/1/1933.

485 Low, *Critical Heritage*, xv.

486 *Scots Magazine*, 1/4/1824.

487 Lewis Grassic Gibbon, *The Mearns Leader and Kincardineshire Mail*, 8/2/1934.

488 John Cairney, *Immortal Memories*.

489 Douglas Dunn, '"A Very Scottish Kind of Dash": Burns's Native Metric', in Crawford (ed.) *Robert Burns and Cultural Authority*, 58– 84, at 84.

490 Edwin Muir, 'Burns and Popular Poetry', *Essays on Literature and Society*, (London, 1949), 57

491 Anon., Burns' 110th Natal Day, 63.

492 Murray Pittock, 'Foreword', in McGinn, *Ultimate Burns Supper Book*, 13.

493 Samuel Johnson, *A Dictionary of the English Language*, (London, 1755), i, 956.

494 A version of this subchapter appeared in *The Drouth*. 'Robert Burns and the Invention of the Haggis,' Winter 2012, Issue, 41, 90-95.

495   William Dunbar, 'The Flyting of
       Dunbar and Kennedy' in Robert
       Crawford and Mick Imlach (eds), *The
       New Penguin Book of Scottish Verse*,
       (London, 2000), 89.
496   François Rabelais, *The Life of
       Gargantua and the Heroic Deeds of
       Pantagruel*, Sir Thomas Urquhart of
       Cromarty (trs.), (London, 1887), 212.
497   Kinsley, III, 1221-1223.
498   Jean Anthelme Brillat-Saverin,
       Physiologie du Goût, (Paris, 1825), 1.
499   President Chirac described the haggis
       as 'unappetising' and warned that 'you
       can't trust people who cook as badly as
       that.' *Daily Telegraph*, 5 July 2005.
500   Charles De Gaulle, *Les Mots du
       General*, (Paris, 1962).
501   *The Simpsons*, 'Round Springfield'
       (first aired 30 April 1995).
502   Kinsley, III, 1221; Tyrrell, *et al*,
       'Feasting on National Identity,' 46;
       Roland Barthes, *Mythologies*, Annette
       Lavers (trs.), (London, 2009), 71.
503   *Greenock Advertiser*, 8/2/1808.
504   McNeill, *Scottish Kitchen*, 24. There
       was some controversy recently when
       an FT reporter called Montrose 'the
       place where nutrition goes to die.'
       John McDermott, *Financial Times*,
       21/2/2014.
505   *Poems*, K.72 'The Cotter's Saturday
       Night.' ll.91 – 99.
506   Nigel Leask, *Robert Burns and
       Pastoral*, (Oxford, 2012), 133 and 223.
507   'To Make a Rich Scots Haggis,' in AF
       Crell and WM Wallace, *The Family
       Oracle of Health*, (London, 1824),
       'when my spouse was in use and
       wont to make a noble haggis for the
       Caledonian Hunt Dinner, she added
       two eggs; two or three shallots;
       a *manipulus*, or handful of sage,
       marjoram, savory, parsley, and thyme;
       some ketchup; and half a mutchkin
       [sc:430 mL] of Ferintosh [whisky].'
       p.155.
508   'Being one of the inferior officer's
       birth day... a dog was killed that had
       been bred on board; the hind quarters
       were roasted; and a pye was made
       of the fore quarters, into the crust
       of which they put the fat; and of the
       viscera they made a haggis.' Sydney
       Parkinson, *Journal of a Voyage to
       the South Seas*, (London, 1773), 122.
       A later commentator suggests that this
       might be 'considered an omen of Scotch

       domination, now long associated in
       popular opinion with the Settlement of
       Otago,' Robert MacNab, *Murihiku and
       the Southern Islands*, (Invercargill, NZ,
       1907), 6.
509   Edward Topham, *Letters from
       Edinburgh*, (London, 1776), 158-160.
510   Benjamin Silliman, *A Journal of Travels
       in England, Holland and Scotland*,
       (New York, 1810), ii, 342. In 1833,
       James Stuart, doing the reverse tour,
       stayed in Boston where his landlord
       'had an Edinburgh cook... and
       sometimes there were Scotch dishes,
       even a haggis, sheep's-head, minced
       collops, &c. but the Americans had
       no great relish for them.' James
       Stuart, *Three Years in North America*,
       (Edinburgh, 1833), I, 307.
511   *The Port-Folio*, vols 3/4, 192. See also,
       Kingston Branch Whig, 8/12/1835.
512   Helen Currie, *Poems*, 58-59.
513   [Bishop John Gleig], *A Critique on the
       Poems of Robert Burns*, (Edinburgh,
       Stirling, London, 1812), 49.
514   *Blackwood's Magazine*, July 1823,
       73-76. *Liverpool Mercury*, 27/6/1823,
       and *Charleston Courier*, 8/8/1823.
515   [Christian Isobel Johnston], *The
       Cook and Housewife's Manual by
       'Mrs Margaret Dodds'*, (Edinburgh,
       1828). One English reviewer was
       particularly antipathetic to the 'horrid
       compositions,' 'infernal mess' and
       'abominable compost' that constituted
       Scots cuisine, including 'the *haggis*, the
       mere description of which is enough
       to do more to ordinary and well-
       organised bowels than ipecacuhana.'
       Devizes & Wiltshire Gazette, 3/8/1826.
516   *The Literary Gazette and Journal of
       Belles Lettres*, (1837), 636.
517   Charles Leslie, *Autobiographical
       Recollections*, (Boston, 1860), 64. In
       Rob Roy, Scott uses a phrase 'to slash a
       het haggis' which is glossed as 'to open
       a dangerous business.'
518   *Blackwoods Magazine*, December
       1828 'On the overflow of a haggis.'
       See also 'Brown gives a haggis to his
       Friends,' cartoon, *Punch*, February
       1859. The dangers have been identified
       in contemporary medical literature
       about potential second-degree burns,
       suggesting 'a warning should be
       issued when a plastic covered haggis
       is sold.' *British Medical Journal*,
       22-29/12/1984, 1777. This has

been an issue afflicting cooks since Aristophanes in 423 BC, 'The first time I cooked [roasted] a haggis [γαστηϱ] ...suddenly it burst, and splattered like piss, and spat fat in my face,' Aristophanes (Clare Porter trs.), *Clouds*, ll.456-459, in David R Slavett and Palmer Bovue (eds) *Aristophanes*, (Philadelphia, 1988), 124. However, care should be taken in identifying γαστηϱ as 'haggis' as its recipe uses blood, which is alien to the Scottish haggis. This presence of blood also rules out the recipe (used by lazy commentators claiming 'the haggis is English') from Gervaise Markham, *Country Contentments*, (London, 1615), 222. Similarly, the absence of oatmeal in 1430's *Liber Cure Cocorum*, Richard Morris (ed.), (Berlin, 1862), 131, counts against that recipe. See also: 'Dick Humelbergius Secundus', *Apician Anecdotes*, (London, 1829), 72-75 or a more recent analysis: Adam Balic, 'The Haggis,' in Mark McWilliams (ed.) *Wrapped and Stuffed Foods: Proceedings of the Oxford Symposium on Food and Cookery 2012*, (Totnes, 2013), 82-93.

519 John Galt, *Autobiography*, (London, 1833), i, 281.

520 Queen Victoria, *More Leaves From the Journal of a Life in the Highlands*, (London, 1885), 29; Alex Tyrrell, 'The Queen's "Little Trip": The Royal Visit To Scotland in 1842', *The Scottish Historical Review*, Vol LXXXII, 1: (April 2003), 47-73.

521 Kirkby and Lucking, *Dining on Turtles*, 46.

522 Anthony P. Cohen says: 'the Burns Supper: as iconic, as symbol-rich a commensal occasion as any national ceremonial could be' in 'Nationalism and Social Identity,' *Scottish Affairs*, 18 (Winter 1997), 1-14.

523 Robert Burns, Andrew Noble and Patrick Scott Hogg (eds), *The Canongate Burns*, (Edinburgh, 2001), 214. Carol McGuirk also sees a penis metaphor in the line 'your pin wad help to mend a mill,' Carol McGuirk, *Reading Robert Burns: Texts, Contexts, Transformations*, (London, 2014), 15. While Burns shared Woody Allen's view that his brain was his second favourite organ, I think that this is a step too far.

524 Robert Fergusson, *New Penguin Book of Scottish Verse*, 274-276, at 275.

525 *New Penguin Book of Scottish Verse*, 'Caller Oysters' pp.268-270; 'Polemo-Middina inter Vitarvam et Nebernam', 192-201; *Poems*, K.72, 'The Cotter's Saturday Night.' Burns mentions haggis in one other poem. He teases Captain Frances Grose in K.322 [Ken ye ought o' Captain Grose'] at ll.9-12, worrying that the subject might have been... slain by Highland bodies... And eaten like a wether-haggis?'

526 Nicholas D Smith 'The Muses O'lio: Satire, Food and Tobias Smollett's The Expedition of Humphrey Clinker', *Eighteenth Century Fiction*, 16:3 (April 2004), article 6, 1- 16. At 13, Smith quotes one verse of Burns, but does not draw the wider connection.

527 Tobias Smollett, *Humphrey Clinker*, (Oxford, 1998), xii.

528 Smollett, *Humphrey Clinker*, 295.

529 Kinsley, III,1221.

530 Brown, *Burns And Tradition*, 119.

531 Robert T Fitzhugh, *Robert Burns, His Associates and Contemporaries*, (Chapel Hill, 1943), 36-37.

532 *General Advertiser*, 30/11/1786.

533 *Caledonian Mercury*, 19/12/1786, 'Address to a Haggice. By R. BURNS.' Never before published.'

534 Brown, *Paisley Burns Clubs*, 61.

535 *Punch*, August 1844.

536 Brown, *Paisley Burns Clubs*, 83-86.

537 www.dalry burnsclub.org <last accessed 1/5/2018>

538 *Dumfries Courier*, 26/1/1830.

539 *Glasgow Chronicle*, 13/2/1813. During the 1859 celebrations, 'haggis bags in Glasgow rose from 2d. to 1s.5d. each and could not be had for love nor money.' *Paisley Herald* 5/2/1859.

540 Mackay, *Federation*, 17.

541 Edmund Eustace Dyer, *The Alloa 1828 Burns Club*, (Alloa, 1928). Alloa Burns Club still serves an extra course of 'tripe an' ingans' at its annual Burns Supper). Thanks to Bill Dawson.

542 Meg Dodds, Part 1, 78-79.

543 *Boston Burns Club January 25th, 1859*, 3.

544 *Lowell Daily Citizen*, 26/1/1859.

545 Tyrrell, Hill and Kirkby, 'Feasting on National Identity' in Diane Kirkby, Tanja Luckins (eds), *Dining on Turtles*, 46-63, at 52.

546 Kinnear, *Albany Burns Club*, 8.

547 The new New York Burns Society appended a note to their truly extensive 1869 banquet menu thus: 'Poor Burns! How he would have enjoyed such a dinner.' Anon., *110th Natal Day*, 9.

548 McNeill, *Scottish Journal* No.5, 5.

549 J[ohn] G[ibson] Lockhart, *Memoirs of Walter Scott*, i, 84-85.

550 Strang, *Glasgow Clubs*, 191.

551 *Georgian*, 18/2/1824.

552 *Evening Post*, 7/2/1848.

553 *New York Times*, 6/12/1890.

554 *Ibid.*, 26/1/1858.

555 *Ibid.*, 26/1/1856.

556 Featherstonehaugh, *Centennial Anniversary*. Menzies had been earlier reported at the same activity, in *Milwaukee Sentinel*, 31/1/1851 and *Inverness Courier*, 20/1/1851.

557 *Bell's Life in Sydney and Sporting Review*, 29/1/1859.

558 Ballantine, 166 (Ardrossan), 345 (Melrose) and 411 (Walkerburn).

559 Ballantine, 345, (Melrose).

560 Note Paisley's tradition of using a fiddler and not a piper to lead the haggis procession.

561 Jackie Kay, 'Burns Supper'.

562 *Report of the Proceedings at the Annual Birthday Celebration January 25th 1918*, (London, 1918). See also 'The Houston Scot', *Newsletter of the Houston Heather & Thistle Club*, 5:6 (2007), 1.

563 Kathleen D Vohs, *et al*, 'Rituals Enhance Consumption', *Psychological Science*, OnlineFirst, published 17/7/2013 as doi:10.1177/0956797613478949; 1-8, (last accessed 1/5/2018) at 1.

564 *Ibid.*, 7.

565 DeLancey Ferguson, 'The Immortal Memory', 443.

566 *Chambers/Wallace Edition*, iv, 445.

567 Kinsley, III, 1221.

568 TMC 'Grace for a Halloween Supper,' *Scots Magazine*, 70 (November 1808), 608.

569 Ballantine, 172 (Badenscoth), 339 (Sydney).

570 McNeill, *Scots Kitchen*, 171.

571 Discussed in McGinn, *Ultimate Burns Supper Book*, 71-76.

572 *Letter*, J D Fergusson to Margaret Morris, 19/10/1915, quoted in Smith, *My Country*, 244.

573 Simpson, *Burns and the Bankers*, 95.

574 Buettner, 'Haggis in the Raj,' 238.

575 Alex Watson 'Thirteen Ways of Glossing "To a Haggis,"' *International Journal of Scottish Literature*, 6 (Spring/Summer 2010), 1-16, at 12. A personal favourite in glossaries is in the Henley & Henderson 1896 Complete Edition: 'Haggis, a special Scots pudding, the *pièce de résistance* at Burns Club Dinners, and an esteemed antidote to whisky.' IV, 143.

576 McGuirk, *Reading Robert Burns*, p.15.

577 *Poems*, K.84 'Love and Liberty – A Cantata,' [The Jolly Beggars], recitativo, ll.7-14.

578 Samuel Longfellow, *Life of Longfellow*, (Boston, MA and New York, 1891), iii, 338.

579 Henry Grey Graham, *Scottish Men of Letters in the Eighteenth Century*, (London, 1908), 7-8.

580 <http://www.thefreemasons.org.uk/tarbolton135/history.htm>. (Last accessed 1/5/2018).

581 *Air Edition*, vi.

582 'The *het pint* is made by warming two English quarts of strongest old ale, either Edinburgh or Alloa, with nutmeg, ginger, and half an English pint of the best small still whisky to it; some add an egg, but this is not always done. A most delicious morning whet it is.' Crell and Wallace, *Family Oracle*, i, 211.

583 *Air Edition*, xxxiiii. That comes to 284 cl, or just over eleven UK standard pub measures.

584 Robert Sanderson, 'Clerical Wits: The Late Rev Hamilton Paul', *Frae the Lyne Valley: Poems and Sketches*, (Paisley: J and R Parlane, 1888), pp.108-116.

585 John Struthers, 'Stanzas Written for the Anniversary of Burns, 1810,' *Poems, Moral and Religious*,' (Glasgow, 1814), ii, 129-131. Similar thoughts can be found in his 'Ode, 29th January 1806,' ii, 154-158.

586 Ballantine, 59, (Glasgow, City Hall).

587 Ballantine, 373, (Perth). As 36 standard bottles would equate to 1,008 standard (25mL) units of alcohol, this represents an unbacchanalian single large whisky for each of the gentlemen present.

588 Ballantine, 95, (Ayr).

589 This legislation reduced drink related crime rates in all major towns in Scotland except Ayr and Elgin. See: Duncan Mclaren, *The Rise and*

Progress of Whisky-Drinking In Scotland, (Edinburgh, 1858), 28.

590 *Currie Edition*, i, 202-203. Currie has received a hearty criticism for his characterisation of Burns's drinking habits. His position may be easier for the modern reader to comprehend, and perhaps, forgive a little, if Currie's attitude to alcoholic consumption is seen in the light of the modern view of cigarette smoking which was ubiquitous in our parents' social life, but anathema to all 'right thinking' persons today.

591 *Poems*, K.57: 'Epistle to J L[aprai]k.' ll.121-126.

592 *Port Folio*, December 1821, p.485, Anonymous, Verses on Burns's Punch Bowl, Written Extempore.'

593 *Greenock Advertiser*, 1/2/1805; *The Monthly Magazine*, 21 (June 1806), 430-31.

594 [Lockhart], *Peter's Letters*, i, 106-43.

595 Phillip Sully, *Robert Burns and Dumfries*, 37.

596 *Centenary of the Dumfries Burns Club*, 107, quoting Holbrook Jackson.

597 James Kennedy, *Poems and Songs*, 115-117.

598 Ballantine reports that bowls of 'punch' were served at Footdee (146), Balmoral (174), Berwick, Red Lion Inn (429), Forres Hammermen (249), Derby (448), and Stockton -where 'the famous "Corporation Punch" presented by the Mayor for the occasion' (485). Bowls of 'Toddy' was served at Aberdour (147), Alloa (158) and Pollokshaws (379.) Mr John Begg, a great nephew of the Poet brought a teapot he claimed as a toddy server to the Burns Supper of Glasgow & South-Western Railway at Kilmarnock (305.)

599 Ballantine, 210, (Cupar-Fife).

600 Ballantine, 18, (Edinburgh, Corn Exchange). Mrs Norton, quoted in Alan Dent, *Burns in His Time*, (London, 1966), 78.

601 Ballantine, 90, (Glasgow, Buchan's Temperance Hotel).

602 Helen Simpson, *Burns and the Bankers*, 96.

603 Robert Crawford, 'The Bard: Ossian, Burns and the Shaping of Shakespeare', in *Shakespeare and Scotland*, Willy Maley and Andrew Murphy, (eds.), (Manchester, 2004), 124-140, at 133.

604 Macdonald, *Mother Club*, 24.

605 Semple, *Tannahill*, 382. 'Letter to James Clark, 2nd February 1807.'

606 Brown, *Paisley Burns Clubs*, 89.

607 Ballantine, 81, (Glasgow, King's Arms Hall).

608 The top 3 around 13% each. *Ye Banks and Braes/My Nannie* (ca 7 per cent each); *To Mary In Heaven/Of a' the Airts/Green Grow the Rashes/Rantin' Rovin' Robin/John Anderson* (ca 5% each).

609 Anon. *Burns Centenary, July 21st, 1896: Record of the Celebration Throughout New South Wales* (Sydney, 1896), 8.

610 *Glasgow Herald*, 26 January 1882. Aberdeen had been previously similarly entertained by 'Mr Braid, a n***o [Ed: elided] melodist and comic singer of no small abilities,' *Aberdeen Journal*, 31 January 1844.

611 James Thomson, *Doric Lays and Lyrics,* (Glasgow, 1884).

612 See Ogden Nash, 'Everything's Haggis in Hoboken or, Scots wha hae hae,' *New Yorker*, 19/5/1951, 36.

613 MacDonald, *Mother Club,* 27.

614 Ballantine, 12-13, (Edinburgh, Music Hall).

615 Wilson's party piece was a burlesque of the psalms in the guise of a Auld Licht minister – see Alan Lang Strout, 'John Wilson's Election', 291-299.

616 William Wordsworth, *Resolution and Independence*, quoted in Low, *Critical Heritage*, 159; John D Ross, *Round Burns's Grave*, (Paisley 1891), see JG Whittier, at 37-41, and Fitz-Greene Halleck, at 9-15.

617 Ballantine, 182, (Beattock). The first record of a three-handed recitation of *The Twa Dogs* can be found at Sunderland in 1823, *Durham County Advertiser*, 1/2/1823.

618 Ballantine, 170 (Auchterarder); 171 (Auchtermuchty); 413 (Weymss W).

619 Ballantine, 202, (Castle-Douglas).

620 First published with a musical setting in Vol.5 of Thomson's *Select Airs* in 1818, with a new score arranged by Sir Henry Bishop. For Dunbar, *Caledonian Mercury*, 28 January 1820.

621 Ballantine, 404 (Thornhill) and 400 (Strathaven).

622 Ballantine, 459, (Liverpool, The Concert Room).

623 Alexandria Burns Club website http://www.robertburns.org.uk/burns_supper.htm (last accessed 1/5/2018).

624   *Poems*, K.55, 'Death and
       Dr Hornbook', ll.182-184.
625   *Poems*, K.68, 'To the Reverend John
       McMath,", l.81.
626   *Poems*, K.264, [The Kirk's Alarm]',
       l.70.
627   William Peebles, *Burnomania, [etc.]*
       (Edinburgh, 1811).
628   *Blackwood's Magazine*, 7 (April –
       September 1820), 321.
629   Low, *Critical Heritage*, 424.
630   Reverend Hamilton Paul to J D
       Douglas, 24/8/1853, MS 587 f.93
       National Library of Scotland.
631   *Illustrated London News*, 10/8/1844.
632   Ballantine,514, (Geelong).
633   John Wellwood, *Norman Macleod*,
       (Edinburgh & London, 1897), 32
       (emphasis added).
634   Ballantine, 54-55, (Glasgow, City Hall).
635   Fergus Ferguson, *Should Christians
       Celebrate The Birthday Of Robert
       Burns?*, (Edinburgh, 1869).
636   *Glasgow Herald*, 2/2/1869.
637   *Ibid.*, 16/2/1869.
638   Thomas Watson, *Poems, Songs, and
       Sketches*, (Edinburgh, 1873), 239-240.
639   *Bradford Observer*, 30/3/1869.
640   *Morning Chronicle*, 27/3/1869.
641   Donald Macleod, *Memoir of Norman
       Macleod*, (New York NY, 1876),
       335; Queen Victoria's Journals,
       14 October 1865, 293, on www.
       queenvictoriasjournals.org <last accessed
       1/5/2018.>
642   Grace Atkinson Oliver, *Arthur Penrhyn
       Stanley*, (Boston, 1885), 349.
643   Arthur Stanley, *Rectorial Address; St
       Andrews*, (London, 1872), 14-15.
644   Speech, Williamsburgh, Long Island,
       25/1/1878, quoted in JD Ross,
       Burnsiana V, 77-79, at 78. Beecher
       was consistent in his 'love the sinner,
       hate the sin' approach to Burns, and
       had been involved in his own adultery
       scandal, Mrs Janet Wood quipped
           A century hence, and wha' can tell
           What may befa' yer cannie sel'?
           Some holy preacher
           May tak the cudgels up for ane
           Ca'd Harry Beecher.
       Janet Wood, *Burns **and** Beecher,*
       Broadside, undated but estimated
       187-, Brown University, Harris
       Broadsides Ref bdr: 295134.
645   *New York Times*, 23/3/1885.
646   *Glasgow Herald*, 20/1/1982, he had
       the reputation of adapting material
       from others' speeches, such that he was
       known by the sobriquet 'the thief of
       bad gags,' *Glasgow Herald*, 26 January
       1987.
647   There remain contemporary, albeit
       minority, critics of the Burns Supper
       on a religious basis: 'James McMillan,
       the composer, has denounced the
       "cult" of Robert Burns, claiming that
       Burns Suppers are parodies of the
       Catholic mass... he claims that Burns
       suppers are a deliberate mockery of the
       rituals of Catholicism. "The Ayrshire
       Burns supper is unmistakably a
       parody mass,"' Scottish Christian.com
       (18/10/2009, last accessed 24/3/2012).
648   Reminiscent of Fergusson's impromptu
       Grace:
           For rabbits young and for rabbits old,
           For rabbits hot and for rabbits cold,
           For rabbits tender and for rabbits
       tough,
           Our thanks we render—but we've
           had enough.
       Charles Rodgers, *Leaves From My
       Autobiography*, (London, 1876), 15.
649   *Poems*, K.532, 'Grace Before Meat' and
       'Grace Before and After Meat.'
650   *Poems*, K.267, 'Grace After Meat.'
651   *Poems*, K.266, 'A Grace Before Dinner
       – Extempore.'
652   *Poems*, K.531: 'Burns Grace at
       Kirkcudbright.' The Scots version
       is not in Kinsley. First published in
       Cunningham, *The Works of Robert
       Burns*, III, 311. James McKay used
       the Kinsley text and received an
       admonishment from a *Burns Chronicle*
       reader: 'Aye weel, ye wad expeck tae
       find the grace translated into English in
       an Oxford publication.' BC (1989), 22.
653   Ballantine, 286 (Irvine); 325 (Lerwick);
       345 (Melrose);.553 (Sydney); 392
       (Stanley); 572 (Natchez).
654   Ballantine,.423 (Aston Hall,
       Birmingham).
655   Ballantine, 193 (Bridge of Weir).
656   Ballantine, 460 (Liverpool Soirée of the
       Working Classes).
657   *New-York Daily Advertiser*, 3/2/1818;
       The American, 3/2/1823.
658   *Manchester Times*, 31/1/1829.
659   Ballantine, 271 (Hamilton).
660   *Poems*, Kinsley, III, 1291.
661   Ann Rigney, *The Afterlives of Walter
       Scott: Memory on the Move*, (Oxford,
       2012), 67-70.

662 Pittock, 'Introduction,' *Robert Burns in Global Culture*, 19-20, at 20.

663 http://www.gla.ac.uk/news/archiveofnews/2009/november/headline_136896_en.html <last accessed 1/5/2018.>

664 *Letters*, L.290: to Mrs Dunlop, 17/12/1788.

665 A. G. Gilchrist, 'Goodnight and Parting Songs,' *Journal of the Folk-Song Society*, vol.7, no.28, (December 1924), 184-194.

666 *Letters*, L.178: to ['Clarinda'], 14/1/1788.

667 *Letters*, L.684 [to James Johnson], [Aug. or Sept. 1795].

668 See Pittock, *Oxford WRB (II)*, 72 and 499 for texts and *Oxford WRB (III)* 7-8 and 156-157 for notes.

669 Nathaniel H Carter, *Letters from Europe, [etc.]* (New York, 1827), I, 324.

670 *Baltimore News*, 25/1/1834; *Portsmouth Journal of Literature and Politics*, 21/7/1838; *Melbourne Argus*, 28/1/1848.

671 Charles Dickens, *David Copperfield* (London, 1850), 178. One rather hopes that after emigrating to Australia (where 'seas between us braid hae roared,' (620) he, as magistrate at Port Middlebay, may have enjoyed participation in Burns Suppers there.

672 William Makepeace Thackeray, Edgar F Harde, (ed.), *The English Humourists of the Eighteenth Century and Charity and Humour,'* (Michigan, 2007), 201.

673 Ballantine, 288 (Irvine).

674 *Centennial Anniversary... Milwaukee*, 54.

675 J.C. Ewing, '"Auld Lang Syne" Again', *BC* (1952), 79-81, at 79.

676 Crawford, *The Bard*, 369, 309.

677 *Poems*, K.45, 'Green Grow the Rashes,' ll.17 -20.

678 *Oxford WRB (I)*, 23.

679 *Currie Edition*, I, 107.

680 *Ibid.*

681 Marshall, *Burns Supper Companion*, 43.

682 WC McLehose (ed.), *The Correspondence Between Burns and Clarinda*, (Edinburgh, 1843), 53. *Caledonian Mercury*, 2/2/1815.

683 Letter, James Hogg to Margaret Hogg, [26] January 1832; *Hogg's Letters*, III, 16-17. See also Mrs Crawford's reminiscences, 'Autobiographical Sketches,' in *The Metropolitan Magazine*, vol. XXXII (September to December 1841), 206-213.

684 'The Cairn', Dalry Burns Club 1863: poem by Andrew Aitkin: the Club also toasted 'The Haggis-maker (Mrs. Willison)' between 1890 and 1897 and from 1900 to 1903.

685 *Rhode-Island Republican*, 5/2/1829.

686 Hepburn & Douglas, 8.

687 *Blackwood's Magazine*, September 1844, 8.

688 *Ibid*, 376.

689 Mackay *Federation*, 44.

690 Brown, *Paisley Burns Clubs*, 192, 243-244: Robert Crawford, 'Robert Fergusson's Robert Burns', in *Robert Burns and Cultural Authority*, 1-22, at 20.

691 Ballantine, 359, (Paisley) carries a detailed report of the Paisley Dinner (not organised by the Paisley Burns Club, which was at that time in 'suspended animation'). It is important to note that, in evaluating Robert Crawford's analysis above that (a) the hall was also decorated with a transparency representing the scene in 'The Vision' where 'the [female] genius of Coila [was] crowning the bard' which must be seen as a positive view of the feminine and (b) the hundred-odd ladies joined the event immediately after Grace after Dinner and in time to hear each of the more than fourteen speeches in full.

692 Ballantine, 145, (Aberdeen).

693 Ballantine, 158, (Aylth).

694 Ballantine, 225, (Dufftown).

695 Ballantine, 214, (Cupar, Fife).

696 *Norwich Aurora*, 19/2/1859.

697 Ballantine, 40, (Glasgow, City Hall).

698 *The Age*, 27/1/1859.

699 Ballantine,.291, (Jedburgh).

700 *110th Natal Day*, 4.

701 *New York Times*, 23/1/1870.

702 *Ayr Advertiser*, 29/1/1885.

703 *Paisley Herald*, 27/1/1887.

704 Leanne M Day, *Civilising the City: Literary Societies and Clubs in Brisbane During the 1880s and 1890s*, (PhD Thesis, Griffith University, 2004.)

705 Ballantine, 158, (Aylth).

706 *Peterhead Sentinel*, 27/1/1893.

707 *ibid*, 28/1/1896.

708 *Berwickshire News*, 3/2/1920; *Dundee Courier*, 26/1/1921.

709   *Berwickshire News*, 27/1/1920;
      Southern Reporter, 31/1/1935.
710   DAJ MacPherson, *Women in the
      Orange Order: Female Activism,
      Diaspora and Empire in the British
      World, 1850 – 1940*, (Manchester,
      2016), 118-121.
711   *Eastern Star News* (1936), 178; (1940),
      11. *Scotsman*, 26/1/1924, reporting
      the Eastern Star Burns Supper in Ayr:
      'Miss Hardwick, Ayr, probably has the
      distinction of being the first woman to
      propose "The Immortal Memory".'
712   Kyle Ladies appear to have been
      unaware of the Peterhead Ladies thirty
      years before.
713   Mackay, *Federation*, 73-74.
714   Irvine Lasses Burns Club,
      Secretary's Report 1976, www.
      irvinelassesburnsclub.org (last accessed
      1/5/2018); BC (1977), 75 – a man gave
      their first Immortal Memory.
715   Anon, *Burns Day in Detroit,* (Detroit,
      1921), 9; Bueltmann, *Scottish Ethnicity,*
      216.
716   BC (2018) lists the following: Annan
      Ladies Burns Club (founded 1928,
      number 393), Dumfries Ladies Burns
      Club No.1 (1930, number 437);
      Langholm Ladies Burns Club (1937,
      number 660), The Poosie Nansie Ladies
      Burns Club (Kirkcaldy) (1949, number
      688) and Irvine Lassies Burns Club
      (1975, number 936).
717   *The Scotsman*, 26/1/1999.
718   Saturday's Royal Naval mess toast was
      traditionally: 'Wives and Sweethearts:'
      with the unauthorised but near-
      universal reply: 'May they never meet.'
719   *Oxford WRB (I)*, 23.
720   Dalry Burns Club 'The Cairn' Mss
      Toast lists.
721   Robert Burns Begg on behalf of
      his mother and sisters in 1859, see
      Ballantine, 56, (Glasgow, City Hall).
722   Ballantine, 89 (Students Meeting,
      Glasgow University). Also 367, (Paisley,
      Drapers' Assistants of Paisley) and 366,
      (Paisley, Mr Russell's).
723   Ballantine records 20 toasts to the
      'Lasses' and five to the 'Lassies' in 1859
      and both styles carry on: the 'correct'

      use of 'Lasses' remains a fetish amongst
      'purists'.
724   110th *Natal Day*, 14.
725   *New York Times*, 26/1/1876.
726   Mackay, *Federation*, 73.
727   Minute Books of London Burns Club
      (Scots), 26 January 1920. President and
      Mrs Rintoul were the first Burnsians
      to be captured on film when laying the
      annual wreath at the London statue
      in 1920. 'Robbie [sic] Burns Statue'
      British Pathe News at http://www.
      britishpathe.com/record.php?id=27870.
      (Last accessed 1/5/2018.)
728   Jean Muir Gourley, 'For Lady Members
      of Burns Clubs,' BC (1939), 95-99, at
      95. Also 'For Lady Members of Burns
      Clubs: The Duty of Happiness,' BC
      (1941), 60-61. Neither article exhibits
      proto-feminism.
729   *Dundee Courier*, 27/1/1940.
730   BC (1946), 50. The first school Burns
      Supper being at Currie in 1944, BC
      (1945), 37.
731   JFT Thomson, *Suggested Lines for
      Organising a Burns Supper, BC*, (1979),
      31-32, at 31. Murdo Morrison, 'Time
      Gentlemen/Ladies Please at Burns
      Suppers,' BC (Spring 2009), 43-44.
732   The author was pleased to assist her
      research. *Evening Times*, 20/1/2016.
733   The earliest reference in print being
      Williamina Dickson's speech, Royal
      Thames Yacht Club January 2002,
      http://www.worldburnsclub.com/
      newsletter/0204/royal_thames_yacht_
      club.htm, (last accessed 1/5/2018).
734   Ballantine, 43-44, (Glasgow, City Hall).
735   Brown, *Burns and Tradition*, 119.
736   Robert Crawford, *Scotland's Books*,
      (Oxford, 2009), 343.
737   Ian Duncan, '"An Unco' Sight": Burns
      and Enjoyment', quoted in *Robert Burns
      Lives!*: http://www.electricscotland.com/
      familytree/frank/burns_lives146.htm
      <last accessed 1/5/2018>.
738   Murray Pittock, 'Nibbling at Adam
      Smith', *Fickle Man, Robert Burns in
      the 21st Century,* Johnny Rodger, and
      Gerard Carruthers, (eds.), (Dingwall,
      2009), 118-131.

Luath Press Limited

committed to publishing well written books worth reading

LUATH PRESS takes its name from Robert Burns, whose little collie Luath (*Gael.*, swift or nimble) tripped up Jean Armour at a wedding and gave him the chance to speak to the woman who was to be his wife and the abiding love of his life. Burns called one of the 'Twa Dogs' Luath after Cuchullin's hunting dog in Ossian's *Fingal*.

Luath Press was established in 1981 in the heart of Burns country, and is now based a few steps up the road from Burns' first lodgings on Edinburgh's Royal Mile. Luath offers you distinctive writing with a hint of unexpected pleasures.

Most bookshops in the UK, the US, Canada, Australia, New Zealand and parts of Europe, either carry our books in stock or can order them for you. To order direct from us, please send a £sterling cheque, postal order, international money order or your credit card details (number, address of cardholder and expiry date) to us at the address below. Please add post and packing as follows: UK – £1.00 per delivery address; overseas surface mail – £2.50 per delivery address; overseas airmail – £3.50 for the first book to each delivery address, plus £1.00 for each additional book by airmail to the same address. If your order is a gift, we will happily enclose your card or message at no extra charge.

Luath Press Limited
543/2 Castlehill
The Royal Mile
Edinburgh EH1 2ND
Scotland
Telephone: +44 (0)131 225 4326 (24 hours)
email: sales@luath. co.uk
Website: www. luath.co.uk